MW01002516

* Bybee - undergrad ~~~~
 . grad
 . prof

* "I've relinquishe

family

THE INWARD MORNING

* Note: Heidegger thinks each
moment has the past, present, &
future in it → v interesting

Kierkegaard

THE INWARD MORNING

A Philosophical Exploration in Journal Form

Henry Bugbee

With a New Introduction by
Edward F. Mooney

The University of Georgia Press
Athens and London

© 1958, 1976 by Henry Bugbee

Introduction by Edward F. Mooney

© 1999 by the University of Georgia Press

Athens, Georgia 30602

www.ugapress.org

Printed digitally in the United States of America

Library of Congress Cataloging-in-Publication Data

Bugbee, Henry Greenwood, Jr.

The inward morning : a philosophical exploration in journal form /

Henry Bugbee ; with a new introduction by Edward F. Mooney.

xxii, 234 p. ; 22 cm.

Originally published: State College, Pa. : Bald Eagle Press, 1958.

Includes bibliographical references and index.

ISBN 0-8203-2071-4 (pbk. : alk. paper)

1. Philosophy. I. Title.

B945.B763I5 1999

191—dc21   98-4177

ISBN-13: 978-0-8203-2071-7

British Library Cataloging-in-Publication Data available

For my father

CONTENTS

INTRODUCTION
Philosophy in Wilderness

This theme of reality as a wilderness . . . is the theme which
unifies my own life. It enfolds and simplifies, comprehends
and completes. Whenever I awaken, I awaken to it.
It carries with it the gift of life.

Henry Bugbee, *The Inward Morning*

I

We sometimes think a dawn of meaning or discovery brings answers to a
restless, questioning mind. But often it opens new vistas and sometimes
boundless ones. Then life's streams and seas lift us bodily, offer glimpses
of worlds too strange to know and sounds of grief or celebration. This is
the tangled and alluring place in which our lives are found, bound in
wonders, urgent and captivating. Here we find the vital ebb and flow of
world as it dawns, new and mobile, ageless and weathered. This is an
inward morning, a home in wilderness. As Henry Bugbee has it, wilderness "carries with it the gift of life" (128).

The Inward Morning contains a philosophy of personal address and
place, played out in a voice that curves in deliberate cadences, precisely
apt to the occasion. The setting may be a talk on Spinoza or a public
hearing on securing wilderness preserves in Montana, a personal response
to Heidegger in France, or an invitation to a fellow artisan of reel and rod
to brave the rush of current to reach just *that* enticing pool. In any case,
Henry Bugbee's address will be first personal. In the philosophical explorations gathered here we find thought always issued from a heart immersed in vibrant life with others. *The Inward Morning* invites us to
traverse this wilderness, a generous space of listening, mutuality of address, and presence.

Wonder greets us through the pages of *The Inward Morning*. Like
great music, its scenes and voice strike home repeatedly: fresh, profound,

and irresistible. Without fanfare, it provides a "phenomenology" or evocation of the human place that stills our will to master all we face. Wilderness defines our place. There we find our lives in question, yet not in ways that undermine. Whatever urgency or danger lies at hand, the writer's voice remains affirmative, sustaining generosity, compassion and respect. Here we live and move and find our being among other creatures amidst the gifts of earth and sky. The place we can inhabit dawns as creation in its manifold simplicity. Bugbee's philosophical explorations parallel Heidegger's and equally fit the tradition of Wordsworth, Melville, and Emerson. *The Inward Morning* is "continental philosophy" in its conceptual and thematic bent, but it is also heir to Thoreau's essay "Walking" and a paradigm of lyric literary philosophy. Andrew Feenberg celebrates *The Inward Morning* as "the only truly original American existentialism," and to catch its open trans-Pacific bent (and defy our pigeonholes), aptly calls it "Zen Existentialism."[1] Bugbee sees his philosophy simply as "a meditation of the place."

A walking meditation of the place evokes wonders even as its words find their ground and stride:

> During my years of graduate study before the war I studied philosophy in the classroom and at a desk, but my philosophy took shape mainly on foot. It was truly peripatetic, engendered not merely while walking, but *through* walking that was essentially a *meditation of the place*. . . . I weighed everything by the measure of the silent presence of things, clarified . . . by the cry of hawks, solidified in the presence of rocks, spelled syllable by syllable by waters of manifold voice, and consolidated in the act of taking steps. (139)

Accounts of streams and snowfalls and life afloat in perilous storms begin to shape a philosophy of wilderness. This is not a wildness apart, however, as if we were safe spectators to a tumult *over there*. Wilderness is a horizon surrounding us, but more important it permeates our existence wherever we are. In some popular depictions wilderness is a distant forbidding Everest, meant to challenge reckless provocateurs or to prompt genuflection or fear among the faithful. But in Bugbee's sense, wilderness is not a wasteland where an ascetic negates temptation; nor is it a danger zone where heroes sharpen willful endurance in adversity. Wilderness lies close at hand and invites our participative response in terms that are everyday. Its vitality calls on what is creative and alive in us.

Wilderness is a place for affirmation and for acknowledging the wonders and the terrors of the commonplace and everyday—and, at times, of the exceptional. Not only is the wildness of hawks and trout and storms brought to our attention but also human fellowship at sea or in a city. And if *The Inward Morning* opens us to the wilderness of things about us, it also opens us to communion with past travelers, say, Spinoza or Lao-tzu, who provide counsel here in a present wild. Depicting the several strands of this "dispersed uncanny" opens us for responsible reply. Wilderness elicits listening and response, becomes an inward morning, a moment with creation.

The entries of *The Inward Morning* move from meditations on Thoreau or Marcel to thoughts on Zen. Heideggerian themes appear. Kierkegaard and Meister Eckhart and Sartre appear as well. Bugbee writes that philosophy can approach the status of a poem (33); and he avers that "Philosophy is not a making of a home for the mind out of reality. It is more like learning to leave things be: restoration in the wilderness, here and now" (155). These thoughts echo Heidegger's *Gelassenheit*. A "return to the things themselves" is a methodological imperative familiar to followers of Husserl, but for Bugbee it has the urgency of a moral, even a religious, imperative. For it is in nearness to the things of creation, including all living things, that we will find our way, our resolution, meaning, and conviction.

We might say that Bugbee sees human beings as alert among radiant particulars, infused by care, answerable to a call, and underway, richly immersed in practices and place. This defines a temporal and finite existence, through and through. We might suppose the influence of Heidegger's "Country Path" and *Being and Time*. Yet the journal was complete before Bugbee encountered Heidegger in writing or in person, and its themes come as much from Thoreau, Zen, and W. E. Hocking as from existentialists.[2]

Gabriel Marcel read parts of *The Inward Morning* in the early '50s. In August of 1955 Heidegger delivered *Was ist das—die Philosophie?* in Cerisy-la-Salle. Bugbee and Marcel attended, and afterward Marcel arranged an evening meeting. Perhaps curious to test a young Harvard professor's footing, Heidegger inquired how one *starts* to think profoundly. What occasion prompts philosophical reflection? He no doubt anticipated a flat American response. Yet he found his question returned in a Socratic reversal. Bugbee simply asked, echoing a Basho haiku, Could the sound of a fish leaping to a fly at dawn suffice?

The counter-question was Thoreauvian, but there was also an impish Zen-like ring to it. As a junior faculty member, it had been Henry Bugbee's task to shepherd D. T. Suzuki, the Japanese Zen Buddhist scholar, from talk to talk along the Northeast seaboard; later the two shared a summer on Long Island. Some years later still, Heidegger would fall in step with a Japanese scholar and acquaintance of Suzuki and publish an account of their dialogue.[3] Without alluding to American wilderness in particular, Heidegger finds thought called out as one traverses paths toward forest clearings where things stand forth in luminosity. Whether or not Heidegger would remember Bugbee's wilderness articulations, Suzuki knew the theme, especially the epiphany in *The Inward Morning* where a trembling line and leaping trout gather vivid definition blessed by stream and glistening pool (86).

The moment of the leaping fish, when meaning dawns, promises a place in and toward creation: but how can this be? The dawn we answer is surely underway, perhaps always already behind us, falling away just as we begin to grasp its shape. Could it be otherwise?

Let us note the mobile style of *The Inward Morning*. In contrast to an essay's argumentative drive toward closure, journal entries track the *flow* of reflection, perhaps by reenacting the motion attended to. Classics deliver results of thought, but also, with luck, thoughts as they emerge, before they are wrenched from movement into finished static format. This is thinking at the edge. Gilbert Ryle could suggest that the origin of our thought is "systematically elusive," as elusive as our selves. Catching thought-as-it-dawns is as tempting and impossible as jumping over our shadows. In *The Mystery of Being*, Marcel argues to the same effect. Yet *The Inward Morning* seems to accomplish what argument would say is unattainable: it seems to give us thought at the moment of its forging or appearing, to give us dawning meaning outright through the sinews of its passages. Like Thoreau who sounds the cosmos and himself through sounding Walden, we have writing that evokes a larger canvas through the particulars it displays. "I could wish for no more than to do justice to the instruction I have received from moving waters" (83). This is thought at the source and on the move.

In Alasdair MacIntyre's view, *The Inward Morning*'s unexpected success in presenting reality outright-and-in-process makes it a classic, a merit also earned by its ease in taking up the creative spirit of founding texts in our tradition. Exemplary text and interpreting-thinker emerge alive together, outside the warehouse where an inventory of concepts or doctrines or arguments accumulate on neatly labeled shelves. We glimpse a philosophical mind on the move through new terrain, finding its unique way with texts. Melville or Plato or Eckhart appear newly framed, their meaning etched as subtle as the coming of a soaring hawk or newly fallen snow. This matters when philosophy gets professionalized and dry and disappoints those who seek a living thought.

II

The sensibility so evident in this journal challenges those who embrace a professionalized, tightly disciplinary conception of respectable intellectual endeavor. On this latter view, philosophy should be straitlaced, scientific, and impersonal. Remarking in the early '60s on *The Inward Morning*, a writer in the *Journal of Philosophy* found the explorations "beautifully told" and "strangely moving," yet quite unacceptable: "I fear that the philosophic point of such a venture escapes me utterly: I should think that it is a function of art, poetry, and literature—or mescaline—to yield up a heightened awareness of objects, of other people, and of reality in general, and that philosophy has quite different aims."[4] To write of wilderness in a philosophic spirit was unthinkable in scholastic cloisters at the time. Bugbee's zest for thought found greater scope along the Clark Fork in Missoula. He moved West to relative academic obscurity for a better blend of essentials: open space for an unfenced range of thought; space where an unrestricted breadth of books could be encountered in the classroom; wild country at one's doorstep in mountains, streams, and dramatic seasonal change; a tempered human pace and graciousness.

Today the presumption that philosophy takes only one, clearly demarcated path is in decline. One can avow philosophy's common aims with art and literature. The distinguished philosopher Stanley Cavell writes across the cultural map, on Thoreau and Emerson as well as on Shakespeare, Kant, and cinema. Cavell was Henry Bugbee's student in the '50s. In interviews, he expresses the need to root philosophy in one's own inner dialogue, disregarding the tacit ban on personal writing that "yields up a heightened awareness" of things. Since Augustine and Plato, philosophy has been testament and confession, not just impersonal report. "In a sense," he confides, "to write your own words, to write your own inner voice, is philosophy. But the discipline most opposed to writing, and to life, is analytic philosophy. . . . This is what my first essays are about—the suppression of the human voice in academic, analytic philosophy."[5]

The Inward Morning suffered early academic neglect, even as it attained a sizable following underground, for its voice was singular and frankly anchored in the vivid particularities of the writer's lived experience. Bugbee reveals how "to write your own words, to write your own inner voice," day by day, and to know in your bones that this can be philosophy.

What leads a person to philosophy? Sometimes it will be a book. *Falling in Love with Wisdom* is a collection of short essays by American philosophers in which they recount how they were led to their vocation. Henry Bugbee's book is mentioned several times. The power of *The Inward Morning* to ignite and cultivate a philosophical bent is confirmed further and in great detail by the essays collected in *Wilderness and the Heart: Henry Bugbee's Philosophy of Place, Presence, and Memory.* In this collection, Albert Borgmann, author of *Crossing the Post-Modern Divide,* explores ways *The Inward Morning* might help us to envision communion across our differences, and Dan Conway writes on Bugbee and Thoreau. A foreword by Alasdair MacIntyre honors the journal as "an American classic." The novelist David James Duncan sketches several portraits of Bugbee in wilderness, a man whom W. V. Quine celebrates as "the ultimate exemplar of the examined life."

A catalog of topics to discuss in a full introduction to *The Inward Morning* would include the shape of meditative, "experiential" philosophy; the place of grief, compassion, and delight; wonder, technology, and daily work; and it would explore the difficult notions of finality and universality. Here I restrict myself to a few words on responsibility and vocation, on perishing, and on the recuperative idea of reality as vivid presence.

Responsibility is appropriately responding to claims on our comportment and being as persons with concern. Another's suffering calls on our compassion; your dignity claims my respect; a job can claim concerted effort; a sense of vocation can claim my long-term aspirations. As apt responsiveness to such claims, responsibility is as multifaceted as the claims it answers.

The Inward Morning evokes moments of address and answer, call and response. Bugbee recalls one such moment: a swollen river pulls a fellow camper from a pool along the river's bank, under a boom, and into the rush of smothering downstream rapids. The man is swept under an overhanging willow branch, and at the last moment he clutches at the trailing, tangled shoots and clings for life. The branch holds, the man holds, and he is swept in a wide arc toward the safety of a muddy bank. Arriving on the run, Bugbee grasps the hands of the man in stunned relief: the nearness of death, the strength found in a will to live, and a gratitude for the gift of willows registers and takes hold. As the moment of alarm recedes, Bugbee finds himself released into a world reborn at the instant it passed the brink of perishing: "Not a word passed between us. As nearly as I can relive the matter, the compassion I felt with this man gave way into awe and respect for what I witnessed in him. He seemed absolutely clean. In that steady gaze of his I met reality point blank, filtered and distilled as the purity of a man" (172).

Here responsibility is grounded in perception and our native sympathy, and it opens toward deep respect and awe. Perception aims at immediate features of a setting—say, the presence of danger—and also deepens in appreciation of "reality point blank," say, the profound presence of "the purity of a man." This appreciation of presence in its bearing on responsibility, sympathy, and respect is twofold. First, there is the particular man just rescued, his presence distilled to his unique singularity: just *this* man, at just *this* moment of encounter and desperate need. Second, there is his presence distilled to his essential universality: this man as reflecting persons in their vulnerability and "innocence," their "purity" *overall.*

This bivalence of radiating presence is rooted in particularities of person and place in such a way that singularity and universality do not undercut but enhance each other. The singularity of the endangered man in his setting does not diminish his standing as embodiment of a broader simplicity, innocence, and vulnerability of humankind; nor does his standing as embodiment of universal worth calling on our respect, compassion, and commitment to aid and comfort diminish his presence as a crystallized individual, here and now. An excess of meaning flows from and through the place, sweeping these potentially opposing vectors in an arc of revelation.

Now if this rich expression of responsibility held fast in the grip of reality resonates convincingly, its authority will rest on the speaker's testimony, on the accumulated respect we have gathered for a voice trued to its experience in a world we can recognize as our own. This authority is thoroughly first personal and does not rest on appeals to abstract reason or "the moral law." Of course interpretation can amplify the case, and our responses to this testimony can be closer or farther from the mark, better or worse. But the case to be interpreted lies before us as the givenness of reality, awaiting our reception. It is not to be mistaken for the production or projection of a detached, omniscient, or imperial self. Nor is it material for a disembodied reason to disassemble into lifeless components. The philosophical accounts of responsibility and compassion in *The Inward Morning* are not haunted by a wish to squeeze out a periodic table of their elements.

Henry Bugbee's work can be framed as a phenomenological project that renders the full reality of things. The appearances recorded are not "mere surfaces," deficient, or illusory. Reality does not lurk *behind* them; nor is the very *idea* of reality a hoax. Bugbee's evocations pay tribute to a "surplus" of reality *gifted in appearance*, even as that reality declares itself ever mobile and awaiting our response. The real is confronted head-on as value-laden (whether "positively" or "negatively"). This makes his moral philosophy both contextualist (we are always positioned, in a place and time, as *this* particular person, *here*) and also realist (we are not mainly in illusion, but confront real pain and are capable of true responsive sympathy). His ethical reflections also hold out for a "somewhat absolute" in experience: not some*thing*—a doctrine, say, or a piece of knowledge or algorithm determining right action (133). What is absolute is an experientially delivered *relational* bond: I find myself gifted with a solid fulcrum on which action and understanding can be raised. This is necessity, the basis for a moral "must" as well as for those inescapable promptings that trace personal vocation.

Alasdair MacIntyre remarks on Bugbee's excavation of necessity, of what we *must* do, as opposed to what we should or ought to do. He suggests that Bugbee's moral philosophy cuts a middle path between Hume and Kant.[6] Hume puts sympathy center stage but finds no deep ground for its necessity—it rests simply on our longing for social approval. Kant finds a deep ground for moral response but locates it, inappropriately, in reason's law-like necessity. Bugbee works to uncover an experiential ground of felt-compassion that carries the necessity not of law but of the heart—what in reality speaks to the person as a whole. Another's suffering is real and calls not just to reason but to the very springs of whole-hearted human responsiveness. An almost Buddhist sense of compassion is grounded in a necessity reminiscent of Spinoza.

If Bugbee can shore up human concern as responsiveness to others and the realities of our setting, then we have groundwork not just for ethics but for a deep environmental ethics.[7] Returning to things receptive to their meaning and cultivating a willingness to evoke those meanings in writing and speech make good sense philosophically, as Edmund Husserl insisted. But returning to things themselves is also a homecoming in a moral and spiritual sense. Responsiveness, responsibility in and to our setting, means restoration to our place as wilderness, where nature and her creatures become far more than a decorative setting or exploitable resource, and in terms of orientation for our lives, such responsiveness opens a place for acknowledging vocation.

A capacity to be called arises in attending to exemplary lives. Philosophical reflection merges with biographical absorption, say in the detail of Thoreau's or Gandhi's life. In *The Inward Morning* the writer himself becomes exemplary. Quine's tribute, that in his friend he finds "the ultimate exemplar of the examined life," dawns on us as apt just as we find the writer grappling to true his life to his reflective vocation in the wild.

We recall Henry Bugbee "weigh[ing] everything by the measure of the silent presence of things." This passage continues:

> It was in the fall of '41, October and November, while late autumn prevailed throughout the northern Canadian Rockies, restoring everything in that vast region to a native wildness. Some part of each day or night, for forty days, flurries of snow were flying. The aspens and larches took on a yellow so vivid, so pure and trembling in the air, as to fairly cry out that they were as they were, limitlessly. And it was there in attending to this wilderness, with unremitting alertness and attentiveness, yes, even as I slept, that I knew myself to have been instructed for life, though I was at a loss to say what instruction I had received. (139–40)

Intimations of vocation can arise from sources at some remove from natural wildness. "It was music which first awakened me to the need for reflection" (139). Yet even musical awakening places one in wilderness: "Wilderness is reality experienced as call and explained in responding to it absolutely" (128). There is a readiness to put one's life in question, to ask *Am I on track?* And there is a readiness to hear a summons to which one can authentically respond. Then we sense our lives as claimed, as called to a vocation, however difficult we may find the task of spelling out what such a claim might at last entail.

III

Listening responsiveness puts us at creation's dawn, full of life yet replete in the perishing of fluid streams and fading light, and in the perishing of our own robust momentum: "It seems to me that every time I am born, the wilderness is born anew; and every time I am born it seems to me that then, if ever, I could be content to die. Surely it is here that I must research for the meaning of coming to be and passing away" (129). As we gather meanings of our setting, our place, it is clear that we are not minds apart confronting a machine in motion or a frozen heap of substance. The real is an ebb and flow that implicates us in its liveliness and perishing. We open to things rising into life and passing from it, and reverence then gains hold in gratitude for a reality "old and new and ageless" (129).

This readiness to see things in their passing vulnerability marks a vantage far from cool detachment or presumed control. It reveals the writer in a distinctive light: "Two dear friends and teachers of mine have said to me, independently of one another: 'You have written here as a man might write only near the end of his life'" (11). This sense of death, he confides, has accompanied him since certain harrowing experiences in World War II, "Not in a way that saps life, but in a way that militates against putting off what one has to do" (11).

Death is a notable theme not just for Sartre or Kierkegaard or Heidegger, but for Plato and the Stoics, as well. Its office is to snap us alert to the present, to the inevitability of our passing. Wittgenstein carried his *Tractatus* in his military knapsack through trench warfare, but his early philosophy denies our urge to speak about life-and-death. Bugbee's journal also matures through war, but in his case awareness of the finite readies the soul for praising recognition of things in their living and their dying. As he has it, "The very perishing of what we love might be an essential moment in the clarification of the worthiness of love of that which perishes." And he continues: "There is weeping and gnashing of teeth; there is stony impassivity; there is ribaldry, and vacuous staring. There is confusion. But there is pure gentleness, and it is in this vein that perishing speaks" (138).

In their praise and recognition, I sense that Quine and others, whose "official" philosophy hardly resembles Henry Bugbee's, are implicitly acknowledging the more-than-academic reach displayed in passages like these. If Quine finds in his friend "the ultimate exemplar of the examined life," it must be in part because Bugbee is attuned to the elusive stream of life-and-death in which a philosophical conversation will move. He pays tribute to a thoughtfulness cognizant of risk and perishing. Such praise pays tribute to thought that gives life density and direction. Following such thought is like traversing an expanse "as vast as the Pacific and the music of Handel" (138). It finds us in wonder, a wilderness; and however tested there, it can issue in compassion and leave us ineluctably alive.

The Inward Morning prompts us to amplify rather than deconstruct or undermine the meaning of our place. The springs of philosophical impulse are completed in a sensibility where arguments play a secondary role: meaning supervenes to quiet minds all too ready to be adversarial. Thus the grand contrasts or options of the philosophic canon—pragmatism vs. idealism, realism vs. anti-realism, absolutism vs. relativism, mystic vs. secularist, monist vs. pluralist, even philosopher vs. littérateur—recede in urgency, cease to be the exclusive levers on which the enterprise is raised. Yet as my colleague Dan Conway wryly observes: "The literalness and boundary-bending nature of *The Inward Morning* can be related to some very traditional philosophical aims and objectives." The evocation and analysis of responsibility makes this clear. And his phenomenology of our place as wilderness not only underlines our embodied placement: it evokes the "ongoingness" of the life of things that mark the place through which we move. This walking in wilderness is participative, for the place we *live* will continually be completed by our responsiveness: it is not some static dot on an abstract map, but depends for its profile on our responsiveness, a life undertaken with others in a creation that is emerging, that is underway.

Our participation is political, but also experiential, reflective, and cultural. As we navigate our tangled paths, the journal's evocation of wilderness seems especially apt. Like much contemporary "postmodern" thought, *The Inward Morning* challenges standard views of agency, meaning, reason, and responsibility, but brute critique is not its final object. Reality is revealed to be affirmed. Beyond cultural chatter and disciplinary conflict there are familiar everyday experiences to be attended to: of love and work, of grief and terror, wonder and celebration. In the work of poets like Rilke and Dickinson, of thinkers like Rousseau and Lao-tzu, and of philosophers like Spinoza, Heidegger and Thoreau, we find these experiences strong and in their element, consummately voiced, even for the first time discovered. *The Inward Morning* amplifies and underwrites the presence of the traditions these names define as a resource for survival. And as a philosophy of wilderness, of place, it sets hubris straight, allowing meanings to dawn toward the listening responsive self. Such an "experiential philosophy" is post-empiricist yet fully realist. Not unlike our contemporaries Alasdair MacIntyre or Martha Nussbaum, Henry Bugbee shows us how philosophy consorts with poetry, biography, and history to unveil our worlds, configuring them narratively and imaginatively. His journal anticipates comparative East-West philosophy and religion in its attention to doctrines of "no-self" and karma as well as Zen, and it is allied to phenomenology and continental philosophy as it intersects American philosophy in the tradition consolidated by Emerson and Thoreau, and sustained in the work of John Muir, Aldo Leopold, Rachel Carson, Wallace Stegner and Gary Snyder.[8] At so many levels, and unerringly, *The Inward Morning* treads our tangled cultural paths.

There were interludes in Paris and Pennsylvania before Bugbee found home along the Clark Fork and Blackfoot in Missoula. In Montana he found solitude and inspiration where teaching and wilderness, swift water and reflection, could mingle, each a worthy measure of the other. Here is wilderness that bespeaks Spinoza's divinity-and-world, Suzuki's flashing Zen epiphanies, and Melville's dark sea and shipwreck. It is wilderness that embraces Marcel's availability to necessary others and Wordsworth's walking, recollective meditations of the place.

It is Christmas as I write these words. Sunlight sparkles through bare and feathery birch limbs, now drenched mysteriously by memories of New England snows. And I hear or see in all immediacy a passage from this journal. It is fellowship at dusk among a crew underway in the Pacific, caught up in war but for the moment caught up in song. "In the closing light of that day, riding to the endless swells, they sang the song of men in our position. And it was Christmas in the wilderness" (71). Like Odysseus, each was far from home, in danger, and full of longing. Yet amidst that awful incongruity, time opened up for thankful memory and melody. I think of him today more than fifty years since that wartime sea-watch. Among family, friends, and the massive Bitterroots where he has taught and fished and climbed for years, he is at home, looking out on falling snow, still against the mountains.

There is the book of tradition, of doctrine and argument, open for any to engage or rebuke; as inheritance it presents a raft of problems to take out, wrestle with, and make our own. But there is also the more private daybook of a philosopher's inspiration and advance, the record of philosophy becoming a vocation for a writer here and now; as testimony it opens uncharted space—or simple sudden spots—where self and world are found. *The Inward Morning* gathers generous worlds of inspiration and advance. This is Henry Bugbee's gift.

Edward F. Mooney

NOTES

1. *Wilderness and the Heart: Henry Bugbee's Philosophy of Place, Presence, and Memory*, ed. Edward F. Mooney (Athens: University of Georgia Press, 1999).

2. Hocking was Husserl's first American student and is the author of *The Meaning of God in Human Experience* (New Haven: Yale University Press, 1911). Marcel dedicated his *Metaphysical Journal* to Hocking.

3. Martin Heidegger, "A Dialogue on Language," in *On the Way to Language*, trans. Peter Hertz (New York: Harper and Row, 1971).

4. George Pitcher, review of *Essays in Philosophy*, edited by the Philosophy Department, Pennsylvania State University, *Journal of Philosophy* (1964): 111–12.

5. Quoted in Giovanna Borradori, *The American Philosopher* (Chicago: University of Chicago Press, 1994), p. 126.

6. Alasdair MacIntyre, foreword to *Wilderness and the Heart*.

7. Bugbee's sense of experiential rapport with things, as it contrasts with a strictly empiricist notion of experience, is discussed by Andrew Feenberg, "Zen Existentialism: Bugbee's Japanese Influence," in *Wilderness and the Heart*. The sense of experience delivering finality is the topic of Albert Borgmann's essay, "Finality and Universality: Bugbee, Heidegger, and Modernity," explored in the same volume. Several essays mark the connections with recent environmental philosophy.

8. Thoreau is undergoing a minor revival in academic philosophy, thanks in part to Cavell's *The Senses of Walden* (San Francisco: Northpoint Press, 1981), which places Thoreau with Wittgenstein and Heidegger. Bugbee's reflection can facilitate the links between Thoreau (as a representative American philosopher) and continental styles of thought.

PREFACE

A life's work takes shape slowly. There is a periodicity about it. At intervals of years there comes a real show-down. Then one discovers, within the scope of his powers at the time, what he has been about.

These pages represent such a period for me. Since they rounded out in the fall of 1953, the period which they represent has assumed its place more unmistakably in the rhythm of years. I could not then appreciate as I have come to do that they would have to stand or fall pretty much as they were written, and why this should be so.

In the first place, I have tried to rework the material here presented. I could see that it left much to be desired. After I had culled out all that seemed irrelevant to the basic undertaking, there were still 'the good days' and 'the bad days.' I could imagine many questions which might be justly raised about my meaning, when it remained far from clear in my own mind. And since the themes which occupied me in these pages undergo as much reflective analysis as they do, why not organize at least some of the ideas which are recurrently developed into a more systematic form? Why not cut free from the bad days and supply a better substitute for the continuity of those days in the overall task? Over and over I tried to act on such considerations as these. And each time the heart went out of the ideas themselves. They lost their actual exploratory cast. I found I was in danger of betraying the very undertaking in which experience yielded them their measure of meaning and support. Finally, I have come closest to establishing continuity with the work of these pages in the interim when I have forgotten about them, when I have worked from where I am— as I did in writing them.

I can therefore say that subsequent trial has confirmed the intimations on which I resolved to act from the outset of this work.

As I would put it now, the guidance of meditation, of the themes received in meditation, is the fundamental feature of the work; and the themes of meditation live a life of their own, perhaps wiser than one knows in their advent and departure, in the things they gather to themselves as relevant to their formation, in the memories with which they visit one and establish their own concrete meaning. It was my work to attend upon such themes, in the very rhythm of daily life; to follow them where they might lead; not to put them off when they came to me, not to bid them stay beyond their actual departure; and not to try to make more of them than I presently could.

The present day—that is the dwelling of meditative thought. Consequently this work is in journal form. Not because it is a philosophical notebook or diary; it is neither of these. It is basically a work which required to be done within the day, from the actual human stance which the day might afford, whatever that day might bring.

And how is this daily character of meditation to be accounted for? Meditation is of the day precisely as the human will is. For meditation is the thoughtful reckoning of the will with its own life: Its concern is that of truth underlying human decision. Cut off from the central nerve of responsible being, the themes of meditation fall dead. My task has been that of overcoming such abstraction, to accomodate the life of spirit with all the mind. These pages may serve as a record of such a tendency of thought, and they may testify with some accuracy to the unpredictable alternation between bondage and freedom in which the ambiguity of the human condition is lived, but now and again resolved.

What I have called finality proves to be the unifying theme of the work. By finality I intend the meaning of reality as realized in true decision. The vein in which it comes to us is the vein of wonder, of faith, of certainty. It is the ground of ultimate human concern with which the will is informed. It comes clearest in every unique deed of purest generosity, in which a man gives of himself without stint and with all care. In this disciplined liberality is true freedom.

The term 'finality' seems to me just: It stands for what is first

*the will → might be connected
* to the "central nerve" of
responsibility/responsiveness
— might mean SlE for *preface* 11
freedom/freedom of the will
— might mean self for freedom of the will

and last with us. It is redolent of all first and last words—words in which human destiny comes to ultimate articulation: words such as Augustine's "life of our lives," spoken as he spoke them; yes, and the simple pair, life and death, as they are ever harbored, tremulously unspoken, behind all that we say. The tone of a final word is the tone of reality as definitively given. Accordingly finality must harbor all that requires expression as genuine in human life, including all manner of contraries, such as those our evaluations so often express, as in speaking of good days and bad days. That meaning of reality which is final and decisive comes to us as redeeming, authoritatively demanding, and promising. A final word cannot be the mere contrary and correlative of others. It must be a word in which all words come to a unity of affirmation. It must be found anew, again and again, as just that word which a man can give now, steeped in all that is unknown and cannot be known in our lives. It cannot be made captive in terms themselves, or in any of the cumulative resources at our disposal. It comes to meet us in our acceptance of the frontier of our daily lives.

Two dear friends and teachers of mine have said to me, independently of one another: "You have written here as a man might write only near the end of his life." Since certain episodes in World War II that has been my sense of life. The present since then has always been close to death; not in a way that saps life, but in a way that militates against putting off what one has to do. Nothing short of eternal meaning can settle the concern of man in whom time has exacted something decisive in life. Even if he only comes up with a stammered word, it better be a word that he means. That others have spoken will not relieve him of the answer he must make, nor will it provide him with his word. It must come straight from him, for all that may help him. As he finds it, he will discover that he, and all beings with him, are blessed. As Spinoza suggests: The true good is discovery of the union between oneself and all beings. Thus the meaning of a final word is universal; it is uniquely spoken, or not at all; and it is never said once for all. For the meaning of reality is not independent of the life of the will. In this life we all move from day to day. The more faithfully we do so, the more ours is an eternal

*note: will = might be responsible for acting
that require decisions

present, and the more we can share in testifying that this is indeed *our* life.

Our basic thoughts come naturally in the first person plural. Their title to do so is to be found in the fulfillment of a common trust.

H. G. Bugbee, Jr.

Pittsburgh, July 28, 1956

* "This is it!"
— This is the present
moment → deal w/
it, accept it, respond
to it

ACKNOWLEDGMENTS

First and foremost I must speak of my debt to Gabriel Marcel. It pervades the pages of this work. The many explicit references to his thought, where time and again things he has said slipped into place, only partially convey the nature and extent of my debt to him. My intense interest in Marcel's writings was the natural consequence of the fact that he spoke to my condition. So much that I had felt began to take on clearer meaning in encounter with his thought. Not only did I find much of his 'vocabulary of reflection' most apt, but still more the spirit and the style of philosophy which had been growing on me found affinity, impetus, and substantiation in interplay with the firm and flexible sinews of his thought. Reading his works assumed the character of reciprocal communication. And Marcel helped me to find my own voice, to form thoughts as I had to form them. He instilled in me courage and patience to go ahead on my own. At the same time, the more the themes of my thought underwent independent development, the more they led me back to his work with fresh interest and understanding.

It was a decisive episode of my life to be able to join M. Marcel in August of 1955 and to confirm with him in detail the mutuality of our work. Since that meeting he has accomplished what I had been unable to approach myself in repeated efforts: a clear and accurate summation of the basic themes of these pages, as set forth in the Introduction. For this, and for the deeply generous and faithful friendship of which it is but one expression, I feel a gratitude continuous with that sense of life with which these pages culminate.

A particularly substantial debt to three other men is also embedded in this work.

The wilderness theme and its human significance represent an orientation which I have shared with John M. Anderson since those days in the late Thirties when we began to walk and talk it out together in the Berkeley Hills. He has continually caught the drift of my thought over the intervening years, brought it out with penetrating criticism, and unerringly suggested things of which I have needed to take account. His help and his own thought were of major consequence to me in carrying out this exploration.

Since 1934, when I became a pupil of T. M. Greene's, his advice and backing have been a boon to me at turning points of my life and work. To Ted Greene, and to W. V. Quine, I owe much of the courage of that conviction upon which I set out in 1953 to follow up the initial stage of this exploration, instead of taking another teaching position, which would have been the surer thing to do. Each of these men in a different way caught the necessity of a venture in which I was then relatively far from clear, and confirmed my belief in it. And they were behind me right through it. To Van Quine, as Chairman of the Harvard Philosophy Department at the time, to my other former colleagues in the department, and to the appointing members of the Harvard Corporation, I owe the appointment to the George Santayana Fellowship for 1953-54, on which the bulk of these pages were written.

Among former Radcliffe and Harvard students to whom I owe so much, I should like to mention my specific indebtedness to three: to Cynthia Green, for bringing to my attention the significance of Proust's "involuntary recall;" to Richard Gotshalk for quickening the appreciation of Spinoza which spurred these reflections; and to Robert Langston, for key insight in approaching the philosophic import of tragedy.

For reading and discussion of the manuscript of which I have tried to take account in editing it, I would like to thank Professors George Burch, W. E. Hocking, N. A. Nikam, and D. T. Suzuki, as well as three readers whose names are not known to me.

I am grateful to Chatham College for a subsidy which enabled me to confer with M. Marcel prior to his writing of the Introduction, and to Melle. Danièle Baule-Vastel for her patient collaboration in translating the Introduction.

Finally, there were three persons who uniquely shared the life with me from which these pages come: Daphne, my wife, and her family, Mr. and Mrs. Marcus J. Clark. For the four of us it was a common venture under one roof, and only as such could it have been done. In a special sense this work is ours.

For permission to quote copyrighted material I am indebted to the following: Bald Eagle Press for permission to quote from John M. Anderson: *The Individual and The New World;* Constable and Co. for permission to quote from Frankfurter and Jackson: *Letters of Sacco and Vanzetti;* the Eastern Buddhist Society for permission to quote from D. T. Suzuki: *Zen Buddhism and Its Influence on Japanese Culture;* Harcourt Brace and Co. for permission to quote from T. S. Eliot: *The Complete Poems and Plays,* 1909-1950; Harper and Bros. for permission to quote from R. M. Blakney: *Meister Eckhart: A Modern Translation;* The Journal of Philosophy and the author for permission to quote Donald C. Williams: "Realism;" Princeton University Press for permission to quote from Walter T. Stace: *Time and Eternity;* Random House for permission to quote from William Faulkner: *The Faulkner Reader;* Regnery Co. for permission to quote from Gabriel Marcel: *The Mystery of Being* and *Homo Viator;* Rider and Co. for permission to quote from D. T. Suzuki: *Living by Zen;* University of Chicago Press for permission to quote from Paul Tillich: *Systematic Theology;* Yale French Studies for permission to use material previously published in *Yale French Studies.*

INTRODUCTION
to the 1958 Edition

After weighing my words carefully, I do not hesitate to say that my encounter with the thought and personality of Henry Bugbee will prove to have been a noteworthy event in my life. This encounter is reminiscent of my discovery more than forty years ago of the major work of another American, W. E. Hocking, to whom, with Henri Bergson, I was led to dedicate my *Metaphysical Journal.*

When I read Hocking's *The Meaning of God in Human Experience* for the first time, I had as yet published almost nothing. This book helped to turn me in the direction of a new realism, very different indeed from traditional realism. Between these two dates, 1913-1955, the bulk of my work has taken place. Though I feel sure of the similarity of the two encounters setting off this period for me, the second one presents some rather unique features which I would like to stress.

I am well aware that Henry Bugbee will be inclined to protest, with the admirable modesty characteristic of him: "It was a one-way encounter," he may say, "in which I was the one to benefit by the invaluable confirmation and stimulating suggestions which I derived from the writings of the French philosopher." I would reply, however, that there is no one-way encounter, or more exactly, that an encounter must be reciprocal in coming to fullness of realization. Such is precisely the case here.

As I said to Bugbee during our long and absorbing talks at Chateau de Cerisy-la-Salle in August 1955, the thing that I find especially striking about his Journal is the extent to which his thought is rooted in absolutely personal and authentic experience; experience as different from mine as it could possibly be, since it is that of a man who has been steeped in the Far West and decisively influenced by his three years at sea during World War II. It would be absurd for me to deny, of course, that my writings have furnished him with some useful supporting considerations or even more. But what interests me in this connection is the impact which the encounter with his thought may have upon mine, in return.

More often than not, I must confess, I suffer a bit in reading the expositions others have presented of what I would rather not call "my philosophy." Not that they are inaccurate; but they do not enrich me very much. In reading them I have the feeling of swallowing something I have already digested. Exactly the opposite obtains in this case. Would it do to say that in this Journal I come upon my thought renewed, as if it had been dipped in some sort of fountain of youth? No, this mode of expression doesn't suit me at all. It puts me in the position of an owner, one who might come back to his own house, for example, and find it renovated by some inspired tenant. Yet I can hardly overemphasize the fact that the categories of possession cease to be relevant in a case like this.

In order to express the matter properly one would have to invoke an entirely different kind of metaphor. I would much rather say that Henry Bugbee and I inhabit the same land, but that it is a land with which neither of us has any proprietary connection. Perhaps we could add that this land we inhabit is benefitted by a certain climate, or better still, that it is illumined by a light of its own. The American philosopher and I attempt to orient ourselves by that light. Since this is a spiritual light, however, it is to be noted that we do not occupy fixed and distinct positions which might be plotted on a well-defined map. The truth is considerably more subtle, and more conducive, I would add, to a joy in which we can both intimately participate. Thanks to the incalculable gift of communication I am able to espouse this point of view which did not coincide with my own to begin with. Let us avoid being taken in by spatial metaphors at this point, however. There can be no question of tracing out a certain route which I might adopt and follow in my turn. A sketch of this sort would inevitably turn out to be an abstraction, while what we have to deal with here is a spiritual itinerary.

Once I happened to visit a museum with a friend more versed in painting than I. His remarks, his very presence, keyed the sensibilities with which I was able to see. I saw more, and I saw in a different way. My capacity to perceive was deeply enlivened in proximity with a more experienced companion in whom I recognized something wholly different from a mere claim 'to know about these things', namely, a real affinity with the paintings we were regarding. Nor does this mean that on my part I simply identified myself with him. To shift the image once again, the accord which arose between us might be compared to that between musical instruments; and though I speak of instruments, it would be better to think of instrumentalists. The first violinist in a quartet is not wrapped up in himself as he plays. A kind of interior reference to one another obtains between him and his partners. In some way he *is* his partners, yet he is inalienably himself; and he is completely the latter only in that he is also the former. In this situation we pass beyond the sphere of relations, and the beautiful German word *Bezug* becomes manifestly appropriate in the sense imparted to it by Rilke in the *Elegies*.

These images may serve to elucidate the deep sense of an encounter which may prove to be of some import, and of an import that I would speak of as transcending both of us more than as it might touch either of us personally, either myself in these last years of mine or even Bugbee.

And now I must try to disengage some themes which may be helpful in guiding the reader into this book, although it is not an easy undertaking.

Let us begin with a question: Why is the work in the form of a journal? Is this form accidental? Might the author have worked out his thought in the form of a treatise? I do not think so. On the contrary, the journal form seems to me directly related to what is most original in the thought itself. I reject as specious the interpretation that Henry Bugbee might have been merely following my example. When I began to keep my own journal in 1913, moreover, I thought of it as no more than a collection of notes in preparation for a systematic work. It seems to me of paramount interest to look for the internal reasons which brought Henry Bugbee to work out his thought in daily form. We must keep it well in mind, too, that this thought is unfolding to itself and that the possible reader does not basically figure in this.

On the very first page (August 26, 1952) the author states that he must find a way of expressing what demands of him his unending research, what underlies this activity of turning over his experience, so like the tilling of soil. The moments when an idea worth considering would occur to him always impressed him by their suddenness. "Insight is earned, to be sure, but it is not steered." It must find its appropriate form, and for this a sustained attention is necessary; otherwise insight would remain sporadic and ephemeral. The attention accorded to insight, however, cannot consist in casting it in a pre-established mould. It is quite possible that one may lose the original element which one seeks to express, precisely in attempting to render insight in the form of a theoretical position. Referring to his work of preceding years, the author concludes that the important thing is for him to set down day by day the minute inflections of his thought, the ideas as they come to him, without concerning himself about adding them up, or even about whether they will come to a sum and form a coherent whole. Let it flow, he says; if there can be a concrete philosophy, give it a chance without rushing it. And if warrant is to be sought for this flowing of thought, it lies in the very way in which experience is charged with authentic meaning. There is nothing in the flow of concrete meaning itself which can be settled in advance or realized through some sort of arrangement.

A philosophy governed by such a sense of fluency cannot be like solving a puzzle from a collection of ready-made pieces lying before one. "It will be more like the clarification of what we know in our bones." (August 27, 1952). Bugbee does not proceed, therefore, as do those professionals who insist upon the necessity of starting from utterly clear ideas and following an equally clear method of inquiry: ". . . the reflection worth indulging doesn't know where it's going, just as the life that is lived underlies anything the individual is able to patent for himself . . . if philosophical truth is engendered in depth, we must not expect it to come to light except out of relative obscurity." Later on (August 7, 1953) he says, "It is as if experience must continue underground for some time before it can emerge as spring water, clear, pure, understood. And reflection is a trying to remember, a digging that is pointless if it be not digging down directly beneath where one stands, so that the waters of his life may re-invade the present moment and define the meaning of both."

Here the author is indeed close to the decisive experience of Proust, to which he makes explicit reference. Yet Proust remained attached to a tradition that was basically nominalistic, and this sometimes involved him in the very significant inconsistency of assuming that his research was concerned with the discovery of certain "general ideas," understood in the manner of the Empiricists. It is clear that nothing of this sort obtains in the present work.

Bugbee carefully distinguishes an *experiential* philosophy — just the sort of philosophy he is concerned to work out — from empiricism in its usual connotation. He suggests the character of an experiential philosophy extremely clearly in connection with the opening passage of Plato's *Republic,* and particularly the stand there set forth by Cephalus. Here is a man whose life is drawing near its close. Bugbee asks (October 15, 1952), "What in the life of a man can place his life in such a light that he can live his last moments in the most profound *affirmation?*" (Italics mine). In other words, what may be forthcoming from a life that has been lived which can substantiate an essential affirmation? Bugbee says on the same date that the whole drift of his positive thought has been permeated by belief in the possibility of such an affirmation; and that he has been concerned above all to understand how an unconditional affirmation is possible, and how it may be responsibly articulated. "I know that in speaking to one another," he writes — meaning oneself and any other — "we sometimes can and do bear witness to that which cannot play us false, and in so doing may help one another in our hours of weakness. This seems to me the ultimate form of help implicit, at least, in all actions of purest service and generosity." This is the most lucid possible testimony to the fact that our lives do not necessarily involve betrayal of our most earnest intent and that the last word does not lie with absurdity. One might even say that we understand reality — in the full sense of understanding — in so far as we can answer with utter clarity for the possibility of unconditional affirmation. But the

ambiguity of our situation is evident in the fact that this very possibility can be systematically ignored or even denied.

In the continuation of these important remarks on October 18,
1952, Bugbee writes that retrospective or recollective reflection may
be interpreted as a kind of interior rallying bound up with our establishing ourselves on a basis on which we may stand firm. But this
basis cannot be artificially produced. It can only be revealed through
a process of disclosure which is precisely experiential, because there
is nothing here resembling the discovery of an empirical characteristic
of an object. This disclosure is of such fundamental import that to
deny its possibility would be to deny the very possibility of philosophy.
Such a denial, moreover, is typical of positivism — of scientism. According to the latter, our thought is either answerable to a process of
observation or reducible to the elements of an abstract system, and
any other mode of thought would be vague, insubstantial, indeed
devoid of authentic meaning.

As opposed to this positivism, Bugbee affirms as fundamental that
there is "somewhat absolute" in our experience, coining an Emersonian
expression. The constant burden of his thought is to elucidate this
"somewhat." We need to work out the meaning of this affirmation
without defining it in a way that would alter its singular character.
When we have its meaning more clearly in mind, we will understand
how it is that the thought of the philosopher is trained upon wonder
and certainty, those two themes which can only be approached in
their intimate connection with one another.

It is plain to begin with that the words "something absolute"
would not do at all. For the "somewhat absolute" here in question
cannot be assimilated to the conception of a thing. The author says
that certainty with respect to it is not a certainty *of*, or a certainty
that: and this, I would add, is because in the last analysis it is not a
certainty which we could have, or possess. I do not think it would
be a mistake to say that certainty is a mode of being rather than of
having. For his part Bugbee remarks (August 28, 1952) that it is a
basis for action rather than a terminus of endeavour. "So far as we
are sensitive to the absoluteness of our situation, we live in the dimension of meaning which is the depth of our experience — we live

in eternity. Certainty involves that simplicity which is true to being in a situation that is absolute and registered as such in depth."

Here we come to the heart of Bugbee's experience and thought, and it would be well to pause over it since the language seems to me to leave something to be desired for the sake of complete clarity. What exactly is meant by an absolute situation? Contrary to what one might believe, it is a strictly concrete situation, and no question as to its actuality could cast doubt upon it: The situation of a sailor aboard ship who must reckon with the elements would be to the point. Any interposition of questions or doubts at this juncture would be not only superfluous but misleading, as irrelevant as it would be for the sailor himself to be suspended in reasoning about the conditions which led to his embarkation. The situation is at hand in its unassailable authority.

Now it is in the terms of just such a situation as this that we must think of the human condition. Pascal's "we are embarked" ineluctably comes to mind, and Heidegger's "being-in-the-world" may occur to one, too. The fact that must be stressed is that this situation cannot be articulated in naturalistic or objective terms. Strictly speaking it is not even describable, since it is the point of departure from which any description becomes possible. One must add, I think, that this situation is constitutive for man, and even that it imbues man with his essential humanity. Approached in this way, the centrality of wonder becomes intelligible. But wonder needs to be carefully distinguished from curiosity, and it is possible that the Aristotelian idea of wonder involves some confusion between the two. In Aristotle's account it seems as if wonder would be allayed when the philosopher comes to comprehend those things which initially evoked his wonder as explicable in principle. I must note, however, that in his discussions at Cerisy during August 1955, Heidegger considered wonder a lasting element in the climate of Aristotle's thought.

As Bugbee sees the matter, explanation cannot allay wonder. Explanation is basically an endless process, and the human spirit is committed to the condition of a wanderer to the extent that it is taken up with the task of explanation. But wonder is not concerned with the *explicable* as such. In wonder the presence of things takes root in us and reality assumes a meaning for us which cannot be reductively assimilated to any sort of process of explanation. In this perspective man must appear to himself as an exile for whom there can be no settled abode (something which would not be true if explanation could be exhaustive even in principle). Of course we can readily enough deny this and represent to ourselves some features of our situation as if they were unconditional and some procedures for dealing with it as if they were patented. Or on the contrary, we may open ourselves to the meaning of a *life in the wilderness* and await with patience the founding of that assurance which may overtake us in the course of our wanderings and make us at home in this condition.

In this way we may understand that wonder contains the germ of philosophical truth, that is to say — of fundamental truth. But the openness of the person in his entirety to that truth is a basic implication of this conception of wonder. We may observe that Bugbee is here very near Heidegger once again, for this openness seems in close agreement with the *Erschlossenheit* of the philosopher of *Sein und Zeit*. Opposed to this openness are contraction, rigidity, inertia, which correspond to the moments of our philosophical failure. Thus one can see how wonder can deepen into certainty without lapse or deviation; how the presence of things can reveal its own meaning; and how philosophy is centrally the experiential discernment of all this.

We can now understand why what Bugbee calls "immersion" cannot be separated from commitment. This connection is of the utmost importance, for it alone can assure the proper ethical bearing of what might be interpreted at first glance as a pure mysticism of presence. Here the articulation of certain concrete experiences, involving both work and play, is at least as instructive as are the allusions to the mysticism of Meister Eckhart or to Zen Buddhism. These experiences and the allusions together form a living tissue from which they could not be dissected without a complete loss of the profound import of this entire research.

"I think of immersion as a mode of living in the present with complete absorption; one has the sense of being comprehended and sustained in a universal situation." (September 23, 1952). But we must take care not to interpret this absorption as if it involved contraction or fixation of attention. The present which is lived in absorption cannot be conceived as a succession of discrete moments. On the contrary it expands into spatial and temporal distances. "It is as if one's perception of everything distinct were engaged in alignment with a center from which one moves to greet each thing knowingly. There is a continuing passage from thing to thing in which a kind of sameness or continuity of meaning deepens, ever confirmed and ever relevant." But this is no process of generalization; things themselves become meaningful. And here Bugbee compares our minds to resilient gourds dancing on the waves. When he speaks of this flow as resolving our mental fixations, he seems to me very close to Bergson. He goes on to say that metaphysics must rise with the dawn — the dawn of things themselves, but adds that this dawn is also that of action, and precedes the diurnal world of morality and immorality. Our reasons for acting, whatever they may be, cannot substitute for true affirmation in its depth. This is not to suggest the slighting of reasons which we may have for acting, but rather to point out that these reasons are derivative and bring us only abstract versions of a responsibility in depth from which the philosopher needs to derive his own fundamental impulse. And the term 'responsibility' used in this connection must be grasped in its literal signification of capacity to respond.

"It is of the essence of authentic commitment that it be grounded behind the intellectual eye and not merely in a demonstrable basis which we can get before us." (October 8, 1952). Thus we could not obtain control of the ground of our actions; and this is to say that our part consists in being at the disposal of the source of unconditional demand; it is not at our disposal. This point is obscured in the thought of Kant by his emphasis on autonomy. Explicitly referring to my own criticism of the complementary ideas of autonomy and heteronomy, Bugbee raises the question whether the term "theonomy' suggests a mode of thought which would transcend and resolve the opposition between these complementary ideas. Resuming one of his basic themes near the end of the work, he says (October 23, 1953), "I think of reality as ever questioning, calling upon us, as if in syllables shaped from a mouth, which issue almost soundlessly. In a noisy soul this call is utterly ignored. But as true stillness comes upon

us, we hear, we hear; and we learn that our whole lives may have
the character of finding that anthem which would be native to our
tongue, and which alone can be the true answer for each of us to the
questioning, the calling, the demand for ultimate reckoning which
devolves upon us."

Starting from an experience quite different from mine and un-
deniably more intimately involved with nature, the American philosopher comes into harmony with what I have formerly written of contemplation. Perhaps he notes more emphatically than I have, however, that in the profound stillness of contemplation it is the full honesty of the human spirit which comes into being. Here we are at the
center upon which all of the author's steps tend to converge, and one
could speak of them as so many concrete approximations through
which definite realization accrues to an affirmation that might seem
far from clear at first.

The point in the last analysis is that true experience is to be
realized, contrary to any philosophy which would appropriate experience as if it could be taken for granted and treated as a ready-made
possession of the mind (let alone a philosophy which would represent
experience materialistically in the manner of Epicurus and his followers, or attempt to give an account of experience in the categories
of traditional idealism). It seems to me necessary to insist on the fact
that we are here in the presence of a philosophy of the open air,
something which could be said of Heidegger's philosophy as well: To
ascertain this one has only to turn to a work like the *Feldweg*. There
is an irreducible opposition between a philosophy of this sort and that
of a Sartre, which I have formerly characterized as showing us the
world viewed from a café. Actually, our deepest thought must be
sensitized to an unobtrusive appeal which certainly seems to emanate
from nature, but without our slipping into naturalism; for in spite of
appearances to the contrary, naturalism rests on abstractions — those
very abstractions by which one is inevitably taken in if one postulates
the primacy of the object. Like Heidegger, Bugbee assuredly refuses
to accept the current dichotomization of fact and value as ultimate.
And without doubt the necessity of transcending this dichotomy is
implied in any ontology deserving the name; as far as ontology is

concerned, the recent philosophy styled 'theory of value' represents something comparable to a degradation.

It will also be evident that the American philosopher especially emphasizes the term 'givenness.' This word ordinarily taken in such a feeble sense is restored here to its fundamental significance. The given is truly a gift. Only reality is given, but it is fully given only in the act by which things are received and welcomed as presences. The author speaks to the same effect elsewhere of "the sacrament of co-existence" — he is very close to Claudel here — illuminating the relevance of a reverential attitude to things, and not only to persons. (August 21, 1953). Precisely because things are given such an attitude is possible with regard to them; the attitude is itself something like a thanksgiving. Along such lines as these one might expect to appreciate the metaphysical ground of a certain kind of artistic creation: I am thinking of Chardin, of Cézanne, as well as of Corot. A philosophy like this, in its passionate concern with experience, might even be said to carry experience to a point of incandescence. In more abstract language, it could be said to restore experience to a dimension aptly called that of transcendence.

The pages in which the author recalls his life aboard a minesweeper during the war in the Pacific — so much akin to some of the writings of Saint-Exupéry — serve to bring out vividly some considerations which might be missed in their vital import on a superficial reading. Above all the meaning proper to necessity is revealed in this material: "You do not choose to be absorbed into the life of the ship at sea, you do not choose your tasks. You become steeped in them, perhaps even in spite of yourself; and the round of definite tasks becomes something from which you can hardly withhold yourself . . . you are not working on a clear choice of means to some ultimate desideratum which explains to you the significance of what you do. Rather, your routine becomes transfigured into the ritual of a true life at sea. An utterly silent blessing of finality teaches you the necessity of the task in hand, dwelling at the very heart of ordinary work. . . . But what a benefactress is the sea in the exigencies she engenders, time and again stealing your attention back to the task in spite of yourself. . . ." (September 4, 1953).

From this passage we can begin to gather the conception of necessity which the author is forming. At times he may appear to be quite near to Spinoza, but this may be no more than an appearance. From reflection on Hume he derives the fundamental point that no satisfactory account can be given of necessity, that it cannot even be acknowledged, if things are approached from a purely spectatorial standpoint. The necessary can only become intelligible from a standpoint in which we no longer abstract from our involvement in reality. The necessary is appreciated as such only in that fundamental engagement with things in their uniqueness already elucidated in our discussion of immersion and commitment. Therefore necessity is properly construed as an experiential category and not an empirical one. We cannot discover the relevance of this category so long as our thoughts are arrested upon the course of events in an abstract manner. Its meaning must be conceived in the light of the very way in which we are responding in a situation. The passages drawn from living experience of work take on their full impact in establishing this very point.

Bugbee reflects on the question whether involvement so conceived may not be foreign to the thought of Sartre. If Sartre finds things incorrigibly absurd, is this not because he treats them as sheer objects? Accordingly, each person would seem cut off from all others. For a person so insularized in an absurd world, others are to be reckoned with mainly as threats to his integrity or independence. Hence Sartre's emphasis on choice and on responsibility conceived exclusively in terms of "self-making." Without defending formalism, Sartre seems to think that the only way of conceiving demands as devolving on the person would be in terms of an alleged necessity of acting in accordance with formulated rules. "It is true that he (Sartre) may have a latent appreciation for the mistakenness of an interpretation of genuine decision which would reduce decision to conformity to rules. . . . But I think he has no positive alternative to formalism, in spite of his protestations that his position calls for each person to act for the freedom of all persons. On his view, what is another person to me? How can I have any responsibility to him? He is chiefly a threat to my own freedom, and as object to me, he is profoundly absurd." (July 31, 1953).

Actually it may be that Sartre has fulfilled the role of making evident the sort of wasteland in which we find ourselves in so far as we lack good faith — that is to say, faith. Bugbee distinguishes from this wasteland, this fallen world, what he aptly calls wilderness, a world ever renewed in its plenitude of possibilities, in all the appeals it holds for one who listens and acts in his true humanity.

Let us make no mistake about the meaning of the wilderness, however; it is no world other than our own; it is reality itself as revealed in contemplation. Even the most simple, the most commonplace thing appears as a gift in coming home to us as a presence; but as we have already noted, this presence cannot be separated from that going out to receive it on our part which is love itself. And when we speak of contemplation in this connection, we must be clear that it is a matter of *active* response. The mode of experience meant is not reducible to what we commonly signify as knowledge; for the more we appreciate things in depth, the more we participate in a mystery only intelligible as such, and the more we *understand* that ours is an unknown world. This word 'to understand' must be taken in its full strength: An understanding in this sense is akin to faith.

May it not be that a mistaken conception of believing has obscured for some time the secular problem of the relation between *believing* and *understanding*? This is the conception that believing is some sort of procedure to be followed in order to attain a certain ulterior state, which would be that of understanding. But to conceive believing in this way is to degrade it by reducing it to the status of an operation, and a preliminary one at that, comparable to turning on a faucet or casting dice. It would be another mistake to interpret belief as an arbitrary commitment; it does not involve commitment without right. On this point Bugbee is firmly opposed to Pascal's "Wager" and to William James' "forced option" as well. Faith is nothing if it is not authentic; in other words it can be neither a device nor an option. "Faith cannot be recommended; it can only be called upon." (September 28, 1952).

This leads us toward a remarkably different conception of truth from that customarily formed with regard to the sciences; different because it is formulated in terms of a conception of response and service. (September 26, 1953). Truth here is not construed in its specialized forms; it involves a person wholly even if he be engaged in a discipline which articulates truth in specialized form. Only as conceived in this way can we speak of serving the truth, and of the truth — in the strictly fundamental sense — as only to be served. Truth is to be understood in and through faithfulness, but we have seen that this understanding must not be confused with what is usually signified by knowing. Reality understood in this way is at the root of responsibility, and it could be said that the deep originality of this entire undertaking consists precisely in its illuminating the co-articulation of the ideas of responsibility, of understanding, and of reality.

It seems to me very important to note a qualification that is added, however: Essential truth only comes to us in conditions which do not permit us to attain any kind of permanent hold upon it. The advent of essential truth does not place it at our disposal; on the contrary, it seems to depend upon our being at its disposal, a matter of interior disposition in which we are subject to a rhythm of ebb and flow, the very rhythm of our ephemeral condition. Of course we are always able to hold forth about reality, responsibility, and so on, but these can become quite empty in our moments of desiccation and barrenness of spirit: This evokes the image of being stranded and left by the tide. In fact it is as if there were a tidal background behind us, but for the support of which things explicit for us could not become intelligible and valuable in their own right.

It would be a serious mistake, however, to suppose that such themes as these lead us back into a kind of subjectivism. On the contrary they assume their proper meaning only from a standpoint transcending the distinction between subject and object, at a level which Bugbee joins me in calling meta-technical or meta-problematic. This is actually the home land on which our common research is developed.

Where does this research lead the American philosopher 'in the domain of religion?' If I am not mistaken, he is not presently affiliated with any particular denominational group. It is evident, nevertheless, that his attitude is fundamentally religious. Near the end of his book he says some things which are revealing on this point. He is recalling a criticism made by Richard Niebuhr at the close of a course on 19th and 20th Century religious thought. This criticism was of the tendency encountered in William James, for example, to concentrate on religious attitude to the exclusion of an objective basis for it—as if religious attitude could be understood in independence of orientation to God. Richard Niebuhr seems to have judged it necessary to conceive God as object, no matter how analogically or symbolically the objective conception of God were to be carried out. Though in accord with Niebuhr in rejecting psychologism and in stressing the importance of what might be called a referential relevance in religious attitude, Bugbee thinks that the intervention of the idea of object would re-instate a mode of thinking incompatible with what is definitive in religious attitude. According to him it is an illusion to suppose that the foundation of religious attitude, in so far as it is not arbitrary, can be 'saved' or established in thought by the introduction of an objective referent apropriate to it. In fact the introduction of this mode of thought would incur the risk of undoing faith. To his way of thinking religious attitude challenges the ultimacy of an objective interpretation of reality, in so far as that involves abstraction from experience in its depth, the depth of responsible—indeed of responsive—being.

"Is this to say that religious attitude is not one of concern *for*, since it cannot be objectively differentiated? No. I think, rather, that religious attitude is one of truly universal concern for things. I do not mean concern for 'things in general.' I mean, on the contrary, a concern which is concretely an experience of things in the vein of their individuality, for this is precisely the vein in which they are experienced as universal." (October 20, 1953). Such experience involves being bound in communion with things; it cannot be insular, it is not possible in isolation from them. Perhaps something like the idea of "*religaçion*" defined by Zubiri in his great work appears here. It is especially important to understand, however, that this attitude of reverence is rather less defined as 'orientation towards,' in its being a mode of concern *for*, and more as 'orientation *from*,' in its source of being; while it is confirmed in the meaning which is liberated from things in response to the very act by which we receive them, the ground from which that act is possible is the very ground of our being.

We must always return to this theme, which Bugbee puts in the image of a closed circuit: "To think experientally is to partake in thought of the closed circuit of reality, in which we live and move and have our being." (August 28, 1953). In this 'closed circuit,' and in this alone, a foundation is afforded for a philosophy of contemplation, along with the possibility of fundamental meaning in our existence. In consequence reflection may pass beyond a philosophy of existence in a restrictive sense; and the central affirmations of an authentic ontology may come to new life.

Gabriel Marcel
de l'Institut de France

THE INWARD MORNING

Tuesday, August 26, 1952

In the chapter of his *Autobiography* entitled "Projective Verse," William Carlos Williams has recorded the notion that in the writing of a poem one perception must move instantly on another; also "form is never more than an extension of content."[1] Now for me philosophy is in the end an approximation to the poem, "a structure built upon your own ground. . . , your ground where you stand on your own feet," as he later speaks of the poem in the same book.[2] He also quotes a sentence from John Dewey: "The local is the only universal, upon that all art builds."[3] This last is something that often comes over me, especially in diners over a cup of coffee. But whether you say "the local" is the stuff that art builds on or philosophy, or how both do, and yet wherein they differ—let's set such questions aside. In the Orient, for example, there have been many who put what they must as best they could, now with brush strokes, and now with the flash of the articulate word.

I have yet to discover how to say what moves me to the endless search and research, the reflective turning over in my mind of experience. The turning over is all so much tilling. It can be restless and ridden, too, with a sense of estrangement from the truth that is one's own. All this tilling can be but a burying deeper of what ought to be coming out. The moments in which something reliable has seemed to come of it all have impressed me as sudden. Insight is earned, to be sure, but it is not steered, and it must find its own

1. *The Autobiography of William Carlos Williams*, New York, Random House, 1951, p. 330.
2. Ibid. p. 376.
3. Ibid. p. 391.

[handwritten annotations in top margin: "poetry is about insight — one insight can obscure another — poetry as a model for philosophy)"]

[handwritten annotation in left margin: "star of technical philosophy"]

articulate form. If it is to become more than sporadic and utterly ephemeral, one must pay attention to it, it must be *worked out*. And to work it out is not to cramp it into a prefixed mould; not to say less, with one's own voice, and then to place the little one says at greater length in a 'relevant' context. For then, as the theoretical setting is amplified, the little one may have had to say becomes dissipated. One may seem to become more and more precise. Theoretical alternatives may be laid bare with increasing analytic finesse. But in the effort to get what one has to say into the form of theory (to make it public, perhaps), one lets it go.

I feel that for me a crisis is at hand. I look back over my writing and I discern hints of what I can genuinely say, but undeveloped for lack of riding them through as they came to me. I look back over the last four years of work, and I feel dismayed that so little is set forth, and shown for what it has been. What is needed, I have concluded, is a record based on just one principle: Get it down. Get down so far as possible the minute inflections of day to day thought. Get down the key ideas as they occur. Don't worry about what it will add up to. Don't worry about whether it will come to something finished. Don't give it up when faced with the evidence of miscarried thought. Write on, not over again. Let it flow. Don't haggle with the naturalists. Don't be stopping to jam the idea down somebody's throat. Give it a chance. If there can be concrete philosophy, give it a chance. Let one perception move instantly on another. Where they come from is to be trusted. Unless this is so, after all is said and done, philosophy is arbitrary and idle.

Wednesday, August 27

Let it flow: Fluency is the stylistic counterpart of the way present experience is *invaded* with authentic meaning. Basic meanings are not anticipated; they dawn on one. This is the point of keeping up

[handwritten annotation at bottom: "Midwest Journal"]

Try not to presuppose/anticipate meaning, let it come to you through 'experience'

poem of a bird vs. biology of class of a bird

the flow: If one works out the thoughts, the perceptions that press
upon him with the demand for completion, as they lead to one another,
in time the actual themes of his philosophy may have a chance to
define themselves. Such a philosophy will not be set up like the solution of a puzzle, worked out with all the pieces lying there before the
eye. It will be more like the clarification of what we know in our
bones. Against the professional insistence that one can and should
be clear from the start about what he starts from (premises, assump-
tions), that the procedure and the direction of thought worth undertaking should be equally clear, I am going to try to be faithful to
the intimations I have had: That the reflection worth indulging doesn't
know where it's going, just as the life that is lived underlies anything
the individual is able to patent for himself. There need be no obscurantism in this; if philosophical truth is engendered in depth, we
must not expect it to come to light except out of relative obscurity.

With a sure instinct in the matter, many reflective minds have
registered the affinity of philosophy with certainty. Even today this
traditional affinity is unwittingly honored by professional philosophers
who may rightfully find the *ideal* of certainty a shibboleth of tender
minds. For some of them, certainty lies in scientific method, but since
the method does not yield particular truths which we would claim
to be 'certainties,' the significance of their unqualified endorsement
of the method readily escapes them. The concern, not only of Posi-
tivists, but of many more flexible interpreters of empirical knowledge,
to fix the idea of the given, as in the conception of indubitable data,
or of basic propositions, or of contents of experience which are certainties, is a variant of the perennial philosophical concern with certainty. Sometimes I have felt pretty sure, too, that people who move
from philosophy in a general way to logic in particular, and who feel
most at home even *within* logic, which is more neat and plotted than
the philosophy of logic, that these lovers of clarity and distinctness
have homed in on the beam of certainty. Working within premises
and procedural rules that are explicit and not in question, one can
be sure of what he is saying. If certainty is to be construed as a matter
of incontrovertible warrant for particular truth claims, if the idea
of certainty is to enjoy the fate of any singled out claim "to be certain

agency = found at every moment (whether instinctual or actual decision making) that . . . so-and-so," then it would be easy to follow in the wake of these enthusiasms for particular little nuggets of truth, however low in carat, and for operations of thought about which you are entitled to be sure within the arbitrary limits you have set up. You might even settle for the certainty of taking little, tentative, cautious steps for as long as you are able to step. But it is not 'the philosopher' who is taking the steps by which empirical enquiry proceeds. He would be busy with finding some certainty in this business of taking steps.

When John Dewey criticized what he stamped as "the quest for certainty," he certainly came close to a central vein in which the history of reflective thought deserves to be reviewed. But I don't recall that it occurred to him to consider certainty, not as something quested for, like a pot of gold for which longing search is undertaken, and not as something that hangs on the fate of isolated truth-claims or of structures of hypotheses, and not as very strong conviction, but rather as pertaining to that animating base on which human enterprise becomes sound.

I would wish to say that certainty lies at the root of action that makes sense. It is connected with the ultimate purport of our lives. Perhaps the last thing we should demand of an interpretation of certainty is that it show how we are entitled to some credo, once-for-all, incontrovertibly. No doubt Dewey was right in challenging the attempt to make good an absolute point of view, an Olympian reading of our situation. But he may have been much nearer to a positive base for an understanding of certainty when he touched on that *sense of the whole* and of *communal solidarity* which he emphasized in speaking of fundamental experience.[4]

Certainty may be quite compatible with being at a loss to say what one is certain of. Indeed I seriously doubt if the notion of 'certainty of,' or 'certainty that' will take us accurately to the heart of the matter. It seems to me that certainty is at least very much akin to hope and faith. And I agree with Gabriel Marcel that it would be a serious mistake to undertake the interpretation of hope and of faith under what I will call the aspect of specificity, as if hope were

4. See, for example: *Art as Experience,* New York, Minton Balch, 1934, pp. 194-5; *Human Nature and Conduct,* New York, Modern Library, 1922, pp. 330-2.

essentially 'hope that,' and faith 'belief that.' Likewise, then, of cer-tainty: Perhaps it too is not a matter of knowledge we can be said to *possess*.

Thursday, August 28

Certainty is profoundly resolute, but I would mark it out in diametrical contrast with complacency or being of a closed mind. It bespeaks a basis for action rather than arrival at a terminus of endeavour. So far as we are sensitive to the absoluteness of our situation, we live in a dimension of meaning which is the depth of our experience—we live in eternity. Certainty involves that simplicity which is true to being in a situation that is absolute and registered as such in depth. It seems to me that I have known men to live with such simplicity for the most part without 'knowing it.' It's not the sort of thing you spell out for yourself step by step or study and strive to attain; there-fore the misconception in a quest for certainty. Perhaps certainty is akin to that poverty of spirit, or disinterestedness, of which Meister Eckhart said that we need not know *about* it, since it is not dependent upon knowing about it.

We might well raise the question, then, whether reflection can bear upon certainty, or enhance it. To this I can answer at once: It has seemed to me that meditation can be continuous with experience in depth. It can be an activity consonant with the absoluteness of our situation, somehow opening and answering to the demands of our situation as absolute.

Friday, August 29

Wonder is a theme which has long preoccupied me. When I have read in Plato and Aristotle that wonder marks the inception of philosophy, of the love of wisdom, I have felt that they were right. Aristotle's connection of the love of myth with the love of wisdom on the strength of their common rooting in wonder also struck me immediately as penetrating. Yet it also seemed to me that Aristotle did not begin to follow up these notions as they might and should be. Ultimately, are not wonder and curiosity poles apart? Yet when Aristotle considers wonder as obtaining in so far as we have failed to see the reason for something which we are nonetheless impelled to investigate, he at least invites confusing the two.

One is tempted to suppose that Aristotle thought of philosophy as allaying the wonder in which it is initiated. For his philosophy is centrally an exposition of the principles in accordance with which he thinks the reasons can be given for things being as they are. Accordingly, the philosopher would come to understand that the things about which he wondered initially are in principle explicable, and having at least the key to their explanation, he would cease to wonder for lack of occasion; his urbanity would have become commensurate with the universe!

In all of Aristotle's philosophy there seems to be but one prominent notion suggestive of a different version of the matter: With the notion of the unmoved mover philosophical reflection would eventuate in an ultimate occasion for incorrigible wonder. Whether or not Aristotle would have concurred in this interpretation of the self-caused, I believe this notion is true to a fundamental meaning which reality assumes in experience, coming alive in wonder. With the deepening of this meaning, wonder deepens into certainty, it is not allayed or expelled. The meaning of experienced reality imaged in the notion of the self-caused may mark our discovery, not of a terminal reason, but of the irrelevance of explanation.

Saturday, August 30

The giving of reasons, explanation, has long seemed to me a discursive affair, a roving of the mind even though not random. Yes, from the standpoint I am particularly concerned to define, it might even be called digressive, though not aimless. It takes as some point of departure that which is to be explained, that for which reasons are to be sought or given, and it presupposes a *context* to which attention moves in the process of explanation: In explanation the mind spreads out from whatever is taken as given for explanation, and roves among a wider range of discriminated factors with which it seeks to connect what has been taken as given. Perhaps even in principle, and in at least several respects, explanation is an endless business. Contextual factors give out on further contextual factors by virtue of qualifying as contextual factors: For example, it seems in principle relevant to inquire into 'causes' as effects, and into 'effects' as causes. Also, systems of interlocking hypothesis with respect to contexts within which the ways of things are typified, are in principle answerable to observations yet to be made. Even what is taken as given for explanation, or as the most minimal and secure disclosure from which discursive thought can warrantedly proceed, is taken, and taken discursively. If not so taken, it cannot provide either a point of departure for explanation, or evidence, i.e. the *data* for knowledge. Judgment can have no access to unjudged disclosures; and judged disclosures involve a mind. The mind is committed to the life of a wanderer amidst whatever it can represent to itself; it is not permitted to rest even within the narrowest limits it may circumscribe for itself.

Sunday, August 31

In wonder, however, it seems as if the presence of things took root in us, and planted in us an intimation of reality not to be understood exclusively by digression, by the ways of explanation. From the time reality has begun to sink into us in wonder, we can begin to realize that our minds are committed to wander. That is, in our discursive thought we are imbued with the condition of exile, which involves some measure of sensitivity to our homelessness. We can busy our-

selves with an attempt to deny this condition, to represent to ourselves some features of our situation as unconditional and some procedures as guaranteed to fit it. Or we can open ourselves to the
meaning of a life in the wilderness and be patient of being overtaken
in our wandering by that which can make us at home in this condition.

If wonder is to be construed not merely as a provocation for
reflection, but also as containing the germ of fundamental truth, we
may do well to mark that it involves an *openness* on the part of a
person in his entirety. As Marcel points out, this openness is much
more than intellectual candour and openness of mind; and it is not
contrived.

Perhaps the openness of a human being in his entirety is a condition of philosophical truth. If this is so, contraction and rigidity and
deadness of spirit would mark the moments of our philosophical failing as surely as our flagrant contradictions.

Friday, September 5

Wonder deepening into certainty: the conclusive significance of presence; reflective discernment of this must be continuous with the experience in which it is confirmed.

With what sort of idea of experience would it be realistic to
proceed in a philosophic appeal to experience? I feel that a concern
to reinterpret experience as the proving ground of philosophic thought
is bound up with my sense of undertaking a work of days. This day
is the place of meeting with the lives of persons, yes, even with one's
own life.

Abstracted from intimacy with the lives of persons, our idea of
experience becomes paltry. Especially as they have failed to maintain
such intimacy in theorizing about experience, many modern philosophers have come to think of experience in the image of objects. They
have conceived man as if he were to be understood in this image.

And so they have failed to appreciate that experience is a tissue of meaning grossly misinterpreted by representation in the image of objects. Realizing that statements about objects can always be called in question, and that we would have to draw on experience (in some sense) in supporting them, they have thought that the experience we may draw upon, at least, is somehow an assured possession of the mind, especially as it is analysed down to its least bits and accorded the most non-committal articulation. And so they have been led further from reflection on experience as a tissue of meaning, to be understood at the mercy of the tides ebbing and flowing each day of our lives, from *behind* and not before our attention.

Experience is permeated with meaning by invasion. If our experience is 'ours,' we are not the possessors of its meaning. We do not predict and control the ebb and flow of meaning in our experience nor do we easily ponder experience with respect to the tides of meaning. I do not think we can be, or would want to be, professionals — experts — in the conduct of our lives. We are not masters of the import of our deeds. *We* are involved, to the soles of our feet, in the attitudes inflecting the meaning which we realize, or fail to realize, in our on-going experience. Experience, then, is not something standing over against us (a *Gegenstand*, an object) from which we are removed to the capacity of observers, about which we are in a position to make assured reports. Experience is our undergoing, our involvement in the world, our lending or withholding of ourselves, keyed to our responsiveness, our sensibility, our alertness or our deadness.

Of the nature of things, objectively construed, we may hope for steadily implemented empirical knowledge, interlocked with teachable techniques. Ability to predict and control is susceptible to progressive enhancement from generation to generation. We can start from the scientific and technological achievements of our predecessors.

Of experience, however, we may hope for understanding in our own time, and in this we do not seem to have the edge on preceding generations of men. Wherever men have articulated a measure of understanding of human experience, whenever they have managed to voice something of the basic meaning of the human situation with authenticity and insight, what they have said tends to remain of perennial interest and relevance to our own endeavour to understand our own experience in our own time. It is not a question of our beginning from where they leave off and going on to supersede them. We are fortunate if we can become communicant in our own way with what they have to say.

Sunday, September 7 — Friday, September 12

Two themes are forming in answer to the demand for marrow-bone truth which I feel these days. They come to me as companion aspects of our true mode of being: immersion and commitment. At the same time certain memories from experience of long ago once again press upon me as if they bore the image of conclusive meaning which our situation may yield if only our mode of being be true. I must try to discern what these memories arise to suggest. I will sketch them out.

SWAMPING

The swamps lay about in the vicinity of our school the year around. But the urge to swamp was sort of a seasonal thing. Swamping was a rather senseless activity, and the urge to it used to come at a rather senseless time of year.

It was that time of year when the snows had pretty much dwindled into the ground: no more skiing. And the ice, what little was left, had become too mushy for skating. Often cold rain or sleet would be lashing about, and there were many grey days.

At school, in the afternoons, you could hear live shouts resounding from the gymnasium; but from the grounds all around mostly only wind could be heard, and now and then a lone car going somewhere over wet pavement. A time of year of least resistance to scholastic claims, even of relative academic contentment. You could readily get buried in a book; you could resign yourself to the routine clearing of lessons. The trout season still lay beyond a month or two of high and roily waters. The burrowing animals were mostly underground.

Around the swamps even a squirrel was hardly to be seen. The birds had not yet returned. Only a crow, now and then, would fly from some pine, to make loud and senseless noise upon the air. In the swamps were dead trees: some just grey poles, with here and there the stump of a limb, and some with girth of size that were many-limbed and twisted. But everything else was also dead, the grass on the clumps in the swamp, and all the twigs that tossed in the wind or just marked themselves out dark in a grey still. Of course there were pines, darkly green here and there, or massed in bunches, but when they spoke it was in awesome chorus of a cold wind and a grey sky. And when the pines said nothing, they just stood around inane, giving way to the visible aptness of the bare-limbed trees.

Moving about in the swamp, sometimes you would find ice, questionable ice that most often wouldn't hold you, and you could smash it with a club or prod holes through it and pry it to make it break up. The grassy clumps would be fairly solid, and you could always begin to move about with the intention of keeping dry, testing out the footing and leaping from clump to clump. Even when there was no ice and the mounds were a bit soggy, you'd never just wade in. But no matter how sure your leaping was, there was always a clump a little too far off for which you would try, or a clump that would roll. Sometimes you'd grab at a branch to steady up, and away it would come in your hand. There was something about the water in the swamps that made it impossible to stay out. Not enough to probe for the bottom with a long stick. It seemed as if there were no way of not getting into the swamp. Once thoroughly in the acknowledgement would come over you that it couldn't be otherwise, and you could abandon yourself to the swamp, water and all. How deep could the water get?

It was not particularly pleasant, as I recall. I can remember the shivering cold. But there was no mistake about the gladness of being in the swamp or the immanence of the wilderness there.

BUILDING A DAM

Walking across a large open meadow near school, you came to a small stream. With only a little extra spring from the calf of the leg, you could step across it. There was a spot where the creek came alongside a long ledge of solid rock. An old maple leaned out over the ledge. It was the only tree in the meadow. Just below this spot one day a classmate of mine and I began idly to build a little dam.

We started it wrong, but then we didn't imagine what we were starting. Instead of giving the dam its bulge upstream, like a professional job, we had it bowing downstream from the very start, trying to catch a little water in a pool and hold it still for a moment, as in a cupped hand. But hours flowed into hours, and day after day we returned to gather boulders and rocks, staggering to the dam with the ones we could carry, and rolling up the big ones. Day by day we tore at the sod with our hands, preparing the beds of sod and mud in which to sock home the rock. We had no idea of its coming to be six feet high and nearly as thick at the base, in the center. It kept getting thicker as we tried to stop off the most elusive seeps; there was so little water in the creek, there had to be no leaks. Well, it made the pond bigger to have the dam bow downstream. What we had started idly deepened into work in earnest without the dam changing its character. We never really had a plan.

How big was it going to get? We wondered ourselves at how big it already was. A marvel, it was, to crouch below the dam and watch the stream pour over a spillway stone, imagining the expanse of the little pond above.

In time we saw the pond rise to where most of the rock ledge came under water, and the very deepest part lay in shadow beneath the undercurve of the ledge. There was a hidden place in under there. And the water reached up to the base of the spreading tree.

Some people heard of this dam; a few would wander over to look at it. "What's it for?" "What are you doing?"

"What a senseless thing," someone remarked, "out here hugging rocks and splattering mud."

I remember feeling a little sheepish about our explanations. "Oh, it's to be a fish pond. We're going to plant fish in it. And you could swim in it; it'll be nice for that in warm weather." Somewhere along the line it occurred to us that we might even skate on it in winter, too; well, figure skate, if you kept the figures tight.

But our visitors usually ended by shaking their heads as they walked off. After all, for fish, for swimming, for skating, we had only to go to any of the nearby lakes.

Perhaps we were a little on the defensive about our pond when we actually went off and caught some sunfish and perch and hauled them from quite a way in milk cans to plant them there. This undertaking seemed something else again from building the dam.

But grass was growing, and some wildflowers too, upon the dam itself. And the fish lived and inhabited the pond and came to belong in it. They came to make known to us the hidden place beneath the ledge: They would dart for it and then you could feel them finning there. Indeed there came to be days of heat, when the surface water of the pond was warm. Then we would toe the moss on top of the ledge and commit ourselves to the cool blur, right down among the fishes. There might have been a spring down there, beneath the maple roots and beneath the ledge of rock.

How brief the flaming of that one tree each fall, reflected in our pond. How instant the touch of each leaf upon the live water. But one leaf in an instant touch upon the water is enough.

We never skated there. The pond was really not big enough.

ROWING

I don't remember what first possessed me to 'go out for' rowing in college, if I ever knew. I'd hardly seen a racing shell before. Of course the water was a lure. And I had seen the bulk of the boathouse squatting on the lake shore, with its broad, planked runway sloping down onto the great float. I had peered through the dusty windows into the silent interior, and caught the gleam of the long slim shells. The place had a charged atmosphere; all that equipment in there seemed to be speaking as in mouthed syllables, but without a sound.

When I showed up at the boathouse with the fall turnout my freshman year, it was like waking up in a strange world. I looked with awe at the sixty-foot eights, watching the old hands marching the classy shells down to the float, tossing them up, and laying them over onto the water. Keeping up a familiar-toned chatter, the old hands would trot to the racks for their oars, then back to the waiting shells: Into the locks with the oars, one foot on the slides and then all together with a shove, out they would go, settling on their seats, leaning forward over their oars to adjust foot-stretchers or shoes. Then at a word, handling the oars, all would come forward, heads up and backs straight, blades touching the water lightly. "Ready all, row!" and away they'd go. I would watch them, confounded. How they did it and what it would feel like I couldn't imagine ever coming to know.

Among the freshmen, too, there were quite a few who had rowed before at school, and they were gathered by the coaches and sent out in shining shells. The rest of us stood around, numb and awkward, eager and mystified. Eventually we were embarked in the broad, clinker-built barges, which had bottoms you might have stepped on without going through.

From watching and trying I am sure we were profoundly impressed that rowing is a skill. Implicit in all that went on, you might say, was a murmuring voice: "Rowing is a skill; we row to acquire it; those of us who have it row to perfect it; and you, dunce, row with a prayer to acquire it." Accordingly there was the ladder, with the varsity as its topmost rung, then the junior varsity, the third boat, the first 150's, the second, the freshman crew, the second freshmen, and so on, down to the very bottom of the ladder, where we beginners stood gathering all this, with the greatest clarity. I got the idea, too, that we would take our ladder in the spring and lay it alongside the ladders of other colleges. There was always plenty of purpose, then, plenty of competition, and a clear standard of achievement. You could point to what we were aiming at, and you could measure where you stood. We had heard, too, in further explanation of our endeavours, that we would win good-fellowship and fine health. Well, as it turned out, it wasn't a bad bunch there, like most anywhere, and the case for health was plain enough, especially with the watch they kept on our hearts. If you dropped into a sedentary life sometime after college, you couldn't blame the consequences on rowing.

In those early days at the boathouse I could take most of this in, especially the business about making your mark, which I'm afraid gnawed at our vitals a good deal. A coach could play upon it in subtle ways; and without even intending to, he could foster an interest in rowing keyed to a pitch of anxiety: What boat are you going to make? What can the boat do that you're rowing in? Will you be recognized or passed over today? Tomorrow? By next spring? Surely no less so for being American boys we were susceptible to such an attitude in a sport. If we hadn't read the sport pages in newspapers much before, we began to scan them a bit then.

But rowing turned out to be something else again, something more and other than anyone pointed to or made prominent. And there was one man there who could help you to understand it. For me he was the awakener. John Schultz, he was— rigger of the shells and coach of sculling. He came out of the eastside of New York, a far cry from Princeton, and he never had much schooling. When he died, whether he went to hell or heaven, you may be sure that when asked for his credentials he must have called for a single shell and a pair of oars and a body of water, and freed from the body's limitations, how he must have astounded them! By now they must be rowing their hearts out, whether in heaven or in hell.

John made his first indelible impression on me during the fall of my freshman year. I was out on the lake in front of the boathouse teetering around in a single gig, frozen to inaction by the threats of capsize ensuing upon every move of my body. Then came that voice across the water: "Hey! You out there! Take a stroke!" A horrified glance revealed no one else about. Again: "Take a stroke!" I stabbed at the water in desperation. One blade knifed deep, the other washed out, and over I went. As I gasped and floundered by the upset gig, the voice roared at me through a huge megaphone: "Hey you! Get around to the other side of that boat! Don't forget, you got a coupla hundred dollars o' equipment there!" With a sense of utter calamity, I swam round to the other side of the boat. Then I looked to shore for comprehension. The explanation was forthcoming: "See, the water's warmer on that side!" With a loud cackle John turned back to his shop, leaving me to shift for myself.

John had a sure nose for lard, the lard about people's souls, you might say. None of us fully escaped pique as a result of his discernment. Some of us listened to him, some of us avoided him. There were those who tolerated him and passed him off as a character. Then there were some who opposed him, and opposed the sculling, which he encouraged. John used to say that if a man can pull his own weight alone, you can be sure he's able to pull it in an eight; and if it has become second nature for him to pull his own weight alone, he's not likely to rest part of his share on the others when he's in the eight. Against this it was sometimes argued that the single-sculler becomes too much the individualist, going his own way with his own ideas about how to row, developing a style of stroke, too, which might not fit with that of seven other men. He might even lose interest in the eights, and it would be heresy indeed to sanction this. There were examples about the boathouse with which these and other arguments could be supported.

I encountered one example in my freshman year whom I found convincing. That was Art Strang, who proved himself the fastest man out of seventy in single sculls. John used to go about the shop muttering to himself with surging emphasis: "That Stran. He's one hell of a man." Indeed he was. I remember well Strang in a single and Strang seated as stroke of the varsity crew. There didn't seem to be an ounce of energy in him not honestly engaged and knowingly applied. I remember Strang for his quietness and his gentle smile. I remember there appeared to be no conceit in him. He rowed with real eloquence. You could pledge yourself with him in every stroke as you watched him row, and it felt like flying.

Of course I thought Strang was fine proof of John's case, and I don't think I appreciated explicity how Strang exemplified something deeper in what rowing meant to John than the relevance of sculling to proficiency in the eights. For John himself was partisan at times and on the defensive about a debatable issue. What you had to grasp beneath his stand was the simple fact that John was interested in rowing wherever it was being done. If he could get people sculling, he could get them deeper into rowing. He could hope to see them row in season and out, and perhaps for the rest of their lives, wherever there might be water. If the coaches registered the quality of John's interest in the races of the eights, they surely knew that his championing of sculling was not subversive. There was never any doubt about John's absorption in any rowing that was being done.

I remember the first time I grasped the quality of his interest with full force. Our crews were racing down on the Schuylkill River at Philadelphia, over the mile and three-quarter course. A drive parallels this course, enabling spectators to follow the race somewhat satisfactorily from automobiles. The freshman race came first. I was seated beside John in his old Model-A Ford, holding his great megaphone for him, as we jockeyed to the front of the line of cars which was forming to follow the race. I remember staring fixedly at the wings on the radiator cap as we sat there waiting. I was a bit low about not being in that race. John was making the engine roar, as he always did when sitting at the wheel, deep in concentration. Most likely he was turning over in his thoughts the make-up of our boat, but he said nothing at all. Suddenly the boats were away. Cars behind began to honk; then John let out the clutch with a lurch, and we never did get out of low gear, as I recall.

At the half mile the boats were even. John shoved the gas clear to the floor, and as we began to move ahead of the procession, jerking past a scattering of cars, I just heard him over the violence of the engine: "When they come out from under that bridge . . . That's where they need me!" We simply left the road at a point where it veered from the river and around a little park. We took off into the park through the trees, dodging and bounding, and came to a stop against a solid tree-trunk. I extricated the megaphone and caught up with John as he panted toward the river bank. He was a bit stout in those last years of his.

Presently the shells shot out from under the bridge. They were well over to the far side of the river, rowing stroke for stroke and deck for deck, the coxswains yelling, and the launches following astern.

John watched them an instant, then, without taking his eyes away, he grabbed around for the megaphone. I put it in his hands. It was like handing the firing plunger to a dynamiter.

He raised that thing up to his mouth and he pointed the wide funnel out over the river at the boats, and then he sent out in one enormous exhalation a sound to appall. The sound seemed to shape a single word: "R-r-r-o-o-o-o-w!" given with such roundness and fullness as lungs and heart can sustain. Our boys knew the voice, and they knew what it said. It reached out and it lifted them in unison, and they translated it inch by inch and foot by foot into a margin over the other shell, — driving her, driving her, understanding better each stroke the meaning in what they did. The more they gave themselves to it, the clearer it became.

For a moment longer we watched them going away, down toward the finish line. Then we returned to the car and sat for a while. It was very quiet there, with the noise of the traffic at a distance.

Later that evening as we crawled up Highway One toward Princeton in the old Ford, I told John it no longer mattered to me that I hadn't been in that race. He peered at me abruptly over the rim of his glasses, then turned back to the road with a nod. "You was there," he said.

You might have thought that the races were the moments of definitive rowing, and there is no doubt that we used to enter upon them with a special sense of being called upon. Perhaps John felt this too, and became even more alert and intent as important races drew near. There was the time in England when he was forced to impart his final instruction during the last workout before the race from a bicycle which he pedaled along a path on the bank of the Thames, with megaphone rattling against the handlebar. While exhorting our boys so extraordinarily, he rode through a hedge and into a table-full of ladies who were having tea upon the lawn of a Henley club. Yet this mishap was probably most due to the fact that he needed both hands, as always, in effectively directing the megaphone. It was thus that he ever met us on our return from the countless anonymous miles which we construed as practice, but which he expected us to culminate by rowing as we had never rowed before.

In fact I wonder if the idea of practice really went very deep with him. It was as if rowing had a kind of ground-bass meaning for him which underlay the constancy of his concern and seemed to him to demand relevance from the oarsman in each and every stroke. And so he momently expected each one of us to wake up on the end of an oar. This infinite expectation of dawn often made him seem very unreasonable. What did he want of us, anyway? At the end of six hard-rowed miles, as you were coming home and giving it all you had anyway, what was that old fiend doing out there on the float roaring at you! Was he insisting on more effort? If you took it that way, he became intolerable, and you found yourself fighting it, and those last few strokes would become the most futile of the day.

There were rare occasions, however, when those six miles would round out into an incorruptible song, and you would be realizing its finality as you flew under the bridge and came up abeam of the float. On one such occasion, as the shell glided to stillness on the water, it came to me that I had heard nothing from John. I glanced toward the boathouse and saw him at work in his shop. A little later, as I passed through the shop on my way out, he was still at his bench, and he did not look up as I came by. As I went through the door I heard him mutter, as if to himself, "You was moving." And indeed he might have been talking to himself. He often did.

John used to tell of rowing with some boys down in Cuba. They would hit the water at five in the morning, and often it was so calm they could row right out to sea, translating into the smooth drive and run of their shell the feel of the open sea itself. And this it seems was a kind of rowing which could have no end.

On with it, then. And let each bud of energy flower into the unchecked run of the shell.

Tuesday, September 23

I think of immersion as a mode of living in the present with complete absorption; one has the sense of being comprehended and sustained in a universal situation. The absorption is not a matter of shrunken or congealed attention, not a narrowing down or an exclusion. One is himself absorbed into a situation, or by it, and the present which is lived in does not seem accurately conceivable as a discrete moment in a series. The present in question seems to expand itself extensively into temporal and spatial distances. And it is as if one's perception of everything distinct were engaged in alignment with a center from which one moves to greet each thing knowingly. There is a continuing passage from thing to thing in which a kind of sameness or continuity of meaning deepens, — ever confirmed and ever relevant. It is not by generalization that omnirelevant, universal meaning dawns. One becomes sensitized to its realization, to its becoming manifest as things themselves. But instead of things being fixed points of reference from which and to which attention proceeds in a succession of steps and stops, there is *no stopping*, precisely because each and every thing is a consummation of fluency. And our minds, in the Zen manner of speaking, are gourds dancing on the waves, resilient, flexible, swift and apt. There is this bathing in fluent reality which resolves mental fixations and suggests that our manner of taking things has been staggeringly a matter of habituation. Metaphysical thinking must rise with the earliest dawn, the very dawn of things themselves. And this is the dawn in which basic action, too, comes into being. It is earlier than the day of morality and immorality.

No reason for acting can supplant the depth of true affirmation. This is not to disqualify the giving of reasons, or the having of reasons for acting; it is only to suggest the comparative 'lateness,' and so the relative force of reasons had or given.

The tendency of this approach to the idea of commitment is to suggest that responsibility is possible *in depth*, and that the conception of goals to which action may be oriented, and the reference to standards for the vindication or rejection of actions, can yield no more than rather highly abstract versions of the meaning of responsibility. These abstractions should not be permitted to dominate our reflection as if they were not abstractions. My intent is surely not to junk them, but to handle them with caution, and not get taken in by them.

The preceding sketches have helped clarify for me the possibility of commitment in depth which cannot be interpreted in terms of goal-oriented endeavour, nor in terms of acquisition or achievement, nor in terms of the fulfilment of explicit moral standard, nor in terms of the realization or satisfaction of the ego. If there is satisfaction involved in the experiences dealt with, it is satisfaction of the demand to be and to act consonantly with the felt universe. The realization and clarification of universal meaning in acting: This is the theme into which I seem to be led. It links with the conception of disinterested interest which I tried to suggest in "The Moment of Obligation in Experience."[5]

But conclusive meaning immanent in experience (or as experience?) does not readily slide to the tip of the tongue. It does not seem necessarily connected with discursive articulateness. Perhaps our truest actions, as Meister Eckhart suggests, are those for which we can give no justifying reasons at all, there being no separation of meaning from the act in which it is realized. If you believe profoundly in what you are doing, this doing itself is the mode of being relevant, and it constitutes your manner of being articulate. When Mallory was asked why he was bent on climbing Everest, and he answered, "Because it is there," one may suppose his mind was on the mountain. Yet from his contribution to *Mount Everest, the Reconnaissance,* one gets gleanings of the man and of what the mountain meant to him; the last thing he is concerned to discuss is the point of what he has to do with the mountain. I think of men whom I have watched while they were lost in scrupulous endeavour, as in holding a small ship to a course in a difficult sea, and I turn to this passage from the opening of the fourth part of Joseph Conrad's *The Nigger of the Narcissus,* in which he is speaking of seamen:

> They must without pause justify their life to the eternal pity that commands toil to be hard and unceasing, from sunrise to sunset, from sunset to sunrise: till the weary succession of nights and days tainted by the obstinate clamor of sages, demanding bliss and an empty heaven, is redeemed at last by the vast silence of pain and labor, by the dumb fear and the dumb courage of men obscure, forgetful, and enduring.

5. *Journal of Religion,* Vol. XXXIII, No. 1, January 1953, pp. 1-15.

Indeed true deeds, even when wrought with the tongue, seem massive with the vast silence from which they emerge. There is this silence which fosters endurance and begets the steadfastness of men: a silence scattered with stars and cloven into rhythmical wash beneath the bows of the ship.

Friday, September 26 [6]

The difficulty of ethical inquiry seems related to the whole issue so central for ethical reflection itself, having to do with our capacity to appreciate various possibilities of human attitude. To what extent and on what conditions may we understand attitudes from which we may be at some remove, either in the moment of ethical reflection or in enhancing that appreciation of our situation on the strength of which we act?

We can choose, contrive, sustain, or reproduce the opportunities for improving or confirming empirical knowledge and technical skill. We may be said to *possess* knowledge of the nature of things and techniques for dealing with them. We call upon knowledge and know-how at will, imparting them, too, under specifiable and controllable conditions. Do we similarly call to mind under controllable conditions what may give fundamental significance to our lives? Can we really fix in mind that of which we would improve our understanding in ethical inquiry? Suppose we would inquire into human well-being, for example. Can we command the experience with which such an inquiry might be concerned? Or have we only to remember, as we remember objects and processes, in order that experience may afford concrete purchase for reflective interpretation of well-being? But if the experiential meaning of well-being were thus at our disposal, should we not also be able to select and control experience so as to

[6]· Editorial note: By this date the academic year 1952-53 was in full swing. A course in Ethics had begun to claim my full attention. Considerations connected with this course are reflected in the current entries here, through that of October 18, 1952.

insure our well-being? Or is it only the resistance of present circumstance which might preclude reversion in memory to an indwelling felicity to be conjured up from former times?

What is more to the point, can we assume that we may deliberately place ourselves in the vein of the categorically imperative flowing in our lives? Can we credit the possibility of realizing the root-meaning of being under obligation, either in thought or in action, according to methods for doing so, no matter what allowances are made about the difficulty of developing the appropriate methods of inquiry or of action?

In the end these two questions seem to go together: What are the conditions of our acting as we ought? And, how is it possible to establish intimacy with these conditions in our concern to understand them reflectively? If these are significant questions, I do not think it is because they appropriately call for procedures to be followed, as in technical operations. Precisely as justified action can hardly reduce to the following of 'correct procedures,' so the availability for purposes of ethical inquiry of the conditions of justified action can hardly be due to the following of 'a proper method of inquiry.' Here we may put the point by availing ourselves of a term of Marcel's: Action and reflection on the point of action are both *meta-technical*, over and above whatever technique may enter into them. And for convenience let us use a similar term, and say that they are both *meta-objective* in the sense that they move in a dimension of meaning over which we cannot exercise the power of representation and control that obtains with respect to things in taking them as objects.

Saturday, September 27

It would seem that faith, in the sense of a certain openness and trustingness on our part, is as essential in ethical reflection as in action. As I image the matter, philosophical truth overtakes us from behind in so far as we are at its disposal. Openness to what presses upon us from behind, demanding thoughtful realization, is something of the element of faith in reflection. It has to do with the possibility of concrete recall of things past.

There are times when one seems to come to himself, to recollect himself, and only then does the granary of experience pour into present reflection at a fundamental level. No one has helped me so much as Marcel to form an idea of this strict connection between recall to oneself in one's true mode of being in the present and the depth of recall in which reflection may become concretely continuous with the past.

The whole of Proust's big work might be examined for the light it can throw on the accessibility to a person of what is essential in his life. We seem to be confronted in this work with the struggle of a person through the most intricate variations of an attempt to possess himself of whatever could be essential in his life, to the point where he has virtually given up and is simply going along from day to day. The discovery of what does come to him as essential occurs to him then in moments of the most sudden and involuntary recall. Proust seems to suggest that only in unanticipated readiness is there decisive deliverance of the meaning of things past. Such involuntary recall appears at the same time as a recall to ourselves in our eternal nature: We discover ourselves to be rooted in reality in a manner which time and change cannot contravene. The recollection in question is 'involuntary' in the sense that one is led to it; it is not a remembrance one ordains.

Unquestionably these thoughts are in the vicinity of a central concern of Marcel's, nowhere more strikingly defined than in the first part of *Being and Having* where he inquires how a man may commit himself to a sustained course of action with continuing fidelity and sincerity if human commitment can have no purchase not subject to the vicissitudes of a life in time.[7] Marcel's entire development of the idea of being may be reviewed in alignment with just this inquiry.

7. See *Being and Having*, Boston, Beacon Press, 1951, pp. 47-56.

Sunday, September 28

Two statements have remained with me for years as reflecting two live alternatives in religious philosophy in the Middle Ages: 'understand in order to believe,' and 'believe in order to understand.' They are beginning to assume fresh interest for me now.

'Understand in order to believe' easily makes sense, while it is not even as clear what might be meant by 'believe in order to understand.' From the position which the former statement so readily commends, the latter may seem quixotic or perverse, even an invitation to dishonesty and obscurantism. Suppose it to be possible to believe what we do not understand; surely we must understand what we can rightfully believe, including the factors legitimatizing belief? How can a responsible thinker think otherwise in good conscience? Must not an examination of empirical knowledge utterly confirm this? And if we may speak of deductive knowledge, or of *a priori* knowledge, or of what Hume subsumed under knowledge of the relations of ideas, then in speaking of such knowledge, too, what sense could it make to say that we must believe in order to understand?

So long as we concentrate on the forms of knowledge alluded to, and the methods of inquiry which yield them, it is hard to make any sense of 'believe in order to understand.' Yet it might prove relevant to consider very closely what is involved in the 'inner activity' of a person engaged in inquiry yielding one or another of these forms of knowledge. A great deal of theory of knowledge in the West is singularly devoid of reflection on the active commitment of the human being in his prosecution of inquiry. Scientists and mathematicians, furthermore, seldom undertake careful phenomenological examination of their *experience* in what they are doing. And this seems natural enough. They are not reflecting on experience; they are studying a subject-matter which exists for study through the activity of abstracting from concrete experience. Yet to abstract from is not to do without. Perhaps the sciences and mathematics do not reveal what they presuppose. Yet when the epistemologists come to expose the structure, the methods, and the conditions of scientific and mathematical inquiry, they rarely seem to be reflecting experientially on the concrete conditions which may underlie the activity of inquiry. They tend to observe what is being done and the manifest yield of the doing. How could it be 'objective' to do otherwise? How else can there be a subject-matter to which epistemological thought can be made responsible?

Can it be, as Professor I. A. Richards in a public lecture once said, that philosophy is strictly devoid of a subject-matter? For him, and for many others, this seems to have meant that philosophy enjoys what may be called a parasitical status, subsisting on borrowed subject-matter premasticated by other disciplines. Or it might emphasize philosophy in the role of arbiter and judge, of collator and systematizer with respect to the methods and results exhibited by disciplines with subject-matter of their own. But one could hold to the justice of what Professor Richards said, and at the same time conceive reflection as answerable to the experience of men. And what would be distinctive of philosophical reflection, thus conceived, would be bound up with the idea of experience itself: Perhaps in all strictness we would have to realize more and more that experience *is not a subject-matter* susceptible to objective representation and deliberate control. Here we are back again to the meta-objective and meta-technical aspects of philosophical reflection.

But to return now to the sense in which understanding may require believing — apart from the possibility of an approach to the matter through a philosophy of scientific activity. Perhaps one of the first obstacles to be gotten out of our way would be this supposition: that believing is something one *does* with a view to attaining a resultant condition, called understanding, the character of which is somehow to be appreciated — as any intelligently sought result must be — in advance of its attainment. Of course the dictum seems to disallow the possibility of such advance appreciation of what it would be to understand. Yet the "in order to" suggests not only that 'believing' is something one elects to do, but also that it is to be done on purpose, that is, with a view to some further attainment. Not only is the idea of 'belief' as comparable to turning on a faucet or casting a die objectionable, but it is a further offense to suggest that something ought to be done for the sake of a result the character of which must remain obscure (by hypothesis) in advance of the doing. I doubt if a 'take my word for it' situation would make this interpretation of the dictum more respectable. Believing itself must be answerable to something more authoritative than someone's say-so if it is to be a condition of understanding. It cannot be induced by a fiat one imposes on himself. And if it is a condition of understanding we must be most careful to avoid supposing that the connection between belief and understanding is to be thought according to the mode of causal connection. If we move explicitly to the interpretation of belief in terms of faith, as perhaps we must, again we should avoid the 'psychologizing variant' of the causal interpretation of that connection (suggested, for example, by talking of "the faith-state" precedent to being "twice-born").

First and foremost I would follow up the idea that faith is not an arbitrary matter; that it does not involve a commitment *where there is no right*, but fundamentally the contrary of this. And perhaps it is to be thought out in connection with the very idea of there being a right to commitment, yet in a sense very different from that of asserting or claiming a right.

Let me note here that I have encountered no attempt to accord the idea of faith a 'sympathetic' interpretation, 'a defence,' more misleading than the kind suggested by Pascal's "wager" or William James' "forced option:" that faith means tipping the scale in favor of a set of beliefs which can be neither established nor disproven conclusively, because we have everything to gain and nothing to lose a) if they are true, by believing so, and b) by believing they are true even if they are not. If faith is a condition of understanding, it must be as authentic and non-arbitrary as the understanding of which it may be the condition. It must be genuine. The last thing it can be and be genuine is a device or an option. Faith cannot be recommended; it can only be called upon.

How naive it seems to talk of "articles of faith" as if their meaning were clear and only their truth were in question.

In passing beyond this point, consider the possibility that the meaning of faith may be clarified by thinking through the idea of assuming responsibility: a study in responsiveness and, as Marcel would put it, in *disponibilité* — availability. Something the recognition of which seems to be seriously lacking in Kant's account of the assumption of responsibility.

Monday, September 29

The believing that concerns us seems to be first and foremost a believing *in*, rather than a believing *that*. It is a believing that centrally involves 'value-sensitization,' and the understanding dependent on it seems to have to do with what is *essential* in the human condition, in our lives. We cannot even conjure up the suggestion of that which may be essential in our lives, however, without placing ourselves in the way of questions fairly ultimate for our line of inquiry. Does one mean to compress the unlimited complexity and variety and diversity of our lives into some provincial simplification of what ultimately renders them significant rather than insignificant, in the end? Are not questions of what is essential pertinent only when raised in limited contexts and where the standpoint from which the essential is to be recognized has been taken into account? And must we not conclude that there can be no absolute standpoint from which it would be legitimate to determine *the* essential in our lives? Why should we suppose that what is essential in the life of one man is a matter in which other men share, even if there were 'something' unconditionally essential in the life of *a* man, or of *any* man?

All these questions may be helpful to the elucidation of the idea of a basic understanding to which faith is germane. They may help us to see what our line of thought cannot be. We might answer them, partially, in this way. Each one of us may attain insight into what may be *essential*, and unconditionally essential in his own life. But the point here strikes deeper than seemingly similar remarks often made about sympathy: that we can appreciate the feelings of others only on the strength of having been in a position similar to theirs and having felt as they do. For that matter, we seem able to appreciate how others may feel without being particularly sympathetic. And even when we are sympathetic in our appreciation of another's position, this by no means carries us to the point at which the unconditionally essential for him or for us becomes focalized in our experience. One can sympathize with a man without being in readiness to stand by him. But the more that which is essential unconditionally becomes focalized in our experience, the more we seem to find ourselves committed to stand by other men.[8] The unconditionally essential may be reflectively approached by concentration in the experience of communion with other men. If we do not find the basis of this communion underlying ourselves, and permeating our actual commitment, we will never find it; if we were devoid of it, how could we understand it? But if it were not universal in its relevance, then how could this basis of communion and community be unconditionally essential *even in the life of one man?* The unqualified endorsement of which each one of us may be capable with warrant can only be an endorsement of a universal meaning in the condition of man.

Surely it is something like this, and this alone, which would substantiate that root-belief of Kant's, for example, in the priceless worth of individual men. It is unfortunate indeed that Kant approached universality as 'rationalistically' as he did. Perhaps the central deficiency of his ethical thought, for all its greatness, lies in its lack of a grasp upon individuality in its connection with universality. In his just concern to elucidate the possibility of human action that would be non-arbitrary in the most ultimate sense and unconditional in its ground, he seems to have failed to appreciate that the idea of universality in its relevance to action can only be developed along with the most penetrating cognizance of what is involved in true individuality. The human individual cannot be understood in his individuality along the lines of a supposal that it sets him apart from other men and over against them in practice. Perhaps we are only truly individual in so far as we are able to acknowledge and act upon a universal significance in our lives which is the very opposite of divisive in its import for our relations with other persons. It seems necessary that such significance dawn upon each one of us out of a life that is his alone,

---

8. I think of meaning as *focalized* in distinction from objects of attention *focused upon.*

and to act consonantly with it is also for each one of us to find a way that is his alone. However similar his pattern of behaviour may be to that of others, such action cannot be construed as an importation of behavioural patterns justified in themselves. The universal in action binds man with man, but in a way rendering each man irreplaceable rather than 'a value of a variable for which any other rational being might be substituted.'

Have we strayed far from the idea of faith? I think not. We might say that the believing conditional to basic understanding is a matter of response to the intimations we receive of an absolute stake in life. To be able to affirm that stake as ours in the life of any man, whether in our own person or in the person of another, provides the key to the resolution of another major difficulty in Kantian thought: Kant saw the well-being of the individual as disjoined from his capacity to meet the demands of universality in action; but if the suggestions here recorded are on the right track, to maintain such a disjunction is to misunderstand both of its terms. In the end, we stand together or fall in separation; as a community of individuals, we stand. As a society of particulars (either collectivistic or atomistic) . . .

As we look to the lives of men for illumination on these themes, let us bear in mind that they are not inductive generalizations, and they cannot serve as ultimate premises in arguments to conclusions which can function as surrogates for live decision. Live decision is never merely 'choice' or 'problem-solving.'

Thursday, October 2

ON SOCRATES[9]

Aristotle credits Socrates with bringing to explicitness a conception and practice of inductive method. Yet I wonder if we ought not to balance this interpretation of Socrates' thought with certain

---

9. Editorial Note: This discussion of Socrates continues through Friday, October 10, 1952.

considerations reflected in Plato. True, Socrates seems to have urged persistent recourse to live situations in order to clarify ideas. But the force of Socratic inquiry might be quite misconceived either in terms of the practice of induction or in terms of an intention to reason out and urge what we would understand by this practice.

If we may believe Plato, Socrates was concerned with a certain examination of life, with man as the center of his concern, and self-knowledge as a paramount demand to be met in the kind of inquiry that absorbed him. The *Phaedo* suggests an explicit disclaimer on Socrates' part of the pursuit of natural knowledge, unless, perhaps, underlying our knowledge of nature, we should find an understanding of man pertinent after all to a basic understanding of reality. Furthermore, Socrates did not leave us a systematically developed set of ideas, or even the suggestion that he would have wished to develop one. He left us with certain questions and a mode of questioning that force us back on ourselves. He left us with certain themes which also appeal to our capacity for reflective interpretation. I doubt if the current significance of these themes is diminished by the progress that has been made either in inductive knowledge or in the conception of it since his day. Finally, Socrates left us the testimony of his life, suggesting in some measure what he meant.

Let us see what we can make of some of the principal Socratic questions and themes.

First, what of the examined life, and the value of it to which Socrates testified? Let us bear in mind that any man might be tempted to say of his vocation that a life worth living involves this vocation; for him this must be true. Perhaps a philosopher is not worth his salt if he is not inclined to agree with Socrates that the unexamined life is not worth living. Yet I think of two day laborers whose daily endeavour with pick and shovel seemed to me tempered to the stature of vocation. Also a particular sailor comes to mind who was remarkable for the scrupulous care with which he fulfilled the tasks coming to his hands. Socrates himself appears to have felt a very close affinity with craftsmen, in whom he discerned competence and steadfastness, and perhaps a minimum of pretentiousness. Perhaps he would have agreed upon the diversity of genuine vocations among men. Whatever may be the ultimate connection between vocation and the examined life, it may be well to entertain the preliminary reflection that the life of man devoid of genuine vocation is not worth living.

Without disagreeing with Socrates, then, we may cull a most important theme from the implicit emphasis on vocation in his appraisal and conduct of the examined life: For each man there is an absolute stake in life, something absolutely essential in his life; the understanding of what is essential is bound up with understanding man as capable of vocation. Think of the import of this theme for ethics if it is taken seriously. Would it not suggest that we must come to grips with the mode of involvement of a whole man through such a spread of action as would afford purchase for an idea of vocation? This would be rather different from seeking in isolated instances of types of action for the characteristics by which to judge actions justified or not.

But now let us consider the stronger version of Socrates' statement of the value of the examined life. Is it that the examined life is to be conceived as a kind of vocation of man? Are we to think of the examined life as the realization of what is essential in the life of any man? Two companion Socratic persuasions seem to support this interpretation: First, that human excellence crucially involves some form of knowledge; and second, that no man knowingly pursues the worse course. These persuasions carry with them the Socratic question as to the form of knowledge which might be constitutive of excellence. Is it a form of knowledge, for example, which might be taught? And how would this knowing enter into the determination of the better course? To what extent would the knowing evolving through the examined life establish this life itself as the better course?

From Plato's portrait of Socrates' last days something more than a thesis is sustained. Whatever we may make of the idea of the examined life as essential for man and its companion persuasions, we cannot readily discount the tone of unshakeable faith pervading Socrates' utterance and bearing as the life in which he took his stand was brought to the test in death. But how to understand his conception of that life, and to what extent we may concur in it, may become guiding issues for ethical reflection to this day.

Saturday, October 4

How could one say that the unexamined life is not worth living,
that excellence in men is a matter of knowledge of some kind, and
yet maintain that he is wisest among us who realizes that his wisdom
is worth little or nothing (to paraphrase from *Apology,* IX)? To some
it may appear that there is little point in dwelling upon vague dis-
claimers of wisdom tricked out as embodiments of wisdom. Others
may say that if Socrates is to be credited with such a disclaimer, we
should consider it in the context of his defence as an oratorical device,
perhaps of a rather dissembling character. We might even reflect that
if Socrates seriously intended to question the possibility of our possessing wisdom and found it the better part of wisdom to do so, Plato
either failed to understand him in this or tended to disagree with him,
and failed to see in their disagreement an issue of philosophical importance. For Plato's whole conception of the development of human
reason to the acme of its proper functioning seems quite sanguine
about the possibility of man's taking command of his situation through
knowledge which he may acquire; which he may employ as an acquisition, moreover, in behalf of other men, who are lacking in the wisdom so necessary to their own well-being. If Plato also entertained a
different reading of the human condition, at least it does not show
up in his social philosophy.

We have already evolved the clue to a way of interpreting the
elements of the paradox mentioned above which may revive our
interest in it and suggest the possibility of resolving it: It may be the
better part of wisdom to realize that wisdom is not a form of knowledge which we can be strictly said *to possess.* Wisdom may better be
conceived as giving us the strength and courage to be equal to our
situation than as knowledge giving us command of it. To the extent
that human well-being and capacity for acting well ultimately turn
upon understanding (I will not say knowledge), the understanding
in question is going to have to be distinguished from powers we can
be said to wield, including such knowledge as we *acquire* and might
employ as an acquisition. I shall use the term 'wisdom' for such understanding.

Better to go at it a little differently. The substantive use of 'wisdom' suggests an 'it,' a 'something,' on which we might be able to try for a hold just in attempting to characterize it.

Let us try to approach the 'worth little or nothing' aspect of wisdom in this way. Understanding may come to us that is bound up with the realization of what is essential in our lives, but it may be antithetical to such understanding to think of it in the vein of an accomplishment. Let us put it strongly: No man *arrives*. Decision can not be boiled down to informed choice. The frontier on which each one of us stands, and beyond which each one of us commits himself in action, is an incorrigible feature of the situation of a man who acts. This needs careful examination.

It may well be that we are trying to get at what may be meant in speaking of men as "equal before God." (Thought: I can appreciate the mistakes of other men without making those mistakes; at least I can learn from detecting them and avoid similar mistakes by being on my guard against them. But can I appreciate evil without being in some way profoundly involved in it? In our respective failures we are separable from one another, but is this true of us in our failings? Why is it that the attempt to institute ultimate evaluative comparisons of men can strike us as invidious, as I believe it surely can? I suspect that these questions cannot be dealt with relevantly apart from the very standpoint of compassion: a most decisive realization of human communion.)

Yes, it is an idea of radical equality, of non-privileged status, that we are bordering on. In all those respects in which we may be legitimately compared with one another it is reasonable to point out that we may differ. In a perfectly intelligible sense we may be said to differ with respect to endowments, skills, giftedness, and our degree of cultivation or accomplishment. One of us knows a great deal more than another of us in a quite testable way. It is obvious that opportunities of all sorts are unequally distributed. Men are of unequal stature according to many ways in which the measure of stature might be taken. And so on. Some men 'go far,' others 'go nowhere.' Some are born with a silver spoon in their mouths; others find themselves holding the dirty end of the stick. Some are called upon to bear adversities which seem out of all proportion with what we would consider their deserts; others seem to slip smoothly along on a sea oiled by good breaks. Men have been taxed beyond the bearing point by what they have construed as the injustice of it all. No less a philosopher than Kant concurred to this extent: that if there is fixed in the grain of the universe and human destiny a balance between merit and reward, it requires an adjustment radically different from any possibility of such a balance disclosed in our actual experience of life. He saw no intrinsic connection between human well-being and well-doing. Surely this would seem the most radical inequality we could make out: that undeserving men might be as well off as deserving ones, or might even fare better than they.

We have already followed a Socratic disposition to question this, but perhaps there are some respects in which we ought to concur with Kant: for example, in this — that an inductive study of the lives of men fails to reveal a clear basis for refuting Kant's thesis of radical inequality. And what could be more obnoxious than either of these views: that human suffering is a sure sign of what the sufferer had coming to him; or, that we hardly need concern ourselves over apparent injustices because really there is no injustice in the universe.[10]

Then what of this radical human equality to which allusion has been made? For the time being, it is not the equality in ultimate worth of human beings (also a Kantian idea) which I would dwell upon. What I want to suggest is that the standpoint from which we can act is subject to demands upon us proportional to our resources, whatever they may be. By 'demands' here I do not mean claims which others levy on us, or claims to which we subject ourselves. I mean demands which go deeper than what others or we ourselves might translate

[10.] Sacrilege: to enact the denial of our being involved in a mystery; for example, to claim to be able to read the purport of the lives of men like an open book. Do not most 'theories of human nature' tend in this direction? Consider Freud in this connection; was he not better than his own theory? Did he not *believe in* men, more ultimately than he thought to explain them?

into explicit claims, even if such translation is quite possible without distortion. We do not place ourselves or each other under obligation; we *are* under obligation. And no man becomes an authority with years regarding what devolves upon him or anyone else to do. Some choices may become easier; we may become relatively prepared to cope with them effectively. But decision and commitment go deeper than choice. The person is decided or committed. And though choices may overlay decision or commitment, in themselves they are made at the level of the optional, or of the problematical and technical. "Try this and see how it works. See if you like it. If it doesn't work, or if you don't like it, try that, or the other." Choice involves alternatives reduced to the terms in which we can represent them to ourselves; and though it means taking up mutually exclusive alternatives one at a time, it does not preclude shifting from one alternative to another without threat to a person's integrity. With decision, or commitment, on the other hand, it seems to me that we *become* this sort of person or that in a more radically irrevocable way. For the person we become by virtue of commitment is indeed a different person from the one who would have evolved through a different line of cleavage. In so far as we may speak of alternatives at the level of commitment, and in so far as these alternatives would fundamentally define the person in different ways, alternatives other than that shaped in his actual commitment would tend to escape him. One tries many things, but one can live only the life of one man. What we might have been is essentially a darker question than what we might have chosen.

Suppose we were disposed to treat alternatives at the level of commitment as if they were alternatives at the level of choice. First of all we would be liable to the delusion that we stand apart from our decisions and perdure untouched by them, retaining the capacity to explore alternatives in succession 'for what there is in them.' Secondly, we would either have to call in question the authenticity of former commitment or steel ourselves to betrayal. Who could claim that this terrible predicament is unknown to him?

I feel sure there must be a great deal to think out with more care in connection with the ideas of commitment and choice just roughly hewn out.[11] Even now, for example, I should be willing to grant an ambiguity to the notion of decision of which I have not taken account in the foregoing passage. Decision involves something of commitment and something of choice. Lurking behind this ambiguity is the whole issue of interpreting awareness in intimacy with action, and it is just this issue in only a few aspects that we have been touching on all along. For the moment, however, let us try to bring the rough idea of commitment to bear upon this matter of the radical equality of men.

Wednesday, October 8

It seems to me that the more we can appreciate the conditions of well-grounded action, the less we will be inclined to suppose that we are in a position to fulfill them as we may fulfill prescriptions for behavior, or for the achievement of results. It is of the essence of authentic commitment that it be grounded behind the intellectual eye and not merely in a demonstrable basis which we can get before us. The ultimate meaning of service lies just here: We cannot gain command of what grounds our actions; there can only be an unconditional basis of action in so far as we are at 'its' disposal and not our own (something Kant seems to me to obscure by his emphasis on autonomy; Marcel sees this, and has helped me to see it).

Again, we might put the matter this way: At the heart of justified action we will not find an explicit vindication of one's actions to oneself, but rather a foundation underlying ourselves and what we do which virtually eludes translation into explicit vindication. In this connection it may be a help to discern what is involved in ethical reflection when it seems most to the point and least adrift. Ethical reflection is bound up with the possibility of becoming critics of our

[11.] Consider the question which Kierkegaard raises: in what sense, and how, may it be possible to choose ourselves?

own lives, and without pretense. It involves a kind of withdrawal, a genuine kind of detachment, but not the withdrawal of increasing abstraction. It should be, at least, a discovery of ourselves anew, at a level of commitment on which a man can stand. Thus the withdrawal, the detachment, of which I speak is not a matter of stepping outside of life, outside of all commitments, and of viewing them while we hold them in abeyance. If it does not involve a fundamental recollection of ourselves, as Marcel puts it,[12] it is in fact a spurious endeavour.

Only if we carry into the moments of ethical reflection that very faith and spiritual candour on the strength of which we may act with assurance and without pretense, is it possible for us to focalize in moments of reflection that basis of commitment in our lives which gives them authenticity. The practical importance of ethical thought lies not in its yielding a blueprint on which we might construct our lives and model our actions, but in the possibility it may afford of immediate clarification with regard to a foundation of life that is absolutely genuine (as opposed to optional, arbitrary, or conditional), and utterly beyond artifice or manipulation. Except as ethical reflection is undertaken in what I must call the spirit of prayer — an utmost form of commitment which cannot be simulated or induced — it cannot be freed from arbitrariness. For in reflection, too, our position is not sound except as we are at the disposal of what we cannot command.

I see that our conception of truth might be deeply affected in those moments when life comes to us as a gift. I share the current philosophical concern with 'the given' as important for our understanding of truth. But there are all manner of relative givens, and they are relative to the modes of receptivity in which the given may be received. But what is fundamentally given, and fundamentally received, in our concern with truth? If this question is begged, as perhaps it must be, we may be nearest to begging it in the right way when we discover and acknowledge life as a gift.

[12.] See, for example, the discussion of "secondary reflection" in Vol. I of *The Mystery of Being*.

Friday, October 10

The upshot of these reflections on Socrates seems to be that we may construe human wisdom to be worth little or nothing in so far as we become involved in a pretension to the possession of wisdom. The work of the love of wisdom, then, is the reflective amplification of truth as it may only be given to us in serving it, and each day anew.

Correspondingly, our true position in action would seem to be this: that it is one of being called upon to act, and not one of calling the moves. Our ultimate stake in action consists in the immediate clarification of its ground. But the ground of action only seems susceptible of clarification that is immediate, and its immediate clarification presupposes that opening of ourselves to it which is faith *in* it rather than belief about it.

We vary indefinitely with respect to the resources which one or another of us may have at his disposal. But we are radically equal to each other, and to ourselves (from time to time), in that the demand to act devolves on us, *such as we are,* and it is never in essence repetitious, or normal, or abnormal, however much we remain constant amidst constants of our situation and resemble, or differ from, other persons. The disclosure of our radical equality seems native to the simplicity and innocence which there may be in us. Sometimes in the moment of our settling into sleep, with what gentleness this becomes clear. Here all of us are, together and alone. In the solitude of each one of us, it is we who are blessed. As Meister Eckhart says, all paths are even; though it may seldom seem so.

For a moment just now I could remember some times at sea; especially the grey Christmas Day of 1944 on our little ship, as thirty-five of us sailed on alone over the endless swells. The land of Manus Island in the Admiralties lay behind us by some days of open sea. The Philippines lay ahead, but far beyond our seeing, like whatever was in store for us there, or from there on. All that we knew of our position was like the ship's position approximately fixed on the chart. It was something else again to be there looking out over the grey sea under the grey sky, steering a course that took its direction more from the world of the chart than from the world we beheld. It was Christmas in the wilderness.

As the day drew to a close nearly everyone not on watch was sitting about on deck up forward of the pilot house. The sound of the engines was muted up there, and the wash of the seas under the bows made it seem quite still. Only the faintest tinge of color crept into the sky as the sun set. The men who talked were talking very low. Someone in a steady, quiet voice began to sing, and there were soon others singing with him. In the closing light of that day, riding to the endless swells, they sang the song of men in our position. And it was Christmas in the wilderness.

Saturday, October 11

Without question it is a pivotal persuasion worked out in *The Republic* that the foundation of right conduct is also the foundation of the well-being of the agent, appearances to the contrary notwithstanding. In the *Apology* Socrates is represented as putting this persuasion rather extremely, to the effect that no harm may befall a good man in this life or any other, if there be any other. There are respects in which I think we may be justly suspicious of such a statement of the theme. If it is construed as the expression of a faith in the common foundation of our well-being and well-doing, well and good. But the notion of "the good man" seems to me risky. It suggests the possibility of 'our arriving,' and does not give due place to the ambiguity of our condition. Even further it may suggest that equally precarious note of insular self-sufficiency which becomes rather prominent in later Epicurean and Stoic conceptions of "the wise man."

Sunday, October 12

Could we ever understand ourselves in the image of the rocklike island or the stronghold, impervious to what surrounds us, living a life of inner containment, perduring incorruptible in solid singleness, or reigning over ourselves to secure constant excellence and tranquillity within this island of ourselves? Are human excellence and well-being to be conceived as states of exemption or immunization from the liabilities of the human condition? Are they, indeed, to be conceived as *states* at all? I think not. For one thing, if they were states, we ought in principle to be able to proceed from the formulation of the conditions of their occurrence to their production and maintenance, as we may do to an appreciable extent with states of the human body.

At the very bottom of any attempt to interpret human excellence and well-being in the mode of self-sufficiency there would seem to be the liability of radically obscuring the bond underlying individuals by virtue of which we can be genuinely available to one another. I do not mean that the mutual dependency of persons will be ignored. Rather, I mean to suggest that the conception of the relationship between persons is liable to be confined to terms of mutual dependence and independence. The ideal of self-sufficiency seems incapable of undercutting the discussion of the destiny of the individual in these terms. Indeed, the more the destiny of the individual is understood to be *communal*, and not merely more or less *social*, the less the temptation will be to indulge such an ideal.

Wednesday, October 15

There is nothing particularly arresting about the remarks of Cephalus in the prelude of Plato's *Republic*. This opening passage leads us with such ease into the provocative discussions ensuing after Cephalus has retired from the scene. Yet there is a tone in the utterance of this man which brings him alive in all his years, and it may elicit our respect even as it calls forth Socrates' admiration in the dialogue. Cephalus voices very simply the idea that a person's position is sound only if he is squared with other men. In retrospect it seems to Cephalus that the character of a person, young or old, will have more to do with whether he finds his lot tolerable than anything else. And in old age there is the advantage that one is less liable to enslavement in passions. Cephalus bespeaks concern about what a man may have done amiss during his life; with advance in years one may feel the importance of making such amends as one can. He ends by speaking with conviction about honesty and rendering men their due, but agrees with Socrates that no automatic rules of judgment or action could follow from these convictions.

Cephalus' remarks seem to me to escape banality in the tone they carry of a man well aware that he is in his last years. His thought is keyed to the fact that his days are numbered, yet the fact does not unbalance him, and in this he shares something of the spirit of Socrates discernible in *Crito* and *Phaedo*.

As Socrates says to Cephalus in *Republic*, the appraisals of a man in Cephalus' position are a matter of the keenest interest to us. What will a man have to say, for whom no future stretches out as an indefinitely extended prospect? What can a man discern from the span of a life so largely behind him that may afford fundamental purchase for evaluation? What can he disclose to us of what may stand a man in good stead, not merely in the long run, but more fundamentally, when the obscurity of death becomes immanent? What in the life of a man can place his life in such a light that he can live his last moments in the most profound affirmation? Or is such a thing possible?

I will not hesitate to say that questions such as these seem to me to set the ultimate philosophical issue in a very clear manner. And the whole drift of my own positive thinking has been imbued with belief in the possibility of such affirmation, with the concern to understand how unconditional affirmation is possible, and with the responsible articulation of that very affirmation. I know that in speaking to one another, and otherwise, we sometimes can and do bear witness to that which cannot play us false, and in so doing may help one another in our hours of weakness. This seems to me the ultimate form of help that we can give to one another, and it is a form of help implicit, at least, in all actions of purest service and generosity. When I think of the meaning of a friend, I think of actions and words of persons in which I have found lucid testimony to this effect: that the lives we lead need not betray us in our earnestness, and that finality is not absurdity. Perhaps the thought might be ventured that the measure of our *understanding* of reality lies in our capacity for the responsible realization of unqualified affirmation. But the ambiguity of our situation is patent in the fact that the possibility of such affirmation can be systematically ignored or denied. Indeed systematic thought is disposed to reflect the unification of complexes of discriminables; it is responsive in terms of *uniformity*; but how will it accommodate simplicity? Yet I suspect that the understanding of reality which I connect with the possibility of unqualified affirmation is more attuned to simplicity than to uniformity. This idea of reality understood in its simplicity might answer to the intent of the Buddhist thought with which I have been so much helped by Dr. Suzuki.

Friday, October 17

These phrases quoted by Ernst Cassirer from Meister Eckhart keep returning to me: ". . . the simple ground, the still desert, the simple silence (der einveltige grunt, die stille wueste, die einveltic stille) . . ."[13]

The awareness of reality in its simplicity or absoluteness does not seem to cancel out the awareness of distinct things, or to vitiate the trustworthiness of discrimination. Perhaps it even underwrites the mind in its forming of distinctions. I believe I was trying to put something like this point in 1946 when I wrote of "the sense of being" as undergirding the scientific enterprise.[14]

13. *Language and Myth*, New York, Harper & Bros., 1946, p. 74.

14. Editorial note: The reference here is to my doctoral dissertation for the University of California, written during 1946 and entitled *The Sense and the Conception of Being*.

The theme that was central for me at the time still seems sound: The *presence* of things in their definiteness is bound up with understanding reality in its absoluteness. As I thought of the matter then, anything definite becomes definitively given as its presence comes home to us; but the presence of things does not come home to us except as presence is completed from within ourselves. Love is such a matter of completion of presence from within ourselves. It is being, understood from within, and this alone, which can make sense of being in discriminable form.

At this point I find myself brought to the reconsideration of John Anderson's idea of the life of man in an unknown world.[15] In what sense shall we interpret ours to be an unknown world? May we not say that in the contemplation of known things, in our experience of known things in depth, we come to understand the very things of which we have some knowledge in a way not represented by the knowledge we have of them? When John Anderson speaks of an unknown world, I am sure he does not mean that our knowledge of the world is very limited, limited though it may be. The world does not become less 'unknown' in his sense in proportion to the increase of our knowledge about it. We might be nearer the mark in saying that the understanding of our position is not fundamentally consummated merely as knowledge about the world. The world is not unknown, for example, as a secret withheld from us is unknown to us. As Marcel would put it, our experience of the world involves us in a mystery which can be intelligible to us only as a mystery. The more we experience things in depth, the more we participate in a mystery intelligible to us only as such; and the more we understand our world to be an unknown world. Our true home is wilderness, even the world of every day.

15. Editorial note: See Anderson, John M., *The Individual and the New World*, State College, Pennsylvania, Bald Eagle Press, 1955. I should like to quote here the concluding sentences of this book: "Man's nature is not attained once and for all, but again and again, hauntingly maintained in an eternal present. The meaning of the unknown, the New World, is to be found in that journey taken into it, a journey which discovers again and again that man's nature is to be reborn."

Saturday, October 18, 1952

To get back to the prelude of the *Republic*, the conversation of Cephalus: It is the orientation of the ethical thought in this passage which impresses me, in contrast with the theoretical tone of the discussion which prevails throughout the rest of the dialogue.

Granted that the sample is slight, we can still note the concrete recollective vein in which Cephalus' reflections move. There is a true note here of the actual man taking stock of what has gained authority over him in his experience. Further, there is a suggestion of the possibility of an intimate relation between such reflection and the emphatic shape which a person's life may assume in a kind of retroactive manner. If faintly, nonetheless unmistakably, Cephalus expresses the concern of a person to define his stand through a re-search of the life he has lived, as if his life had been given to him in trust, and as if it behooved him in taking stock of his trusteeship to define his present stand in the light of those demands which have gently but irresistibly pressed home to him the acknowledgment that he *is* in the position of trusteeship, and not at his own disposal. Once reflection is instituted from this standpoint it makes sense to think of two possibilities: that one has, perhaps, usurped prerogatives in a way implying the denial of the position of trusteeship; second, that a trust so abdicated might yet be redeemed while the conditions of the trusteeship still hold. Again it seems to me clear that recollective reflection can be interpreted in its practical import as the gathering together or rallying of ourselves on a basis which affords a stand. Such a basis, of course, could not be artificial. It could not be of our own making. To become clear with respect to it would be strictly a matter of discovery, and of the kind of discovery to which philosophical thought is peculiarly answerable. I will call this mode of discovery experiential in deliberate distinction from 'empirical.' For it is not a mode of discovery to be interpreted as a disclosure of the nature of objects. I do not think it is subject to cultivation by experimental method.

To accentuate this point: The denial of the possibility of *experiential* discovery would be the root denial of the possibility of philosophy. Isn't this denial in its clearest form just the point to which so much of Positivism has come? That our thought can be responsible only to empirical discoveries, or to the elements of an abstract system, and that thought in any other mode would be vague and irresponsible, devoid of authentic purchase: This is 'scientism,' the antiphilosophical persuasion so evident in our time.

I have mentioned the possibility of a kind of retroactive or redemptive force which one may come to understand in recollective meditation, having noted the suggestion of this idea in the standpoint of Cephalus. In Oscar Wilde's *De Profundis* there is some very interesting material for reflection concerning the relation between what it means to assume responsibility in the fullest sense and the capacity to review one's life in the spirit of truth. Indeed one may discern in these pages flashes of the interplay between a kind of spiritual candour and the capacity to assume responsibility in the fullest sense. For Wilde this involves the acceptance of responsibility for his past life to his dying day, evaluated from a standpoint that tends to free him from a defensive, apologetic approach to the past, and also from an intolerable burden of suffering and shame. In this book we come to the verge of the theme of liberating truth: the very spirit of truth.[16]

Wednesday, July 8, 1953

Two days ago I settled down to resume work and I have only managed to avoid getting in my own way by reading. On the first day I happened once again upon those opening lines of Claudel's *Tête d'Or* quoted by Marcel:[17]

16. Editorial note: From this point on, through the remainder of the academic year 1952-53, what I was able to write proved to be spade work for my courses, and diverged considerably from the venture represented in these pages.

17. Marcel, Gabriel, *The Mystery of Being*, Chicago, Regnery, 1950, Vol. I, p. 90.

Here am I,
Weak, ignorant,
A new man in the face of unknown things,
And I turn my face to the year and the rainy arc, my heart is full of
   weariness,
I lack knowledge or force for action. What shall I utter, what shall I
   undertake? How shall I use these dangling hands, these feet of mine
   that draw me on like dreams?

These lines come near to expressing the condition in which I found myself. As I read them now, I relate them immediately to Marcel's own essay in *Homo Viator*, "The Ego and its Relation to Others." In this essay Marcel helps to expose the matter of getting in our own way, and the egocentricity underlying it: the anguish of self-consciousness, of feeling the need to prove oneself to oneself, and the connection of this frame of mind with the asphyxiating atmosphere of the competitive situation. I must have sensed the fittingness of Marcel's essay to the condition expressed in Claudel's lines in turning from them directly to the essay on that very day.

That was the first day in which I faced the crucial year ahead. What would I do? Here I am in a situation about which I feel the need to set down a few words; it is the actual situation which I must somehow work through and beyond.

For five years I have been writing in an exploratory way, gradually forced to recognize that this was the case and I must accept it, along with its professional consequences. My task has been to learn to write in a vein compatible with what I can honestly say in the act of trying to discover what I must say. It has been a precarious business. I have found myself thinking quite differently from the majority of men who are setting the style and the standard of philosophy worth doing. Only when lost in my own work, and especially in communication with those students who have shared the venture with me, have I been able to transcend the uneasiness and the defensiveness incurred in diverging from the main trends of thought in current academic philosophy among English-speaking circles. It has already become apparent that the thought which I am concerned to define is not easy to produce on demand. Often I do not know what I am trying to say. By now I bear a considerable burden of not having spoken out among my colleagues at times when a protesting response to what they were saying would well up in me. I think I have known what it is to fail to bear witness. Perhaps one aspect of the task before me is to clear my conscience on this score. The point is not that I was, or was not, entitled to think them mistaken in what they were saying. The point is that a person must make known where he stands. And if it be philosophy that he is engaged in, he must speak out. In so far as he fails to do this he loses reality and he loses his community.

I am now free to speak my mind in a fairly sustained way. It is something I have wanted to do since those days in World War II when I used to dream of the possibility of a period free for reflection, to work things out for myself. Yet already I have savoured the danger of being afloat on a sea of possibilities, 'at liberty' to take any direction. There is no true freedom in this.

On the second day of facing up to this situation I felt the first faint stirrings as of a breeze in the sails of a becalmed ship, brought to me in the voice of Meister Eckhart, while reading the "Talks of Instruction." He imparts the sense of working with what you have and from where you are, and not straining. Here are a few of the passages which especially impressed me:

> As I have often said, if a person were in such a rapturous state as St. Paul once entered, and he knew of a sick man who wanted a cup of soup, it would be far better to withdraw from the rapture for love's sake and serve him who is in need.[18]

> There is no way of making a person true unless he gives up his own will. In fact, apart from complete surrender of the will, there is no traffic with God. (One may note that this does not prevent Eckhart from entertaining a conception of good will.)

> The light shines in the darkness and there man becomes aware of it. . . . It is when people are in the dark, or suffering, that they are to see the light. The truth is that the more ourselves we are, the less self is in us. (My note: integrity cannot be self-imposed.)

> . . . God never tied man's salvation to any pattern. (My question: must not each man actually fulfill a *unique* destiny?)

[18.] *Meister Eckhart: A Modern Translation*, Trans. by R. B. Blakney, New York, Harper & Bros., 1941, p. 14. The ensuing quotations are from pp. 16, 17, 23, 32, 34, 38, and 38, in that order, respectively.

There is no stopping place in this life — no, nor was there ever one for any man, no matter how far along his way he'd gone. This above all, then, be ready at all times for the gifts of God and always for new ones.

Know it or not, the storms of unrest come of self-will.

We are to have what we have as if it were loaned to us and not given . . . (My note: it is false to act as if we could endow what we do with authority.)

. . . all blessings and perfection begin with being "poor in spirit." In fact, that is the only foundation on which any good may rest . . . (My note: isn't this poverty something akin to living in the presence of the universe?)

Thursday, July 9

It seems to me that Meister Eckhart talks like a reasonable man. No doubt there is much in what he says that I do not understand; on whole pages I sometimes draw a blank. Yet there is this reasonableness about his utterance and the calm assurance of a man talking from experience.

It just occurred to me that one might get a fresh slant on the topic of reason and faith by pulling it down off the pedestal on which theoretical treatment has placed it and handling it a bit more intimately to see if it is not, indeed, a kind of philosophical idol. In reading Meister Eckhart, for example, one encounters, not reason and faith, but the reasoning of a man whose reasonableness, in its groundedness, manifests faith. Might one not think of faith as a concrete condition of having something to do or to say? Isn't faith akin to that "poverty of spirit," that non-self-willedness, that disinterestedness so central in Eckhart, which is a concrete condition of reasoning being reasonable? Instead of trying to formulate the respective characteristics of propositions articulating truths of reason and truths of faith, we might therefore reflect on reasonable thinking and doing, such as the reasonable thinking of Eckhart. And we might find that we can fix upon faith in at least this sense: As a condition of the flow of authentic meaning in the consummation of understanding. But we will miss the point if our reflection fails to dwell in and on the *act* of reasoning. If our reflections about 'reason' keep getting focused on statements instead of partaking of the experience of live thought, we would do better to reflect on the experience of playing a reasonable game of tennis, or even of perceiving a game played with some measure of alertness and gracefulness and absorption. That which is alertly and gracefully done can teach us of faithfulness, and of reasonableness, in their connection.

An example comes to mind apropos of this matter.

The lower reaches of the Rogue River were mainly accessible by water, by traveling on the river itself. There used to be a mailboat which made regular runs upriver to a point thirty miles above Gold Beach, which is at the mouth. The boat took passengers, and it would drop you off or pick you up wherever you liked along the way.

No doubt the river is never exactly child's play to negotiate. Even in those lower reaches it is more like a mountain river than anything else. As I remember, the boat used was powered with twin Packard engines. It was solidly built but as light as possible, and maybe twenty-five feet long. At the time of which I am speaking the river was low, and I remember particularly a technique which the boatman employed while descending over the shoalest spots, especially just at the break above rapids, at the tail end of the slick below pools. With the drift of the river accelerating our pace over the ground, instead of inching down over these spots, our boatman would apply full power upon approaching one of them. Down through the pool we would shoot at an alarming pace, and just as we would come upon the shoalest spot, our boatman would cut his power. Overtaken by its own wash, the boat would be lifted up and over into the rapid below, as neatly as could be. Of course I suppose the boatman had to remember without even calling to mind just where he had to come out at the head of the rapid. Even though he steered standing, there were quite a few drops which precluded a perspective of what lay below until you were over and into the run. In general, you might say, he had to be steeped in the river, constantly alive to it in its ever-unfolding. There were the protruding boulders and snags which had to be just grazed in holding to a channel. For the passenger these were the breath-taking perils. But I imagine the boatman welcomed them, with which he knew where he stood, compared with the up-reaching but unobtrusive thrusts of rock, sometimes scarcely told on the surface, which had to be taken equally close aboard.

As the Indian boatman stood there in steady communion with the flowing river over mile after mile of deeply remembered bottom, as the full-throated engines sang along the river bars and through the pine-forested valley, as we labored up in the teeth of the constantly opposing current and then turned back down with it into the accelerated decisions of descent, the lasting impression was built into me that without a reasonableness instant with faith, this thing could not be done. I can feel that Indian standing there handling the boat aright. And to this day, from some fifteen years ago, this man has seemed to define the condition of man as it should be, and as it should be understood.

Remembering this river and the man in the boat upon it brings me home into the midst of my work. The very revival of the reality of a river carries with it the sense of reality as I would do justice to it. I could wish for no more than to do justice to the instruction I have received from moving waters. Even as I think of the Housatonic River, the Gualala River, the Eel, of the Truckee and of Rising River, of the open sea itself, the care of the situation which so lately cramped me washes away. It seems that there is a stream of limitless meaning flowing into the life of a man if he can but patiently entrust himself to it. There is no hurry, only the need to be true to what comes to mind, and to explore the current carefully in which one presently moves. There is a constant fluency of meaning in the instant in which we live. One may learn of it from rivers in the constancy of their utterance, if one listens and is still. They speak endlessly in an univocal exhalation, articulating the silence.

This calls to mind something Max Picard has to say: "Spring does not come from winter; it comes from the silence from which winter came and summer and autumn."[19] Here, quite concretely, we

[19.] *The World of Silence*, London, Harvill, 1948, p. 113.

get the shape of the thought which it is most imperative to think. I shall try to set down one or two more ideas and references which may be cognate with it.

Friday, July 10

From Picard I retain the idea that sounds, distinct sounds, make sense only as heard articulations of silence. Perhaps sounds are only so heard as we are still. Otherwise they are only abstractly heard, and no matter the order noted between them, they would tend to become merely a sequence of noises. There are philosophers who would give us reality as a series of noises, raising their glasses, perhaps, as does Hume, with such graciousness that one may be quite taken in. Yet if reality be noise, this comprehends human utterance in the end, and pleasing or mannerly noise makes no more sense than does unpleasant, or vulgar.

We might be disposed to say that only man-made sounds can make sense, as in music and in speech. Yet it seems to me that man-made sounds, different though they may be from sounds at large, involve that peculiar stillness in ourselves which partakes of a silence in things at large, of which they are the composed articulation. As sounds at large articulate silence, so what we utter from inner still-ness is authentic human sound. Perhaps we could say that it is in this regard that true words match reality. True words do not originate from antecedent words construed merely abstractly in serial order. True words flow from that stillness from which antecedent true words have flowed.

I find the shape of the thought which I am trying to define loom-ing out of Spinoza's *Ethics*: An infinite number of things follow in infinite ways from the divine nature. If one tries to conceive the di-vine nature in distinct terms, one can conceive of nothing but what can be numbered among the infinite number of things which Spinoza speaks of as following from it in infinite ways. The divine nature is not another thing from which things follow. Nor is their "following from the divine nature" itself modal. The "following from" is non-relational and non-sequential. From the standpoint of Spinoza's second kind of knowledge, the systematic knowledge of the order of distinct things, there can be no acknowledged reason for speaking of the divine nature; that is, things are not taken into account as expressing the divine nature. As Richard Gotshalk has seen better than any commentator on Spinoza whom I have read, we need to exercise a greater caution in moving to the subject of a third kind of knowledge, in terms of which things are concretely appreciated as expressing the divine nature, than Spinoza himself is given to suggesting. From the standpoint of the second kind of knowledge, the third kind of knowledge is not a kind of knowledge at all. Perhaps we could speak of it as concrete understanding of things. Yet if we would *represent* things to ourselves, we must represent them in terms of the second kind of knowledge. There can be *no thing known,* and no thing to refer to as known, apart from the distinctly and systematically known. Yet to understand reality concretely is not merely consummated as the comprehension of the distinct. It is to appreciate the distinct, not as the expression of *some thing* which is indistinct (i.e. vague!), but rather, precisely as one appreciates the distinct sound (i.e. "a mode," in Spinoza's terms) as an articulation of silence.

The genius of Spinoza lies eminently in his development of the idea of power, as the concrete essence of a man, *so as to suggest* the connection between human action and the possibility of reality in its final significance dawning upon a man: The understanding of reality and human fulfillment are bound up with effective action. We come to *understand* the reality which we know according to the second kind of knowledge in the moment of effective action. In this moment of effective action. In this moment the matter of "following from" is clarified. Thus, apart from one's own commitment, one's own complete commitment in action, the distinct things which we know, however systematically conceived, must remain as noise; they fail to make ultimate sense.

The authenticity of our deeds is the basic condition of our concrete understanding of reality.

Saturday, July 11

I recall mornings, at the crack of dawn, on the Gualala River when we would walk up along one or another of the long gravel bars. As we approached the water in the gathering light, we sometimes perceived all up and down the length of a pool, such as Miner's Bend, the breaking and swirling of a fresh run of steelhead trout. The day before there may have been only occasional fish showing, the vestigial fish, darkened from having already spent some days in fresh water. But on this morning the lower river is alive with new, silvery trout, fresh from the sea. On such a morning as this there is a temptation to dissipate one's attention over too many fish and too much water; one makes a cast above where a broad back has just shown. But even as the drift begins there is a resounding smack on the smooth surface twenty feet upstream. Then two swirls appear forty feet below. Meanwhile your partner clear down at the tail of the slick is backing out of the river, his rod nodding in sweeping arcs, and a gleaming ten-pounder ascends from the water almost into the branches of that overhanging pine on the bank opposite him. It is a glorious thing to know the pool is alive with these glancing, diving, finning fish. But at such moments it is well to make an offering in one's heart to the still hour in the redwoods ascending into the sky; and to fish in one place, for one fish at a time. On such mornings, too, one may even catch nothing at all.

It takes many, many days to learn of what may and may not be in the river. Let us wade right in and keep fishing where we are, with our fingertips touching the trembling line. It is just in the moment of the leap we both feel and see, when the trout is instantly born, entire, from the flowing river, that reality is knowingly defined.

Now the river is the unborn, and the sudden fish is just the new-born — whole, entire, complete, individual, and universal. The fisherman may learn that each instant is pregnant with the miracle of the new-born fish, and fishing in the river may become a knowing of each fish even before it is born. As he fishes the ever-flowing current, it teaches him of the fish even before it is born, just in so far as this alert fishing involves "abiding in no-abode," or the "unattached mind."[20] If one is steeped in the flowing river and sensitized through the trembling line, one anticipates the new-born fish at every moment. The line tautens and with all swiftness, the fish is there, sure enough! And now, in the leaping of this fish, how wonderfully, laughingly clear everything becomes! If eventually one lands it, and kneels beside its silvery form at the water's edge, on the fringe of the gravel bar, if one receives this fish as purely as the river flows, everything is momently given, and the very trees become eloquent where they stand.

Here, as concretely as may be, lies a basic point, one so strongly grasped in the reflections of Gabriel Marcel: Individuality and universality come hand in hand in experience. Either they are appreciated simultaneously and concretely, or not at all. Perhaps they might be spoken of as experiential ideas, to dissociate them from categories germane to a more abstract and theoretical, indeed a more *typological*, frame of mind. Is it not the typological frame of mind, in its abstractness, which fixes the character of the Aristotelian categories, by the way? If so, then individuality and universality as experiential ideas would be more cognate with Aristotle's own thinking in the *Poetics*. For here Aristotle seeks to interpret tragic drama in terms of universal significance expressed in the actions of individuals. As a matter of fact, I would like to think out the ideas of individuality and universality in connection with just such experience as seems to have about it that "catharsis" in terms of which Aristotle sought to analyse tragic consciousness. I think at once of Robert Langston's study of tragedy with reference to *Lear*,[21] and his suggestion that catharsis be thought of as a kind of catharsis of "self."

To hear a sound as an articulation of silence, is to apprehend the distinct as individual and as universal. This is the cue to what I mean.

[20] For the use of these phrases, see e.g. Suzuki, D. T., *Living by Zen*, London, Rider & Co., 1950, pp. 66-67.

[21] In a course paper written at Harvard University during 1952.

Sunday, July 12

If one finds a persistent obstacle in his way, a tenacious difficulty in which he is involved, a liability which seems more serious to his undertaking than anything else with which he repeatedly copes, perhaps it is as well to be explicit about it in following his way and in trying to be explicit about that way, even though in so doing one may not be rid of the obstacle. I would simply record the fact, to begin with, that I am sensible of being my own chief obstacle in this attempt to follow the way of philosophic truth.

In "The Ego and its Relation to Others" Marcel sets forth a penetrating analysis of this matter of being a liability to oneself. At points his analysis is strikingly close to the work of Dr. Karen Horney,[22] and his reference to Meredith's *The Egoist* has proven extremely apt upon following it up. Marcel is concerned with what it means to be self-centered, cut off within oneself. This, he says, is not a matter of spatial enclosure, but of a certain emphasis or accent which one places upon an image of oneself. Not that one is particularly aware of that image in attempting to foster it. The image has to do with what one purports to be, and the claims through which one attempts to support it must tend to disguise their function in so far as they are to contribute to the deception one is attempting to practice on oneself. Even more exactly, what one pretends to be one must obscure from himself, so that the obscurity in which "the idol" is safeguarded extends to the claims by which one attempts to support it. If the latter were to appear in explicit connection with the former, if one were clear, that is, about what he is pretending to be and how he is attempting to establish this pretense, the whole business would collapse. Thus despair may well mark our passage to renewed candour.

22. Editorial note: see especially Dr. Horney's development of the concept of "the idealized image" (*Our Inner Conflicts*, New York, Norton, 1945), and her final version of the same matter in terms of "pride systems" (*Neurosis and Human Growth*, New York, Norton, 1950).

The following quotations from Marcel seem to me so helpful and suggestive that I must write them down:

> Burdened with myself, plunged in this disturbing world, sometimes threatening me, sometimes my accomplice, I keep an eager look-out for everything emanating from it which might either soothe or ulcerate the wound I bear within me, which is my *ego*. This state is strikingly analogous to that of a man who has an abscess at the root of his tooth and who experiments cautiously with heat and cold, acid and sugar, to get relief. What then is this anguish, this wound? The answer is that it is above all the experience of being torn by the contradiction between the all which I aspire to possess, to annex, or, still more absurd, to monopolise, and the obscure (latent?) consciousness that I am after all nothing but an empty void; for, still, I can affirm nothing about myself which would be really myself; nothing, either, which would be permanent; nothing which would be secure against criticism and the passage of time. Hence the craving to be confirmed from outside, by another; this paradox, by virtue of which even the most self-centered among us looks to others and only to others for his final investiture.[23]

> From the very fact that I treat the other person merely as a means of resonance or an amplifier, I tend to consider him as a sort of apparatus which I can, or think I can, manipulate, or of which I can dispose at will. I form my own idea of him and, strangely enough, this idea can become a substitute for the real person, a shadow to which I shall come to refer my acts and words. The truth of the matter is that to pose is always to pose before oneself. "To play to the gallery . . ." we are accustomed to say, but the gallery is still the self. To be more exact, we might say that the other person is the provisional and as it were accessory medium, through which I can arrive at forming a certain image, or idol of myself; the work of stylization by which each of us fashions this image might be traced step by step. This work is helped by social failure as much as by success. When he who poses is scoffed at by his companions, he decides, more often than not, that he has to do with imbeciles and shuts himself up with jealous care in a little sanctuary where he can be alone with his idol.[24]

> Maybe there is no more fatal error than that which conceives the *ego* as the secret abode of originality. To get a better idea of this we must here introduce the wrongly discredited notion of gifts. The best part

[23]. "The Ego and its Relation to Others", *Homo Viator*, Chicago, Regnery, 1951, p. 16; parenthesis mine.

[24]. Ibid., pp. 17-18.

of my personality does not belong to me. I am in no sense the owner, only the trustee.[25]

Does it, however, follow that this *egolatry*, this idolatry of the self, must necessarily be met by a rationalistic and impersonal doctrine? Nothing, I believe, would be farther from the truth. Whenever men have tried to put such a doctrine into practice we must own that it has proved itself extremely disappointing. To be more exact, such an experiment has never been and never could be effective. Actually it is of the very essence of this doctrine that it cannot be really put into practice, except perhaps by a few theorists who are only at ease among abstractions, paying for this faculty by the loss of all real contact with living beings, and, I might add, with the great simplicities of existence. For the immense majority of human beings, the entities which such a rationalism claims to set up as the object of everybody's reverent attention are only shams behind which passions incapable of recognizing themselves take cover.[26]

Marcel goes on to identify such rationalism with ideologies, and I am reminded of the fact that we are presently engaged in this country in manufacturing counter-ideology, as if there were nothing suspect in ideology as such.

I cannot resist setting down just one more passage, which also touches the nerve of my present interest:

As I hinted just now, one cannot strictly say that personality is good in itself, or that it is an element of goodness: the truth is much more that it controls the existence of a world where there is good and evil. I should be inclined to think that the *ego*, so long as it remains shut up within itself, that is to say the prisoner of its own feelings, of its covetous desires, and of that dull anxiety which works upon it, is really beyond the reach of evil as well as of good. It literally has not yet awakened to reality. . . . I would go further: it seems to me that each of us, in a considerable part of his life or his being, is still unawakened, that is to say that he moves on the margin of reality like a sleep-walker. Let us say that the *ego*, as such, is ruled by a sort of vague fascination, which is localised, almost by chance, in objects arousing sometimes desire, sometimes terror. It is, however, precisely against such a condition that what I consider the essential characteristic

25. Ibid., p. 19.
26. Ibid., p. 20.

of the person is opposed, the characteristic, that is to say, of availability (*disponibilité*).[27]

Undoubtedly these passages may occasion very legitimate questions. They verge upon one question, in particular, with which I wish to deal eventually at length, namely: What does it mean to assume responsibility authentically, as opposed to that semblance of the assumption of responsibility which suffers the illusion of autonomy?

But the point I wish to accentuate now is that of the concrete epistemological import of such ethical reflections as these of Marcel. The philosopher wishes to understand reality. Wherein must he conceive his fundamental difficulties to lie? Are they of the sort a speculative mind would be apt to indicate, when taking stock of the respects in which we are liable to be mistaken, as Descartes does in his *Meditations*? Or must we suspect that our availability to advent of essential understanding, essential truth, is chiefly smothered by ourselves?

Wherein can a reflective concern with reality find a purchase, then? Surely not in some immaculate principle abstractly set up as a touchstone for philosophical truth. The purchase can be none other than that experience which is our involvement with other living beings acknowledged in their own right, and "with the great simplicities of existence." But these only dawn on our reflection as we are able to open ourselves to their reception, and in all manner of situations besides those of a dominantly reflective character.

I think of those lines with which Thoreau closes *Walden*, which return upon me again and again to test my belief: "Only that day dawns to which we are awake. There is more day to dawn. The sun is but a morning star." I place my trust in this simplicity, not knowing where it may lead; and as I may do this with deep consent, I find I am relieved from the burden of myself. And once again, the ideas of individuality and universality come back to me, hand in hand. Earlier this day they were utterly lost to me, like empty word-shells.

[27]. Ibid., pp. 22-23.

Here is a poem written in the Sung dynasty which stays with me:

> Misty rain on Mount Lu,
> And waves surging in Che Kiang;
> When you have not yet been there,
> Many a regret you have;
> But once there and homeward you wend,
> How matter-of-fact things look!
> Misty rain on Mount Lu,
> And waves surging in Che Kiang.[28]

When the anticipated trout leaps, how wonderfully matter-of-fact it looks.

Now where is it that one may not yet have been? Surely one is not speaking of rain on Mount Lu and waves in Che Kiang without having been in the place to begin with, in the very place from which things come to look so matter-of-fact, once one *is there*. I do not think the poet speaks of travel from one place to another. One is in this place all along. Wending homeward is not leaving the rain on Mount Lu and the surging waves of Che Kiang, not leaving them behind. It is, rather, a coming to meet them, a welcoming of them, an acknowledgment of them. Yes, they are there, just as before. But as one comes home to them, they are *realized;* and therefore, how matter-of-fact they look, how wonderful they are! One knows that they could not be other than they are. Such is the necessity of the divine nature, from which follow an infinite number of things in infinite ways.

I think there is no surer criterion of truth, in so far as truth defines man's ultimate concern — though this criterion is necessarily immanent in experiential realization — than the utter clarity and delight in the commonplace, just in its matter-of-factness. As I write this, the leading theme of Professor Nikam's talk on the *Bhagavad Gita* slips into place: "the delight of existence" was the phrase he used, the "ananda" of "sat-chit-ananda."[29]

---

28. Quoted by Suzuki, D. T., *Living by Zen*, London, Rider, 1950, p. 15.

29. Editorial note: Professor N. A. Nikam, of Mysore University, gave a memorable talk on the *Bhagavad Gita* to a seminar in Philosophy of Religion at Harvard University during the Spring of 1953. The reference is to this talk.

How much of the sense of this is in these lines of Donald Williams':

REALISM[30]

It's good to know
the earth is there,
compact below
the actual air,

its substance kept
immune, opaque,
when I have slept
as when I wake.

The clay commutes
its dark duress
to feed the roots
of consciousness,

and, thought or sensed,
the spirit's act
is shaped against
the stone of fact.

The levers set
by our purpose lock
with a purchase let
in the living rock.

The world's uncouth
old lengths decree
what chains of truth
shall make us free.

Reading this poem from my present standpoint, it seems to me that the fourth verse is off a bit, and perhaps even in conflict with the trustfulness and the gratitude with which the earth is received in the rest of the poem. Conflict or not, however, I find that "the spirit's act is shaped against the stone of fact" puts me off, inviting me to conceive of fact as over against spirit, and spirit as over against fact. It is just such a conception that I feel impelled to undercut, connecting it, as I do, with the subject-object dualism emerging so pervasively in Western thought. Here we have 'object-mindedness' in just that

---

[30] Williams, Donald C., "Realism," *The Journal of Philosophy*, Vol. XLII, No. 21, October 11, 1945.

form which I have found to be the most serious obstacle in the development of my own reflections, and in the communication of any possible mode of thought that does not begin from this object-mindedness.

Now the place where one is at home is no object, or congeries of objects. If one abstracts from experience of being at home in a place, however, then things tend to assume the aspect of being "over-against:" *Gegenstand*. And it may seem that "the spirit's act is shaped against the stone of fact." Perhaps we may say that the stone of fact is but an abstraction from the living rock.

On the subject of understanding reality nothing seems more important than to take care over the prepositions we employ, and to be wary of the way we let spatial relations enter into our mode of thinking about our mode of being in and of reality, knowingly. Two loci in the history of philosophy come to mind as affording opportunity for instructive studies in this connection. One is the climax of the interplay of the correlatives, internality and externality, in the thought of David Hume. Another, less obvious and less widely appealing, would be the development of the notion of inwardness in the thought of Kierkegaard, which is closely associated with his claim that truth is subjectivity. May not this claim presuppose just that object-mindedness in terms of which the subject-object dualism is perpetuated, in the case of Kierkegaard leading to a celebration of truth as subjectivity that is bound to rot in the stifling atmosphere of a soul that has insisted on severing itself from reality? There is, indeed, a from-withinness of essential truth; we are invaded by it "from within," in a sense that we must be watchful for the chance to define with care. Understanding of reality indeed seems peculiarly 'reminiscent,' as Plato suggests. But from-withinness, or inwardness comes to worse than nought in an isolated and despairing self, and this is just the position of one who insists on abstraction and at the same time seeks to make himself the possessor of truth in its inwardness. Nowhere in Kierkegaard have I noted a love of place, or even more explicitly, an acknowledgment of the commonplace in its wonderful matter-of-factness. In his pages one may seek in vain for a sense of the locking of our purpose "with a purchase let in the living rock." In Kierkegaard's tortured preoccupation with the salvation of the insular soul, what place may be found for the baking of bread and the breaking of bread? And what is another man to me, but someone to whom I deduce allegiance from the axiom of God's command?[31] I must allow that I may misread Kierkegaard. In any case what I wish to say is this: Give me the inwardness of partaking of fresh bread with living men; in this is reality enough.

Tuesday, July 14

I warn myself of the need to take care over the prepositions we employ in discursive thought on the subject of understanding reality. Yet I bespeak more an uneasiness over the matter than any adequate appreciation of it. If there is a dance of thought here through which we may rightly move, I do not know how to call the figures, and could hardly show the premises on which it might be safely performed.

There can be no caution without trustingness; one must try to embody some of the salient considerations in which he places trust if his questioning is not to be gratuitous. (Did not Descartes place trust "in the senses" in calling them in question: How else maintain that "they sometimes deceive?" Did he not place trust in the distinction between dreaming and waking in a way to belie the question, how may I be assured that I am not utterly consumed in dreaming?)

It seems to me that we might rightly say that we *know* reality as spatio-temporal, but that knowing reality as spatio-temporal does not of itself consummate understanding reality. And it is the latter, of course, which makes for philosophical business. This is not to say that we might articulate understanding of reality without speaking of reality as known, and in terms of such knowledge of reality as we may have. We may suppose all too readily, however, that the reflective task

---

[31]. The reference here is to *Works of Love*, which I remember as having much to say about love, the neighbor, and loving the neighbor, but little in it to quicken the understanding with respect to these.

of attempting to clarify the meaning of reality consists only of the extension and further organization of our knowledge about it. We seek to be exact in the formulation of philosophical issues, which I distinguish as matter to be resolved in concrete understanding, and in so doing we often take these issues as if they were susceptible to demonstrative settlement. Out of sheer intellectual conscience one may find himself belying the birth-right of philosophy, and ignoring the testimony of the history of philosophy. The latter, to my mind, suggests that philosophy is not a matter of successively revised descriptions of a kind with respect to which there has been evidenced a clear-cut possibility of demonstrative advance. Either a Hegel or a Positivist might dispute this; and anyone might say, philosophy is yet in its infancy, evidence may yet decide against you. I freely admit to reading the history of philosophy philosophically, and differently from those who think of philosophy either as a forerunner or as a continuation of systematic knowledge about reality on a footing with the yield of scientific investigation.

What I wish to suggest now, however, is the possibility that a philosophical interest in knowing, in action, and in reality might be served by thinking of these as matters we wish to understand, as matters about which our position is less akin to that of knowers' and more akin to that of testifiers, witnesses. We must learn to bear witness to meanings that dawn on us with respect to them, and this may be quite different from advancing propositions which we can claim to demonstrate.

With respect to knowing, then, what I think I want is an understanding of knowing rather than what I might call knowledge about knowing, even though a reflective discussion in this interest may inevitably proceed somewhat misleadingly, as if one were formulating a systematic account of knowing and of knowledge. Let this general statement pass, however, contestable as it seems. For the nub of the matter, with respect to knowing, as something I want to undersand, applying the principle I have tried to sketch, would be to call in question the relevance of such phrases as "within the mind" or "outside the mind," which are so prominent in establishing a problem of our knowledge of the external world, for example. I do not doubt that there may be something phenomenologically quite apt about these phrases, but without going into them in their metaphorical character, I ask myself: Why should I permit my thinking about knowing to be controlled by such phrases taken literally? Why should I suppose that I will understand knowing any better if I try to nail it down in terms of a would-be knowledge about it, taking it as a peculiar complex that happens, of which I offer, or more insidiously — presuppose, a *picture*? In a word, I would suggest that we may be even seriously impeded in our reflection on knowing, if our reflection be in the interest of understanding knowing, if we are taken in by the thought of knowing as a spatio-temporal phenomenon. To be sure, I am here, and the lamp on my desk is external to me, but just in the sense in which I am external to it, as spatially related. It does not seem to me that optics, as a branch of physics, or physiology, have much to do with the understanding of my knowing, such as my knowing of the lamp, or of whatever I would detail in terms of optics or physiology. To be sure, my experience of knowing in these instances might provide matter for reflection in the interest of understanding knowing. But can I say that my experience, *qua* knowing, as matter for reflection is tantamount to a complex happening which I observe and describe? What I wish to understand is the knowing that enters into all observation and description, and I want above all to understand the abstraction this knowing involves, and to appreciate what abstraction is from.

There is knowing, then, of a world with respect to which the ideas of externality and internality are correlatively pertinent, and I think one must insist on their correlativity. But there is no world in which things are external to me in any strict sense in which I am not equally, and in the same sense, external to them, as one thing spatio-temporally related with others. But a world within which I am spatio-temporally related with other things, is a world that so far forth includes me on a par as a knowable with the other things of the world which I know in these terms. I cannot *understand* my knowing of myself and the things with which I conceive myself in such relation *in these terms*.

So much by way of a preliminary effort to free my thinking from that naturalism which breeds ghosts (i.e. disembodied knowers, trying to know their way into an hypothetical external world), and then raises a ghostly world (i.e. the "phenomena" of phenomenalism, among which no knower can be found) to dispel the illusion of ghosts.

Wednesday, July 15

It is often suggested that Kant's work can be conceived as mediating between the extremes of Rationalism and Empiricism. Yet I am struck by the possibility that he ought to be considered as equally opposed to both in a fundamental respect. Both these traditions seem to embody a claim to look at reality and tell us what it comes to. Their conceptions of *how* we look at reality, inflected by the emphasis now on sense experience and now on the inner eye of reason, are manifestly different. But where Rationalism and Empiricism seem in essential agreement is in the reportorial vein in which they proceed. Now Kant conceives himself to be engaged in defining an alternative to a dogmatic philosophy, and it is just the reportorial attitude in philosophy that lies at the bottom of philosophical dogmatism. The reportorial attitude is just that of one who claims to be looking and telling you what is going on, what is there, without editing or interpretation; you can leave him out of it. He is being objective, no more and no less. What he is talking about lies before you.

Perhaps we are always to some extent *talking about*; but a philosopher must get over thinking that what he wants to talk about can ever be reduced to something lying before him, which he merely talks about as a reporter might, leaving himself and his mode of involvement in reality out of account.

Friday, July 17

Even the rationale of coherent thinking seems to involve 'something' which is indispensable to the *de jure* force of a system of coherent propositions which cannot be reduced to a mode of relationship between the propositions explicitly entertained. It is as if there must be a background, necessarily implicit, from which whatever becomes explicit for us can derive intelligibility and *de jure* force. Without the backing of 'implicit mind' explicit mind is adrift, or astray — aberrant. If what is explicit for awareness is taken in abstraction from basic mind, our awareness of it is like a potential electric circuit which has not been closed — or like one which has been opened, in which current has ceased to flow. Or what we are thus abstractly aware of might be likened to a set of iron filings randomly disposed, awaiting the drawing near of a magnet before they can come into significant alignment. Yet 'the magnet' here is only disclosed in the alignment of the filings, which it makes possible. Again, in the Platonic metaphor, things become intelligible by virtue of a certain light in which they may be seen; but here I persevere in the thought that it would be absurd to seek for the source of such light as if it might be seen, or to disclaim that such light is a condition of seeing because it is not among the things seen by virtue of it. In these respects the analogy with the sun seems to break down.[32]

The demand for proof can always take the form of an insistence on abstraction. It can conceal the dislocation of explicit mind from immanent reality, whence alone what we attend *to* can come under an evaluative perspective in which *de jure* force may obtain. This *whence* is not a direction we can turn attention upon. We cannot rub each other's noses in immanent reality by argument. Adversary attitudes entail argument which can be resolved only by conversion of attitude. An argumentative attitude, as we know, is as inflexible and unrealistic as can be.

The kind of 'objectivity' of mind which distresses me philosophically is that kind of abstractedness of mind from immanent reality which entails the reduction of what is explicitly attended to, to an exclusively *de facto* status.

This is a matter in which I am surely groping my way.

[32] Editorial note: The reference implicit here is to *Republic*, VI, 507-8.

Saturday, July 18

We do not believe that a tide rises and falls behind every man which can float the British Empire like a chip, if he should ever harbor it in his mind.[33]

We might think of the waters of this ever-fluctuating tide as drawn from the watershed of one's entire life-time. Their ebb and flow in the moment of present experience is the adventitiousness of meaning constitutive in our experience. Their ebbing and flowing is a cue to the ephemerality of our condition.[34] One moment we understand, the next we may be lost. One moment we are lifted gratefully along the gentle stream, another we are stranded, gasping and writhing, estranged from the element in which it is given to us to live. The stream comes upon us laden with the twofold aspect of responsibility: *the demand and the capacity to respond;* if we swim with necessity we discover power. Faith is trusting ourselves to the stream which makes responsibility possible, and reasonableness a swimming smoothly in the stream.

Without commitment, or but for commitment, in depth, reasonableness even in thinking would not be possible. Yet commitment is not a separate and isolated inner act: It is responding as one who accepts responsibility in the very moment of meaningfulness that is the deliverance of a situation within which one may act with relevance. And this commitment in depth involves wholeheartedness.

Apart from our involvement in a meaningful situation there could be no being relevant or irrelevant to it in thought and deed on our part. Yet our mode of involvement in a meaningful situation seems

---

[33.] Thoreau, H. D., *Walden*, New York, Random House, 1937, p. 296.

[34.] I have in mind as I do so often Pindar's eighth Pythian: "Day-creatures! What is any one, and what is any one not? Man is a shadow in a dream." See the discussion of this in Hermann Fränkel's "Man's 'Ephemeros' Nature According to Pindar and Others," *Transactions of the American Philological Assoc.*, Vol. LXXVII, 1946, pp. 131-135. Editorial addition to this note: This article was of major consequence to me throughout the writing of these pages. I want to acknowledge my debt to Professor Fränkel very warmly here. His elucidation of the line quoted is surely definitive.

to be that of receiving it in its meaning in instant flow from a tide that rises and falls behind us. Therefore there is reason to suspect that a reflective understanding of reality is bound up with a reflective understanding of responsibility, in the concrete moment of willingness and fulfilment. The real is none other than the necessary, in a *de jure* sense. If something like this is so, could we understand any situation in its reality apart from a response in which its necessity comes home to us?

To anticipate the leaping trout is not to expect an event; it is to perceive the leaping trout truly, as an expression of the divine nature, from which follow an infinite number of things . . . One must leap with the trout. Reality is the deliverance of true decision.

●　　●　　●　　●　　●

I must try and try again to clarify the standpoint from which I have been calling the reportorial attitude in question.

Sunday, July 19

In February, 1950, while driving from Massachusetts down deep into Mexico, I became so thoroughly steeped in the experience of things that I found it a most pressing concern to think out a protest, which kept gathering force, against theoretical interpretations of experience by which the experience of things becomes 'denatured.' It seemed to me that faithful reflection on the experience of things must resist the attenuation of experienced reality which comes of ignoring concrete realization; for example in the interest of explicating our title to empirical knowledge of a world of objects. Mr. Lewis on the subject of the foundations of empirical knowledge[35] provided the phi-

---

[35] The reference is to Lewis, C. I., *Analysis of Knowledge and Valuation*, La Salle, Illinois, Open Court, 1946, especially Chs. VII and VIII.

losophical text in which I found exemplified the sort of theoretical removal from experienced reality that I felt might be fatal to reflective understanding of experienced reality and of action. Through criticizing what he seemed to be doing I tried to clarify the basis of my objections. It was mostly spade work, at best, that I did then. As always with such critical work, it contributes slow increment to swift truth, which must sleep in us for a time before it can clarify the tendency of a reflective concern. The reflective concern to which I was then devoted keeps recurring, as I think it did yesterday. I want to set down in direct sequence upon yesterday's notes a paragraph which I jotted down during March, 1953, when the remembrance of that drive to Mexico came freshly upon me:

With what immediacy everything became present. Coming up, coming up, falling abeam, falling abeam, fading past, fading past. At first distant, distant still, suddenly near, then distant again, just as before (cf. Chekhov's windmill, waving its arms, in *The Steppe*). But what a seamless world, what a constant world, what a sameness and all-alongness, each thing being so — just as it is. How welcome everything is, apprehended with such constancy in the immediacy of the flow of meaning, how fluent the articulate world. It is as if it all flowed directly and simply from within oneself and one were receiving the world 'from within' as much as 'from without.' As silence is to the spoken word, so being is to everything distinct. Things are definitively given as the issue of silence. They *are, are,* eternally *are.* To experience them as being is to know them from within; this knowing them from within is concrete experience. Thus one hears the bell even before it rings, and one sees the tree in the field even before it appears; not in so far as one is prepared for what one hears and sees, except in so far as the very expectation of these things is a rehearsal of their birth in experience. But each thing seen and heard stands out (i.e. exists) in the instant light of a dawn from within; everything appreciated is involuntarily remembered, remembered out of no-thing and no-where, remembered out of dark night and deep sleep, springing forth complete in instant dawn and awakening. Things truly perceived are old, and new, and ageless. This is the wonder of them, the full depth of which is certainty. Faith is responsiveness to things in their wonder; grace the gift of things in their agelessness. Whatever, then, is truly given, truly perceived, is loved; to love is to understand what is perceived as eternal. Only the truly received is truly given; true reception is active contemplation; it involves completeness, that is purity of response.

Monday, July 20

How to develop the idea of reality, and how to develop the idea of action, these are the strains of thought which keep mingling and leading me on, laden with the sense of their intrinsic connection. Again and again I have tried to fix the purchase for the development of these ideas in their connection by dwelling upon abstraction as at the nerve of our philosophical difficulties in the development of both. At times I have written as if I were free from the attitude I was trying to criticize, yet it would be well to acknowledge freely that this must be far from the case. The very attempt to develop ideas of reality and of action undoubtedly incurs a measure of the attitude which I am calling in question.[36]

It seems that what is needed is a style of thought which can *bespeak* that 'something' by virtue of which thinking can be concrete. The 'aboutness' of our thinking obscures the 'fromness' of thinking and acting, which is the constant theme of my reflections. Detached from their 'fromness,' there can be no appreciation of the necessity of the explicitly stated or of the explicitly done. The 'fromness' of the necessary, it would seem, cannot be appreciated apart from the appreciation of something we may refer to as necessary. Yet we cannot exhibit the necessity of anything we refer to and focus attention upon, in terms of an explicit relationship in the field of attention to which we refer. If description were no more than what we can in turn describe, could any description have *de jure* force? Could there be aspiration *to* if aspiration were not also aspiration *from*? Yet by "aspiration from" I do not mean to suggest anything to be conceived as an antecedent event, for example, as the cause of aspiration.

That which enables anything to be necessary is *no thing*, no super-thing, no ghost of a thing, yet it dwells in the necessity of things.

---

36. Editorial note: It is what Marcel calls "the spirit of abstraction" that troubles me, and not abstraction in a more generic sense applicable to all thinking. By "the spirit of abstraction" I understand an attitude in which elements of insensitivity, indifference, and sometimes of repudiation figure so as to cut our thought off from the life of spirit.

And for us it is at the heart of our earnestness, saving our earnestness from deadliness, enabling our belief, and the lightness of heart of our true belief and decision. Our freedom lies in the realization of what must be. Whatever we find beautiful, whatever we find right, whatever we find true, invites disbelief in arbitrariness, and calls upon us, each in his own way, to come to the root of the matter (as Spinoza puts it), and to discover how it may be that reality cannot be tampered with.

The Greeks believed in harmony, in order. Yet any field of attention with respect to which discriminations are possible, any complex, may exhibit order of some kind.[37] Harmonious order seems to presuppose reality in its basic simplicity and necessity. We live in a universe which is universal by virtue of the omnirelevance of simplicity and necessity. Anything we understand in its simplicity and necessity we therefore understand in its universality. But the necessary — whatever can be appreciated as necessary — is not necessary as an instance of a class. We do not appreciate necessity from the typological point of view, though we must think typologically in some measure in thinking of anything, as Plato makes clear. The necessary is individual, and whatever is appreciated as necessary is appreciated as individual, unique. It is in this way that I seem to connect the thoughts of universality and of individuality, respectively.

Tuesday, July 21

It might be fair to say that such reflections as yesterday's, on 'fromness,' represent an attempt to give shape to the thought of origination, of genesis, of becoming, in the light of which the finite appears as individual, as universal, and as necessary. It has been suggested that the understanding of reality is not a systematic canvassing

rial note: I recognize in this sentence a specific lesson which I learned Professor W. R. Dennes, and for which I am grateful to him.

of the finite taken as 'in itself;' our discourse about reality is bound to be inconclusive, revisable, endlessly discursive. But can we say that the understanding of reality fits into a conception of the finite as 'in another,' *esse in alio* — to use the Scholastic phrase? I have supposed that this would be misleading, that the 'fromness' of anything that may be distinctly recognised is not reducible to 'from-anotherness.' No doubt there may be an affinity between the way of thinking which I am trying to clarify and the tradition of Christian thought which insists that creation can only be conceived by analogy. But analogy here could not rest on 'objective similarity.' Perhaps it would be well to think of it as phenomenological aptness: the aptness, that is, of analogies in terms of which we might try to grapple with the experiential meaning of creation.

To say there is more to reality than meets the mind's eye, is always to incur the temptation to demand an account of that 'more' which is alluded to in terms of what does, or might, meet the mind's eye, and to banish the thought as pure obscurantism upon failure to produce in this manner. One has endless occasion to doubt himself. Perhaps it is only rarely that one is so positioned in his reflection that this thought may revive as a firm challenge to speculations formed against it, and to the speculative attenuations into which one's thinking time and again trails off. I have noticed, however, that this central thought, elusive though it may be, does tend to revive and receive nourishment in those various moments of reflective life when remembrance of things past takes the form of what Proust called involuntary recall. And the meaning of past experience emerges as if having undergone filtration profoundly below the bed over which rush the quick run-off waters of day-to-day. No doubt something of pure spring-water is in them, too, but perhaps not often noticeably so.

The reflective understanding of reality, then, has seemed to me helped by the incursion into the present moment of remembered situations from which one gains his bearings and his stance as a human being. Thus the recollective understanding of one's actual experience is intimately connected with the reflective understanding of reality. And it may be that the vein in which one undertakes the responsibilities of reflection also determines the depth from which the filtered

meaning of past experience can come home to one, here and now.
There is a believing with all one's heart, in no wise contrary to care-
fulness of thinking, upon which alone it would seem possible to understand reality as grounding our belief. Above all else, then, I trust in
the remembrance of what I have loved and respected; remembrance
in which love and respect are clarified. And I trust in such remembrance to guide my reflections in the path of essential truth. Here I
seem to differ somewhat from those whose thoughts are taken up with
suffering and despair as helps along the same path. With Whitehead's
use of the term in mind, I can say that I am most at home in reflection when the *importance* of things becomes unmistakably clear.

I think of sayings of Meister Eckhart to the effect that we have
only to be empty to be filled. May not tragedy (and I mean tragedy
as a sifting of the meaning of our experience) be a lesson in what
this 'emptiness' is? Is it not akin to being devoid of pretense, and in
this sense, to being simply ourselves? Eckhart's 'emptiness' bears
thinking upon in connection with Zen 'no-mindedness' and that 'vast-
emptiness' which is the wilderness of things appearing just as they
are. As one is redeemed, reality is manifestly given to him as a wilderness, and he rediscovers it as such; it has been so all along. But a
wilderness is a place of infinite importance, and it may be that we
can seldom appreciate it as such.

Now I am inclined to say that the importance of things is indeed
intrinsic to them; we know them in their importance in respecting
them, in appreciating them as deserving of respect. Yet their deserv-
ingness of respect is just as difficult to think out as their derivativeness
is: their origination, their becoming. One thing seems clear. You cannot place yourself outside it and hope to understand it; it can only be
nonsense. Perhaps the existence of things, the standing out of the
distinct, can only make sense, as we stand forth ourselves, as we are
made to stand forth. In *ecstasis* (literally a 'being made to stand forth')
the meaning of the existent becomes clear, and the infinite importance
of existent things becomes clear. Thus in doing what is necessary we
can understand our condition. How apt are those Chinese scrolls which
show men in harmony with all nature, men and things emerging *together* and not as over against one another.

Thursday, July 23

I have connected the appreciation of things in their importance with the understanding of them in their reality, once again arriving at the thought that both turn upon a person's fulfilment of what is demanded of him, not merely in reflective act, but also as action of any sort may fulfil the requirements of his situation devolving upon him. If this thought obtains, then the life we lead and the philosophy we believe in our hearts cannot be independent of one another. I speak of the philosophy we believe in our hearts (following Peirce), however, with the reservation in mind that it seems most difficult to learn what we believe in our hearts. The philosophy we write is not necessarily an explication of what we believe in our hearts. To be sure, where it is not, we may *reveal* something of what we truly believe, and this may turn out to be somewhat at variance with much that we have explicitly said.

For example, the case of John Stuart Mill comes to mind: It has seemed to me for some time that the theme which he formulates as the ultimate "internal sanction" of "the greatest happiness morality" is the real center of his ethical thought. He talks of this feeling of unity with men, or fellow-feeling, as if it were to be construed wholly in causal terms: as the product of influences conceived on the pattern of associationist theory, and as the most powerful cause, in turn, disposing men to accept and act upon the principle of utility. Yet he seems to me to bespeak a *de jure* force in behalf of the proper concern of man for man which, in fact, lends what substance there is to the "greatest happiness morality." To the theme he bespeaks his description of the causes and effects of this feeling of unity with men is simply irrelevant. No doubt it would be fitting to remark here on the development of Utilitarianism in the Christian tradition, but my point is to suggest that there is a discrepancy between the stated and the revealed philosophy in Mill's ethical writings, and so to illustrate what I mean by such a discrepancy. For my part, I have drawn the conclusion from this sort of affair that it is better to try to learn what one believes in one's heart, and to be patient in the effort to bespeak a ground of evaluation and of criticism, than it is to proceed as if one's philosophy from beginning to end were to be conducted as a theoretical continuation and emendation of a purely theoretical inheritance, with a free-wheeling intellect in command of the task.

It is sobering to experience the extraordinary difficulty of coming to grips with one's own beliefs, and yet also to suspect that one can say nothing worth saying that must not stem from what he believes in his heart. It is even more damaging to some of the conventional suppositions on which we are accustomed to philosophize, to entertain squarely the likelihood that our appreciation of things in their importance and the understanding of them in their reality cannot deepen reflectively beyond a depth from which we are prepared to act. The ephemerality of our condition as active beings also spells the ephemerality of philosophic thought. Each day's thinking seems to be at the mercy of the man one is. Yet as Pindar says, what is any one of us, and what is any one of us not, even within the span of a day? Perhaps we would be disposed to think of this as an adverse situation, however, only as we fight against it, failing to accept ourselves.

The final chapter of Jung's *Modern Man in Search of a Soul* is fresh in my mind as I use this phrase, "to accept ourselves." This surely does not mean "to issue ourselves a *carte blanche.*"

Friday, July 24

After a long dry spell we have had two days of rain. During the dry spell there were some very humid days, when it would make up as if to storm, and there were occasional flourishes of thunder and lightning. But only local scatterings of a few pelting drops would ensue. A sort of silent pressure of the need of rain kept building up, something quite independent of noticing and commenting upon the condition of the grass and plants. This need of rain, the feeling of which persists unobtrusively, imparts a tone to one's sensibilities. One needn't be paying attention to the weather and the state of the crops for it to prevail. Indeed this unobtrusive feeling might be thought of as a human parallel to the condition in which vegetation is immersed. The feeling itself is made known in the release from it, wrought by the rain.

Now, on such a clear morning as this, with new sunlight and air welcome among the leaves, it seems well to acknowledge what seems so plain: a rapport with vegetation so gently taught by the weather in which we are steeped, as to differ quite entirely from the lessons we study, such as a lesson in which we might recite the similarities of men and vegetables. We are laid hold of.

•　•　•　•　•

This matter of being laid hold of suggests the need to inquire about our control of belief and attitude. People often talk about belief as if believing were like something we elected to do, or might elect to refrain from doing. There is much talk about adopting beliefs, or of accepting them because of their convenience, or of suspending them for a while — all suggesting that we are, or can be, in a position to exercise jurisdiction over what we believe and whether we believe, at least in part and at some times. We must examine such notions of the possibility of choosing to believe or disbelieve, or to take up an attitude which is neither that of believing nor of disbelieving.

Shall we say that we decide our own attitudes? This is a question which arises with beautiful clarity from a study of the writings of the later Stoics, for example. In Epictetus no question is more prominent or persistent than this: What is and what is not in our power? He is always arguing that we should give paramount attention to the control of our own responses and attitudes, and it is interesting to note the stridency with which he voices contempt for those of us who may fail to grasp his point. Epicureans and Stoics alike are penetrating in their appreciation of the liabilities of our attachments to the world. We are only vulnerable in our relations with things to the extent that we care about them. Thus our desires, our passions, our will to get and to avoid, our being pleased and pained, are all forms of a kind of conspiracy arising in our own nature. But for our caring we could not become the victims of anything that might happen in the world.

Accordingly, these Hellenistic philosophers develop a practical philosophy of self-control, dedicated to the task of helping us to put down the conspirator within our gates, by dwelling insistently on the proper attitudes, which we should concentrate our energy and attention in achieving. Both the Epicureans and Stoics also supplement their practical philosophy of self-control from their interpretations of reality. The Epicureans, for example, insist that the fear of death rests on an illusion which a proper understanding of reality will dispel. They also insist that their picturing of reality is in principle complete — there can be no surds, such as the interfering will of the gods, to confound our command of the scene of human destiny. The Stoics — with varying degrees of authenticity and depth, no doubt — develop the notion of a reality acceptable in all its permutations as the expression of a divine Logos, rendering all happenings beyond human control in accord with man's true interest, defined by this Logos in himself.

When I draw nearest to this Logos-theme at its best in Stoic thought, I wonder if it does not harbor a challenge to the practical philosophy of the later Stoics. While the theme accords primacy to what I really am, in my basic affinity with all things, the later Stoics tend to substitute for this reflective acknowledgement of my true mode of being an emphasis on the activity by which I fashion myself according to the portrait I am able to form of what I should be. The Logos-theme then appears in the guise of a model of human attitude, as an attitude of acceptance and affirmation I should strive for in the act of determining my ultimate responses to the course of affairs, and to its immediate impact upon myself. But what is this devising and shaping of my own attitudes, and what *do* I believe in at the heart of this activity of self-control?

No doubt there must be some perfectly genuine sense in which self-control is both possible and not to be discredited. The point I am after, however, comes to something like this: Who am I in controlling myself? In what attitude do I undertake to determine my own attitude? And in what attitude do I ascertain what my attitude should be? *Is* my attitude arbitrary or not? To the extent that it is arbitrary, what real understanding is embodied in the portrait I hold up to myself of what my attitude should be, even supposing that I might bring myself to be this person whom I represent to myself? And to the extent that my present attitude is not arbitrary, would this be because I have seen to it? These questions may serve as a reminder that any controlling which we may undertake, whether of our own attitudes or not, presupposes an attitude on our part which *is* our attitude at the time; it is our actual stance, firm or flimsy. And now a second reminder fits into place: A firm stance presupposes firm ground.

It is all very well to image our proper independence as responsible beings by talking of standing on our own feet. But this image, by itself, leaves us hanging in air. Let us not neglect to think of the ground being under our own feet; and let us not talk as if we placed the ground under our own feet. A ground which our *feet* do not *discover* is no ground.

At this point I am moved to consider the possibility that we must rethink our idea of feeling precisely in connection with our mode of being grounded. I must put the matter cautiously: It seems as if our being grounded, our discovery of ground upon which we may stand, in standing upon our own feet, is a matter of feeling. Somehow, feeling and having a footing need to be thought out together. And if this is to be done, one must be able to hold at arm's length the modes of thinking of traditional rationalism or empiricism; for example, the psychologizing about feeling typical of the latter, and the intellectualist version of reason typical of the former. I do not suppose that whatever may go by the name of feeling will stand to criticism. In fact the key idea of disinterested interest recurs at this juncture in its relevance as a guide in the thinking that needs to be done.

Perhaps reflection on feeling will prove crucial in the development of such themes as: the importance of things; the understanding of reality; the possibility of action (and not merely judgments about action) making sense; the immediacy of the flow of meaning and 'the channel of the necessary;' reasonableness as requisite to the *de jure* force of the offering and receiving of reasons; and now, last but not least, the theme of belief, which I am approaching as I put it the other day in saying that reality cannot be tampered with.

To revert to those earlier questions today about belief, I would be inclined to say that if we can control belief then, indeed, whirl would be king; or, we would be kings over a vacuum. But we might think of belief as precisely our mode of involvement in reality. In the belief that we do not know, we can suspend judgment, yes; we can consider; we can be of an open mind; we can fend off irrelevancies and be patient of discovering what would be relevant. But what shall we think of these if they are *make-believe?* It would seem that we can, indeed, pretend. But when we pretend to belief or disbelief, whom is it absolutely necessary for us to try to convince, if not our-selves? Why should it be such an effort when we try?

We speak of making up our minds and deciding. Yet it seems as if we participated in the settlement of no issue which does not "settle itself." Perhaps the most somber aspect which necessity can wear arises in the ghosts of issues we have "settled," but which nothing short of genuine decision can lay. How does Shakespeare get away with his ghosts?

Saturday, July 25

Last night the humidity kept dropping, the air cooling off, and a full moon rose. At mid-morning the day is still as clear and fresh as it might be in the High Sierras. The effect of this day, and of Beet-hoven's Opus 135, to which I have just listened, is to make me con-scious that the readiness to receive is all. Without that what can be given?

o   o   •   o   •

If generosity is the mainspring of true action, is it not 'wound' in the reception of things given in their importance?[38] I think of the reception of things in their importance as contemplation, and it seems to me that contemplation may be twofold: It may be perceptive and it may be meditative — reflective. We might speak with precedent

---

[38] Whitehead's use of this term, as in his *Modes of Thought*, keeps echoing upon me.

of the former as aesthetic and of the latter as philosophic. Both presuppose ingatheredness,[39] an alert openness, on our part, like that
of which I was speaking when talking of fishing and of keeping our
fingertips right on the trembling line. And the heart of true contemplation is disinterestedness.

We sometimes run into questions about the practical importance
of art and of philosophy. I want to set down one possible answer to
this kind of question, and it seems to me an answer to be confirmed
again and again from experience. In so far as art and philosophy are
consummated in contemplation, they are kindred ways in which reality
nurtures in us the soul of generosity; and it is from this that we are
enabled to act truly. It may seem very ill-advised to talk of reality
nurturing in us the soul of generosity, in this connection. Yet I would
not stop short of putting it this way. Marcel says "that contemplation
is a possibility only for somebody who has made sure of his grip on
reality,"[40] yet the contemplative act is just that in which reality makes
firm its grip on us, and here is where I start in thinking of contemplation. In aesthetic and in philosophic contemplation I learn of a sustaining ground in which I am rooted; I could not say that I inspect
this groundedness, pulling up roots and soil to have a look at them
and report upon their relation, as it were; though a lot of speculative
questioning seems to insist that if there be anything to such talk
about being rooted in reality, we better have those roots up and show
them, and show how they are planted, and what they are planted in.
Let us regard the tumbleweed.

One reason I take a stand in contemplation is because I discover
in contemplation what it means to be able to stand. One stands independently and at the same time together with everything other than
oneself. Contemplation is governed by omni-relevant meaning. Yet
one may respond upon a conclusive meaning of things without being
able to say what that meaning is. How can we do better than trust

[39.] Editorial note: Marcel's use of this term and his whole disc
templation in *The Mystery of Being*, Vol. I, were of inestima'
and remain so.

[40.] *The Mystery of Being*, Vol. I, p. 123.

our understanding of reality, as far as it may go, as it comes and goes?
No doubt it grows, if it grows, at its own pace. And our sleeping
seems to be not the least important period of its life in us, as when
sleep restores us to simplicity.

Sunday, July 26

What may it mean not to have lived in vain? How is it possible
to accept dying? Let me try to set down some of the context of
thought in which these questions come back to me and suggest the
direction I am trying to take in these gathering reflections.

These seem to me questions which challenge the vein in which
one is thinking: If he does not feel up to them, if they seem ridiculous
or pretentious, for example, do they not take his measure? They are
congenial, on the other hand, to that vein of thought which one may
find, for example, in Thoreau; he seems to put his finger on this vein
when he says: ". . . not suppose a case, but take the case that is . . ."[41]
It seems to me that the writers of theoretical ethics and "value theory"
are for the most part prone or driven to "supposing a case." But taking
the case that is, who is not feeling his way along? And what understanding of our situation can fit our dying? How can we be fit to die,
possibly willing to die? What in dying might we discover? Saint-
Exupéry helped to teach me these questions, as in the fifth section
of Part IX of *Wind, Sand and Stars*, under the heading "Barcelona
and Madrid."

The letters of Sacco and Vanzetti are a part of the context which
comes to mind with the questions from which I began today. There
is, particularly, Sacco's letter of February 26, 1924, to Mrs. Jack,[42]

41· *Walden*, New York, Random House, 1937, p. 294.

42· See *The Letters of Sacco and Vanzetti*, London, Constable & Co., 1929, pp.
14-16.

which seems to express a meaning Sacco found in his life that enabled him to stand up to the death that he faced. Then there are those more declamatory words with which Vanzetti, in his characteristic manner, expressed his assimilaion of the sentence on April 9, 1927; I set them down here because they are conveniently brief:

> If it had not been for these thing, I might have live out my life talking at street corners to scorning men. I might have die, unmarked, unknown, a failure. This is our career and our triumph. Never in our full life could we hope to do such work for tolerance, for joostice, for man's onderstanding of man as now we do by accident. Our words — our lives — our pains — nothing! The taking of our lives — lives of a good shoemaker and a poor fish-peddler — all! That last moment belongs to us — that agony is our triumph.[43]

Something that Whitehead said on his seventieth birthday keeps coming back to me:

> If you get a general notion of what is meant by perishing, you will have accomplished an apprehension of what you mean by memory and causality, what you mean when you feel that what we are is of infinite importance, because as we perish we are immortal.[44]

Perhaps *Process and Reality* would be worth struggling with if it helps to clarify this; he says it is the one key thought around which the book is woven.

Aristotle sets the basic ethical question, in the *Nicomachean Ethics,* in a way that has led many a man in his footsteps since: He asks the question, what is the good for man? From Professor Richard Niebuhr I learned a question that may turn out to be more basic than Aristotle's: What is a man good for? May it not be that we can only learn what is good for us in learning what we are good for? Maybe Aristotle himself is not so far from this emendation of the question: What does he mean in talking of man as "having a function," and of his realizing the good for himself in the fulfilment of his function? The key idea here is that of doing what it is fitting for us to do (and let us note that Ross, who is especially steeped in Aristotle,

43. Ibid., Fly-Leaf.

44. *Symposium in Honor of the Seventieth Birthday of Alfred North White'* Cambridge, Mass., Harvard Press, 1932, pp. 26-27.

is squarely representative of present-day Intuitionism in stressing the "fittingness" of right action). But better than the notion of "function," seems to be that of *vocation*, calling, and it leads directly into the consideration of responsibility. We learn of our position what it *is* crucial to learn, by responding to a call, in truly vocational action. The trouble with the Intuitionists is that they veer off into supposing a case, instead of taking the case that is. They try to deal with fittingness as if it could be elucidated by an appeal to a property, or character, of specific actions, considered in abstraction from the life of man. They supernaturalize concrete reality. But naturalism for naturalism, the Naturalists have the better of the Supernaturalists, and that is a tide of battle that is not likely to change.

Let us reflect, then, on our experience of vocation, such as it may actually be, and drawing on all that has spoken to us with authority in our actual lives. If we have looked upon the mountains time and again, and they have called upon us, and we have responded, let us remember that we have looked upon them with the eye of faith. Let us credit such experience in our reflection as may have prompted us to extend credit to the world. That which carries real weight with us always seems to come "by accident" (to use Vanzetti's phrase). Why, then, should we try to reason out our position on terms we would impose? Why should we try to fathom what necessity there may be to deeds and things as if necessity were something we conferred upon them? as if we might appreciate the necessary and wherein necessity lies — what it means — by abstracting so far as possible from our involvement in reality? From Hume we may learn well enough: Nothing is necessary that is *merely looked at*.

Monday, July 27

I was saying that we must trust in experience that comes to us in the imperative mood, thinking of it and thinking of it, and giving ourselves time to understand. Someone refers to a state of affairs with which I have no intimacy and asks: How does your philosophy deal with that? Another, with a few casual strokes portrays a situation as a scene for action and then wishes to know: How, in terms of your position, ought a man to act in this situation, and why?

But how will I appreciate or bespeak the meaning of the necessity of anything that may be referred to apart from an intimacy with it, and an intimacy that ought not to be confused with mere familiarity 'with that kind of thing, or situation, or state of affairs?' In our reflective exploration of the meaning of necessity, must we not reflect in the very vein of the experience in which things have actually commanded us? And it seems to me utterly foreign to this vein of experience to count ourselves the masters of it, as if we had on tap what is needful to us in philosophical inquiry. Necessity does not seem to me to invest itself in ideas enabling us to seize upon things at random and wield them as bludgeons, *forcing* acknowledgment of the necessity of the things upon which we seize with them. I would be inclined to say that where the use of force is to the fore the appreciation of necessity is absent. Thus, for example, when we are imperious, reality withholds its instruction from us. We learn of necessity in all gentleness, or not at all.

The instruction of which we seem to stand in most need is the instruction to be received from whatever we actually love. It seems plain enough that our part in this loving is no stable matter; of that we need scarcely remind ourselves. Our condition is indeed ephemeral, even within the course of almost any day of which we might choose to speak. That loving has to do with understanding reality, I do not doubt, and it is just in this connection that I have in mind the notion of necessity: It is supported by our experience of things in the imperative mood. It may be of help to bear in mind that the imperative mood is not the mood of assertion. It is the mood of affirmation, the mood in which we truly respond. It seems to me that I have to discover over and over again that I am wrong when I insist; decisiveness is quite other than insistence. Only reality in its necessity can give finality to what we say or do. It is conceivable that our entire lives may require to be spent, as with Joe Christmas in *Light in August*, before the issue of our lives can become really clear and settled. Only as he dies does Joe come to understand his situation and himself.

In Faulkner's *The Old Man*, which I have been perusing again, there is an incident worth setting down at this point. Throughout this entire story there are swift alternations on the convict's part between doing what must be done and resistance; but in the main he holds to the stream of necessity which flows in his life. Time and again his actions *stick*, and he does not peter out.

The incident I want to set down occurs while the convict is in the Cajun country. He has been hunting alligators and has built up quite a pile of hides. The boat which he received early in the period of the flood, when he was assigned to rescue some people with it, is still with him. The woman he rescued is still with him. He has been striving to get back to deliver himself up again to the prison authorities, to return the boat, and to leave the woman and her new-born baby in proper hands. The flood has carried him far down the Mississippi. Having fallen in with the Cajun alligator hunters, he has had a taste of a proper life for a man; he has liked the work right well. He has gone on hunting with the idea of earning money that will help him on his way back. But perhaps he has gotten a little side-tracked. Yes, he likes the work mighty well. The Cajun with whom he has been staying and working has left the night before, after trying to convey an urgent reason for the convict to follow suit. But the convict has stayed on, opposing to the sense which he had gathered of what the Cajun tried to convey, the fact that the Cajun had spoken in an unintelligible tongue. He returns from an abortive attempt to hunt, filled with misgivings. There is a launch with five men alongside the platform of the shack where he has been lodged. He sees the woman preparing to board the launch. He tells her to take back the bundle she has handed to one of the men, to carry it back into the house.

> "So you can talk English, can you?" the man in the launch said. "Why didn't you come out like they told you to last night?"
>
> "Out?" the convict said. Again he even looked, glared, at the man in the launch, contriving even again to control his voice: "I ain't got time to take trips. I'm busy," already turning to the woman again, his mouth already open to repeat as the dreamy buzzing voice of the man came to him and he turning once more, in a terrific and absolutely un-

bearable exasperation, crying, "Flood? What flood? Hell a mile, it's done passed me twice months ago! It's gone! What flood?" and then (he did not think this in actual words either but he knew it, suffered that flashing insight into his own character or destiny: how there was a peculiar quality of repetitiveness about his present fate, how not only the almost seminal crises recurred with a certain monotony, but the very physical circumstances followed a stupidly unimaginative pattern) the man in the launch said, "Take him" and he was on his feet for a few minutes, yet, lashing and striking in panting fury, then once more on his back on hard unyielding planks while the four men swarmed over him in a fierce wave of hard bones and panting curses and at last the thin dry vicious snapping of handcuffs.

"Damn it, are you mad?" the man in the launch said. "Can't you understand they are going to dynamite that levee at noon today? — Come on," he said to the others. "Get him aboard. Let's get out of here."

"I want my hides and boat," the convict said.

"Damn your hides," the man in the launch said. "If they don't get that levee blowed pretty soon you can hunt plenty more of them on the capitol steps at Baton Rouge. And this is all the boat you will need and you can say your prayers about it."

"I aint going without my boat," the convict said. He said it calmly and with complete finality, so calm, so final that for almost a minute nobody answered him, they just stood looking quietly down at him as he lay half-naked, blistered and scarred, helpless and manacled hand and foot, on his back, delivering his ultimatum in a voice peaceful and quiet as that in which you talk to your bed-fellow before going to sleep. Then the man in the launch moved; he spat quietly over the side and said in a voice as calm and quiet as the convict's:

"All right. Bring his boat."[45]

It seems to me that the convict shifted from insistence to decision. To speak here of decision as "true" would be redundant.

Tuesday, July 28

We need to distinguish the wanting, the willing, which is *affirming* from that which is assertive, appropriative; in the latter do we not

[45]. Faulkner, William, *The Old Man*, as printed in *The Faulkner Reader*, New York, Random House, pp. 418-19.

discover the taking up of a dogmatic position? It is this distinction which has seemed to me painfully lacking in the ethical thought of Kant. And lacking it, how could Kant reconcile the idea of unconditional imperativeness devolving upon us and that of human well-being? How could he even bring the notion of human well-being to a level commensurate with his wonderful saying: "It is impossible to conceive of anything anywhere in the world or even anywhere out of it that can without qualification be called good, except a Good Will."[46]

If only he had been able to let himself go in *Religion Within the Limits of Reason Alone,* when at last he comes to entertain the idea of grace. Instead of worrying about the deleterious consequences of a *doctrine* of grace (might it not encourage men to lean on their shovels?) might he not have given voice to the authentic vein in which we can come to acknowledge liberating truth? But what a challenge might have swelled, like an anthem, from the experiential theme of a liberated will, to confound his conception of autonomy, and to confound a conception of human well-being which could so separate man in his well-being from man in his well-doing as to require 'God' and 'an after-life' as theoretical devices to bring these into accord.

Again, in the thought of the Stoics, and to a remarkable extent it is the same with the Epicureans, there is an acute appreciation of the fact that it is our interests, our inclinations, our *caring,* which get us into trouble, but a failure to appreciate that only a mode of caring, of interest, can lift us out of trouble. The upshot of study in Hellenistic Philosophy which I undertook in recent years came to me as a philosophic lesson marvelously expressed in the lines of T. S. Eliot's *Ash Wednesday*:

> Teach us to care and not to care
> Teach us to sit still.

How many are the philosophers who turn the truth of "teach us care" against the truth of "teach us to care," and is it not from sitting still?

\manuel, *The Fundamental Principles of the Metaphysic of Ethics,* Manthey-Zorn, New York, Appleton-Century, 1938, p. 8.

I remember how my heart went out to William Carlos Williams when he prefaced the reading of some of his poetry with some remarks so genial and unassuming, so quiet, and so ordinarily phrased, that one might readily have missed what he was saying. It has just dawned on me what he was saying, after some two years. He was talking about listening to poetry, something like this: "Relax! relax. Enjoy it. Poetry is to be enjoyed. Do not try to make something of it. Don't try to batter down the doors and take possession of it. Take it as it comes. Poetry is for pleasure. If one understands it in time, that will be fine!"

What was he saying? It is conceivable that philosophy students wrote down in their notebooks: "has a hedonistic theory of value." But I think he was saying for the benefit of the Protestant conscience in us, his autonomously-minded audience: "Sit still!" . . . And it may be that some who have defended pleasure have wished to say as much.

There is a good Zen question of which I am reminded at this point: What would you say now? And along with it this answer, to be found in one of the stories in which Zen is at home: a snowflake on a burning stove! We will not let ourselves believe in ease. Instead, we insist. But insistence, however learned or proficient, is not graceful.

We must see to it! We worry. We hurry along. We translate necessity into anxiety and effort, trying to take charge. We are swimmers flailing the water to keep from going down. We try frantically to swim in a relaxed manner, or taking relaxation to be inaction, go down like lead. We take everything that may be said of our condition as instruction on how to go about dealing with it, alert for the cues to success.

Yet there are times when waves overtake us from behind, lifting us up and along; from these we may take courage and be thankful. But it is not always so. For we may claim as our own the power of the wave in the exhiliration of swift swimming, and this is demonic swimming, in which we suffer the illusion that we are not fallen into flailing: We have become the masters of our element.

Then there is the even stroke informed by the sea that carries us all alike; a sea of which trough or crest are but undulations. Now and then we swim a few even strokes and know where we are.

With that phenomenological image of the even stroke I felt that I was drawing near to the meaning of Thoreau's utterances on the theme of free labor. Steadiness and steadfastness are alive to the constancy of our being sustained. They guard against the illusions of elation and depression; such are the undulations of our sea while we ignore our being sustained.

How much of current philosophy of value, and of evaluative criticism, is taking the undulations 'at face value,' also bespeaking a 'faith' in man that is faithless with respect to reality.

First of all the suspicion occurs to me that much of current philosophy of value is voicing the persuasion that when we are up our position is good, and when we are down, our position is bad. Let joy and suffering serve as instances, or satisfaction and dissatisfaction; the terms may not matter too much here. Now it will be clear from the image I have been using that I am trying to say that our position is not necessarily good when we are up and not necessarily bad when we are down. In their own way Plato and Aristotle seem to suggest the same thought when they say that there can be false pleasures, or that what matters is not that a man is pleased, but what manner of man is being pleased. Further, they do not mean merely that 'false' pleasures eventuate in greater pain. And when I try to understand Eckhart's emphasis on the importance of suffering, if it is to be interpreted as free from perversity, I find it plausible to surmise that he found in the trough a clearer corrective for evaluation than on the crest of the wave. He is guarded about our moments of joy, suggesting quite clearly at times the profound illusion we may suffer in elation. It is as if he wanted to say, as men have said in all religious traditions, that we learn to give ourselves up to the sea, and come finally to trust in it, only in the abyss of the deepest troughs. And here is a saying of his which has stuck with me since I first read it, and no doubt it has not a little to do with the way my own thoughts have taken shape: "All ways are even," he says. And he adds, I believe, that we can only confirm this in realizing our own way. (Cf. Sir

Thomas Browne: "Swim smoothly in the stream of thy nature, and live but one man.")

An even clearer indication of what I am getting at, but strikingly in the vein of Eckhart in its theme of purity, emerges in a comment on the story of Hyakujo, as related by Dr. Suzuki.[47] There is not much to the story. Hyakujo has undergone enlightenment (*satori*) — I will not relate the incident; in the sequel to it we are confronted with the report that Hyakujo is found laughing on one occasion, and crying on another. Dr. Suzuki remarks: "Before his satori his crying or laughing was not a pure act." Here we have the Buddhist idea of wholeheartedness, which so attracted Dr. Horney, by the way. I will not try to expand upon it now. I only wish to say that the undulations of our condition do not in themselves serve to indicate the trueness of our position. Joy and sorrow are not necessarily pure. If our evaluations are not subject to the very purification of joy and sorrow themselves, how can evaluations reached in joy or sorrow be trusted?

I feel I must speak of our position, say with respect to joy and sorrow, as requiring consideration, reflectively, in terms of whether it be true or false. I think we must enlarge our conception of truth and of falsity so that it becomes intelligible within the framework of evaluative intent. Whenever we are engaged in the criticism of *attitude*, it seems to me that we take for granted the legitimacy of some such 'enlarged' conception of truth and falsity. It will not do to appropriate those correlatives to an interpretation requiring their reduction to the status of properties of propositions.

I want to set down now one version of what it may mean to be in a true position: The sense of the sustaining sea is bound up with the sense of communion with all the creatures swimming or floundering in it, as may be. The joys and the sorrows deserving our affirmation are those in which we affirm our togetherness with fellow-creatures. These are true joys and sorrows, and as men have ever borne witness, they are true in their concrete understanding of reality and of our togetherness in reality.

So much by way of following out the first part of the embryonic idea from which we began today — the part having to do with taking the undulations of our condition at face value. Now as to the second part: what of a 'faith' in man that is faithless with respect to reality? And what is the connection between this second and the first part of our line of thought?

Thursday, July 30

Last night I was awake for a while after a duet of cats under the window had been silenced, and there was scarcely a sound. I was uneasy about what I had written yesterday about the undulations of day to day experience. Not that there was no point to it. But I was overcome by a sense of how vastly experience eludes the reflective exploration of its meaning; what a vast 'forgetfulness' limits and distances one's reflection from the concrete. Here I am following up traces of thoughts, yet often, no doubt, I am talking more in the tone of assertion than in that of affirmation. This thinking, this writing, this talking I am doing is steeped in the ambiguities about which I am trying to become clear; I want to define a style of thinking, of writing, of talking which is true to this fact. No doubt it may take years before I may express affirmations that live in the traces of thoughts, without falling again and again into the assertive vein of a disquisition. But as I was saying a couple of days ago, now and then one takes a few even strokes and finds where he is and what he is about.

Marcel has this to say about the kind of reflection in which I find myself engaged:

> The man who states a mathematical formula, even if he does not judge it necessary to go over the proof that has established the formula, is always in a position to do so if he wants to. I have expressed that elsewhere, in a metaphor which perhaps sounds rather frigid in English, by saying that round the cogs and springs of mathematics the golden watchcase of demonstration, a sort of handsome protective covering, is never lacking. And it is the same with all the laws of nature. It is

always at least theoretically possible to repeat the experiments from which such laws have been inductively arrived at. But this cannot be the case for us. Existential philosophy is at all times exposed to a very serious danger; that of continuing to speak in the name of various kinds of deep inner experience, which are certainly the points of departure for everything that it affirms, but which cannot be renewed at will. Thus the affirmations of existential philosophy are perpetually in danger of losing their inner substance, of ringing hollow.[48]

I would prefer to use the phrase 'experiential philosophy' in this connection, incidentally, for the key idea here does seem to me to be that of experience, while 'existential' is laden with complex connotations from among which 'experiential' may well deserve extrication. I should wish to handle the idea of experience very differently, however, from the doctrinal manner of those whose philosophy of experience goes by the name of 'empiricism.' Experiential philosophy would seem to be foreign, on the whole, to the empiricist point of view. Yet one would caricature Hume if one pressed this too far; and there is Wittgenstein to remind us that empiricism pushed to its limit by a reflective thinker in earnest may burst into experiential thought. One may come in time to take his involvement in reality into account, too, if he persists hard enough in a contrary vein.

Now to get back to yesterday's question: what of a 'faith' in man that is faithless with respect to reality? By such 'faith' I mean to suggest an attitude as old as Prometheanism and as new as Sartre's humanism. I am interested in this attitude as it arises within the range of philosophical reflection, though we may hardly dream what it might be to be quite devoid of it; and thus we may not dream of what may be implicit along with it, capable of transmuting it. The reflective drama of the ideas of self-power and other-power sketched by Dr. Suzuki is suggestive on this point.[49]

At any rate, the theme which I think I want to develop can be simply stated: It is that "faith" in man is unfounded that is not a facet of faith in reality. I sense the cue to the whole matter, for reflective interpretation, lies in the notions of being made to stand forth (com-

[48.] *The Mystery of Being*, Vol. I, p. 213.

[49.] Suzuki, D. T., *A Miscellany on the Shin Teaching of Buddhism*, Kyoto, Shinshu Otaniha Shumusho, 1949.

mitment), of believing, of affirming, of decision. And apart from the experience of being made to stand forth, apart from one's commitment as an active being, there can be no understanding of the existent — literally 'the standing forth.' This is to say that there can be no conclusive meaning to our situation so long as it is abstractly considered. Necessity can have no meaning, then, except as we act upon it.

Here I find it instructive to turn to Sartre, even though I am working from impressions of his thought that may be far from adequate. For in Sartre's philosophy there seems to be a place for arbitrariness, but no ground of necessity from which man might act. He exhorts us to throw off hypocrisy and stand on our own feet, and yet this standing on our own feet turns out to be precisely standing on nothing. There is all the difference in the world between leaving it at that and getting the sense in which he who can stand on his own feet must be standing on everything, or better, *with* everything on no-thing. No-thing is not nothing, yet it is nothing apart from things. The question is whether we can rejoice with things, or whether we find them simply inane. Sartre finds them inane, absurd. Even this would be all right if he rejoiced with them in their absurdity, as Camus rejoices at the close of *The Stranger*. One can celebrate a world in which things "just happen," as does Chekhov, and in so doing he may open himself to the understanding of reality as mystery. This seems to be the vein in which essential truth flows. But for Sartre, in the name of honesty, the real is reduced to something I stare at, and what is there becomes a mere object.

Yet this 'mere object' teases at the fringes of his thought. It has about it something he thinks men lack. It has an 'in-itselfness' about it which challenges man in his self-consciousness (his 'for-himself-ness'). If man could only become like an object in the sense of losing self-consciousness! This is what he seems to say. How can that which he takes to be inane hold out to him the suggestion of what is needful for us? From Sartre's abstract point of view I do not see how he can fathom his own hint. What would be the human equivalent of the 'in-itselfness' of a thing? Good faith. But from the point of view of good faith, are things inane?

Friday, July 31

Just one or two more notes on Sartre. A central theme of his is that for which he uses the term 'involvement,' or 'engagement.' My hypothesis is that his idea of involvement is not awakened to the meaning of involvement, and that, contrary to his own proclamations and to the usual interpretations of his thought, he is really an *essentialist* thinker in his basic point of view. The cue to this is his doctrine of the absurdity of things. Things are ultimately senseless for him precisely because his view of them is merely a view. He takes them as merely objects. They are over against us, as he sees it, and that is the final word. From this standpoint, it seems clear, the insularity of a man follows. Each person is cut off from everything else where everything else is simply looked on at. Now when Sartre talks of involvement it seems to me that he begins with the situation of a person so construed, I mean construed as an insular one in an absurd world, where even other persons are to be reckoned with chiefly as threats to one's integrity and independence. We shift to the experience of man as an active being from within a perspective of the world in which man is estranged from environing reality. And 'involvement' turns out to be the anguish of estrangement.

What Sartre has to say about action fits into this perspective. He connects freedom with *choice*, and thinks of responsibility as self-making, and of the assumption of responsibility as autonomy. In this case autonomy seems to mean being absolute law to oneself. And there seems to be an intellectualism about action linked with the objectivism about environing reality. Sartre's intellectualism about action seems to me revealed in two emphases: one upon choice as the essence of action, and his confusion of character-formation with making oneself (a man is his own artifact): the other emphasis requires careful detection, and it involves the confusion of moral necessity with a formalistic version of moral necessity.

Sartre does not defend formalism; but he seems to think that formalism, the placing of the necessity of action in formulated rules of action, is the only way in which one might think of demands as devolving on the person. It is true that he may have a latent appreciation for the mistakenness of an interpretation of genuine decision which would reduce decision to conformity to rules. He sees that we may shirk responsibility by leaning on rules. But I think he has no positive alternative to formalism, in spite of his protestations that his position calls for each person to act for the freedom of all persons. On his view, what is another person to me? How can I have any responsibility to him? He is chiefly a threat to my own freedom, and as object to me, he is profoundly absurd. Sartre's 'involvement' seems more akin to the anguish of bankruptcy, poignantly articulated, than to anything else. An involvement which does not mean the extension of credit to things other than ourselves is simply stewing in our own juice. That is where we are left to stew, it seems, so long as we take up a position of detachment, the presiding spirit of which is the spirit of abstraction. It is scarcely a step from the atomic individualism in which object-mindedness seems to have landed Sartre to a collectivistic social philosophy, and I wonder if Sartre is not now taking that step. But that would be another story. Meanwhile I wonder what turn Sartre's thought would take if his understanding of honesty were to deepen. Would he still emphasize role-playing and self-consciousness as definitive of the condition of man as an active being? Would his café waiters remain mimics and imitation men? Would he find "bad faith" writ so large across the face of humanity? He has laid bare the wasteland in which we find ourselves in so far as we lack good faith — faith, that is. And this can also be a step upon the threshold that opens out into the wilderness that is the reality of faith. It is to this theme of reality as a wilderness that I want to move.

This, so far as I can tell, is the theme which unifies my own life. It enfolds and simplifies, comprehends and completes. Whenever I awaken, I awaken into it. It carries with it the gift of life. And it lives in the authenticity of every authentic gift, every true blessing confirms it deeper; it is always with me when I come to myself. Through it I find my vocation, for the wilderness is reality experienced as call and explained in responding to it absolutely. It is the experience of things in this vein, reflectively amplified, which has led me to doubt that object-mindedness against which I find myself struggling, basically in myself. I want the truth, marrow-bone truth, and

I find the intimations of it whenever I am alive to things, even the most familiar and commonplace things, for the wilderness I take them to comprise. It seems to me that every time I am born, the wilderness is born anew; and every time I am born it seems to me that then, if ever, I could be content to die. Surely it is here that I must research for the meaning of coming to be and passing away. Anything understood as reality is understood as old and new and ageless. And this is reverence, the heart of action.

Saturday, August 1

As I take into account once again this color reproduction of Cezanne's "Rock Landscape" hanging here in my study, I am prompted by it to reflect on the way in which I would speak of things. If I were asked to say a word, quick, of this painting, this response leaps into the breach: Here is reality manifestly rock; it is the living rock, quarried intact.

But what underlies this response?

The painting seems a paradigm of things truly perceived. What is needed, then, is a companionate articulation of a notion of things with a notion of true perception — of the perceptive moment of awareness of reality in its concreteness. Yet reflection must move in the very vein of such perceptive experience. This painting seems to summon me to the perception of things with love and respect, and as warranting perception in such a vein. Yet it is clear that neither things nor the love and respect in terms of which they are realized as finally intelligible can be so understood in abstraction from such experience of them. There could be no appeal to what we might conceive as demonstrable characteristics of things as warrant for construing love and respect as their due. Neither reality manifest as things, nor its ultimate mode of intelligibility, can be pocketed by the mind. Only as we may be ripe for it in our entirety does it seem that reality may dawn on us concretely and anew.

What I want to reckon with as a matter for experiential reflec-

ing

forth (literally, the existence) of things in
recognize now that it was this very exper-
istence of things which I was trying to arti-
on July 11th. What I take to be challenged
by the experience from which I was taking guidance then might be
called the dogma of the ultimacy of a merely *optical* mode of thought
in the conception of manifest reality. What needs to be accommodated
seems to be a kind of feeling discernment of emergent definiteness,
of the standing forth of the distinct thing. The thing that does not
touch us, the merely 'looked at,' the mere object, cannot be manifest
reality basically understood. In the ancient Hebrew sense of the
word — that with which there is not the intimacy of touch is not
truly "*known.*" No intimacy: no revelation. No revelation: no true
givenness of reality. The diremption of "fact" and "value" seems to be
the most ultimately ruinous philosophical dogma. Yet all objectivism
seems forced into it. For in terms of an objectivist mode of thought
'feeling' must be construed in one of two ways, either as a threat to
objectivity which requires neutralization, or as merely of the order of
phenomena requiring to be taken into objective account. Of course
without feeling, nothing could be appreciated as *required!*

[margin: (separation)]

[margin: ✱ against objectivism bc of lack of feeling which leads to lack of appreciation]

The enormous potential power of naturalistic philosophy seems
to me to lie in its emphasis on sticking to existent things, to the point
of learning respect for them, and not for this thing as opposed to that
thing, but for this or that thing as *existing.* But respect for things as
existing is a vision of things, a realization, which tends to clarify the
inadequacy of naturalistic doctrines (including *super* naturalistic
ones), even if it does not bring with it an alternative set of doctrines.
Indeed it is about doctrines that one may find himself in doubt. To
respect things *qua* existing, may indeed be *vision,* but it is vision
enacted, a 'seeing with the eye of faith.' At its heart existence and
decision interlock. One is himself the leaping trout.

Everywhere there is talk of the need for "vision," for a fundamental evaluative perspective, yet on all hands we tend to think in
terms which drive us to regard vision as concocted, cooked up — even
those of us whose intent is not disparaging.

Tuesday, August 4

A sense of what governs this task to which I am held may be suggested by use of a phrase in the manner of Emerson: There is *somewhat absolute* in our experience. All my thinking is haunted by it and bears the burden of thinking it out. If this were not the case, I would not think of our condition as ephemeral, and would not find reflection partaking of this condition. ⌐short-lived

Now you begin to understand and now you don't understand — that is what seems ephemeral about our condition. But as understanding comes upon us and deepens from time to time, strengthening however fleetingly our appreciation of finality, one becomes aware of its relevance to our everyday situation all along. At the same time one becomes aware that much of the time he has been dormant or obtuse with respect to it. Furthermore he becomes aware that understanding is not something he possesses, and that the spirit of claiming to possess it is contrary to the spirit of understanding. And the very essence of understanding is that it does not come as the solution to a problem, but (in Marcel's words) as the appreciation of a mystery as such. These things being so, one also understands his condition as basically ephemeral. And he can no longer place stock in what men claim to have to sell. What they can give is another matter; this they do not have, but it is given them. Finality establishes the conditions of its own disclosure; we cannot hold them fast and place them at our disposal. A man who talks of planning for a dam, or for a house, can be talking sense. But a man who talks of planning for value is at some remove from reality. True valuing and understanding go together, and it is reality that makes this possible.

Wednesday, August 5

Every time I retrace the course of my reflections since 'their beginning' in my undergraduate years I discern as central this preoccupation with 'somewhat absolute' in experience, with a kind of central unconditional meaning which always introduces a harmony and simplicity into the complex and otherwise inconclusive. Its reconciliatory power is suggested as inexhaustible. Its relevance has seemed omnirelevance; its significance truly universal. There is that which is final, the very soul of certainty, yet the reflection to which this sets me is not something with which I expect to have done. I say this not merely because it is so hard to begin to do justice in articulate thought to the interpretation of finality, in which we must adjust interminably to the traditions and increments of human thought. More particularly I have in mind the periodicity with which one seems to alternate between exile and homecoming with respect to finality. It is as if finality filtered through to us in periods of estrangement from it and aroused us to reflection as activity pertinent to our resoration. It is as if we vaguely remembered, and the point of reflection lay in clearing our memory. Plato and Proust have helped me especially in shaping this thought. Yet the remembering that is essential, that is our homecoming, that is the reflective experience which sets one to thinking firmly in terms of the idea of grace. If philosophy wants to form the thought of basic truth in its givenness, it needs to come to grips with this experience of becoming permeable with respect to finality. The reflective experience seems to clarify more than itself. It seems revelatory with respect to all experience of givenness. I have said this before of late in terms of the cognate character of aesthetic and philosophic contemplation, and speak of aesthetic contemplation and of true perception synonymously. There is finality in aesthetic contemplation, in true perception.

Now objectivization as a mode of thought, tending as it does to the familiar dichotomization of fact and value, shows up in the attempt to interpret givenness in independence from that finality apart from which there is no true givenness. It makes givenness correlative with 'discreta,' basic data, from which, supposedly, we elaborate such conceptions of reality as have foundation (Empiricism typifies this). It seems to me that the philosophical interpretation of givenness should be liberated from the supposition that the givenness of reality is coincident with our taking possession of minimal discrete disclosures on the strength of which we can claim to make assured assertions. It has been observed that these data are 'abstracta,' but little seems to have been done to reinterpret the givenness of reality apart from the pressure of the demand to make this givenness of reality coincide with a legitimate occasion for making absolute statements about what is given (usually qualified with the utmost nicety and not a little ingenuity!). But why should we suppose that in so far as reality is truly given, we ought to be able to state unqualifiedly what is given?

It has seemed to me that when things were given to me with finality, this had little to do with my being able to make absolute assertions, unqualified assertions about them. It leaves my 'knowledge about them' just as correctible as before. I cannot countenance the translation of their experienced finality into a claim to make unqualified assertions about anything, however minimal or abstract. Neither can I countenance a denial of the experienced finality of things which proceeds from the confusion of their finality with the possibility of making unqualified assertions about them, coupled with what seems to me the legitimate denial of the possibility of making such assertions.

In short, the 'somewhat absolute' in experience does not seem to me tied up with any legitimate claim to absolute knowledge, and it is just on this point that my thinking turns. And I connect this point with the following: that the necessity of the real cannot be interpreted as bound up with the possibility of demonstrating the necessity of anything. And I suspect a corollary to this: that the thinking we might undertake in order to demonstrate the necessity of anything, and to show the meaning of necessity in so doing, is liable to place us at furthest remove from the appreciation of the necessity of anything. Only the truly given is experienced as necessary; this is the contemplation of reality, whether perceptive or reflective (meditative).

But here is an essential point: Nothing can be truly given to us except on the condition of active receptiveness on our part. Our capacity for estrangement from reality, in all its permutations, is to be marked in all our indecision, our insistence to have things on our own terms.[50] If this incapacity to receive is writ as large as it seems to be 'across the face of our experience,' what can possess us to think that givenness should be ours to interpret any old time, as if we were always and equally permeable with respect to reality? It is said that we have eyes to see and ears to hear, and yet do not see and do not hear, and this seems true. Yes, we see and we hear, no doubt, but in large measure there is nothing conclusive about our seeing and hearing. There is always finality in conclusive seeing and hearing, as there is also in truly decisive action. But again, this does not mean that the meaning of conclusive seeing and hearing, or of decisive action, should be confused with a claim to have conclusive knowledge about something. The true certainty which reality fosters in us does not seem to supersede or contravene hypothesis. And in the spirit of those occasions, which seem comparatively rare, upon which it comes clear, it comes clear with the implication that a lifetime of thought and deed are required in its fulfilment.

I think of John Dewey's *Quest for Certainty* once again, and again I agree with his criticism of the quest for absolute knowledge. But I cannot recall that he entertains the possibility that certainty is nonetheless at the heart of the philosophical enterprise, but must not be confused with claims to absolute knowledge, or the quest for absolute knowledge. I am inclined to think that his disillusionment with respect to Absolute Idealism was fatal in this regard. I doubt if his understanding of that disillusionment ever fully matured. Could it have done so unless he had come to appreciate something genuine in his attraction to this philosophy beyond the temptation to succumb to its appalling confusion of certainty with the claim to absolute knowledge?

By 'somewhat absolute in experience,' whatever I have in mind, I do not have in mind 'absolute knowledge' or 'knowledge of the absolute.' I have never felt tempted by Absolute Idealism, though I have read such a work as Hegel's *Phenomenology of Mind* with interest and some care. I have too strong a belief in things in my bones.

50. Editorial note: I have subsequently come across a profoundly suggestive statement of this sort of interpretation of indecision in Martin Buber's *Good and Evil*. See especially the last three chapters of Part Three.

But because of this very belief, I have never been strongly tempted by Materialism either.

Nor have I longed for something permanent, something impervious to change. It is not fixation and possession of reality that I want; no, nor immunity from the vicissitudes of change. What I seek to clarify is a perennial meaning of things, by virtue of which things are experienced not merely as old, or as new, but also as ageless. It is this which I have sensed those to be driving at who have invoked the image of the cyclical character of events (e.g. Nietzsche's "eternal return," and the Pythagorean "here I was once, even as I am now, leaning on my stick and prattling away to you"). Everything that strikes us through and through with wonder, deepening into love, however, should teach us not to confuse things in their eternity with some realm in which time's arrow is stopped.

his aim

Thursday, August 6

No passage in Spinoza continues to interest me more than the autobiographical prelude to his *Essay on the Improvement of the Understanding*. And the crux of this passage comes with his expression of the philosopher's resolution to "go to the root of the matter," having reviewed the respects in which we seem to expend ourselves inconsequentially, to engage in inconclusive pursuits, and to suffer the bondage of desires and craving of esteem. His bill of particulars against folly adds nothing to that which we find in Plato or the Stoics, to refer to classic examples. And his conception of our "true good" is coupled with a very Stoic conception of an ideal human character to be striven for with every nerve, in the attempt to possess it. Neither of these strains of thought appears as thought through, and I do not find them, as they appear, particularly illuminating. But Spinoza does define the ideal character to which he alludes as knowledge of the union existing between the mind and the whole of nature, and this does suggest a merging of the concern for salvation with a concern for the truth, and truth as having to do with our union with the whole of nature. Our "chief good" is thought to lie in the realization of this union. This theme, too, bears an obvious affinity with what is expressed in the annals of Stoicism, but I find Spinoza more solid and replete with intimations of how the theme should be thought than I do the Stoics.

I want to draw on the intimations which I have gathered from Spinoza of how this theme might be thought, and bring them to bear on one or two things he says in this prelude to the task which his *Ethics* undertakes. The interest of the passage, indeed, lies in bringing to bear an impression of the gamut of his more mature thought in weighing the adequacy with which he puts his basic point at this earlier juncture.

After his summary of the disturbances of the mind, he says of them: "All these arise from the love of what is perishable, such as the objects already mentioned. But love toward a thing eternal and infinite feeds the mind wholly with joy, and is itself unmingled with any sadness . . ."[51]

Here is the question which Spinoza has taught me to ask of the Spinoza who wrote this: What thing is eternal and infinite other than perishable things themselves? And what is this love of that which is eternal and infinite a love *toward*, if it is not a love toward those things with which we coexist in union? And what is this love, filling us with joy and unmingled with any sadness, but our realization of the union existing between ourselves and the whole of nature? What is our love toward, if it is not toward the modally manifest? What is our union with, if not with the finite? Apart from the finite and perishable nothing is manifest *toward* which love would be possible. Our failure to appreciate our union with the whole of nature is our failure to love the finite truly.

The whole of Spinoza's effort to distinguish between bondage and freedom, between what are referred to as passive and active emotion, respectively, may be considered as an attempt to distinguish between

---

51. *Philosophy of Benedict de Spinoza*, trans. by R. H. M. Elwes, New York, Tudor, 1936, p. 3.

false and true caring for things, and things which are none other than perishable things. True caring for things is bound up with the appreciation of them as modes; that is, as infinite and eternal in existing finitely. For existence is the expression of the divine nature.

Just a little later in the *Essay* Spinoza says, "Nothing regarded in its own nature can be called perfect or imperfect . . ."[52] What is this regarding things "in their own nature?" It seems to me very close to what I have called naturalistic thinking, or more basically, objectivization as a mode of thought. It is a regarding things 'in themselves,' abstractly, and in abstraction from experiencing them as *modes*. So thought of, evaluation has no relevance to them; that is the point. Of course this is not to say that whenever we think evaluatively of things we also think adequately of them in our evaluations. At the bottom of adequate evaluation there must always be an appreciation of our union with them. But our union with them cannot be thought out as merely a relational union, since this union is founded in existence — our standing forth with things in a unity of expression.

To love things as modes is to avoid idolatry, and it is to love *them*, nonetheless; and to love them *for what they are*. Yet what they are, their meaning, is only defined as we realize our own existence.

And now I would like to bring these reflections back to perishing. As we cling to things, as we fail to realize them profoundly, no doubt perishing strikes us as to be fought against with all our might. Perishing, accordingly, robs us of what we love, and our vulnerability lies in loving anything likely to perish. The premium we place on permanence is a fixation from which we must free ourselves in the attempt to think that which cannot play us false.

At times another standpoint on perishing, and on the perishing of what we love, has hinted itself to me. It has seemed on such occasions that the very perishing of what we love might be an essential moment in the clarification of the worthiness of love of that which perishes. Thus the death of someone whom we have loved, and loved very likely in a thoroughly ambiguous way, may clarify the strain of that love which has been true with regard to that person. And it

---

52. Ibid., p. 4.

seems that in so far as this is so, our affirmation of that person becomes definitive. As never before, perhaps, we understand their reality; that is, in them we come to understand reality concretely. But for their perishing we might not have become clear with respect to their importance. Is Whitehead right in suggesting that only that which perishes can *be* of infinite importance? He opens the way to a vista of reflection as vast as the Pacific and the music of Handel.

There is weeping and gnashing of teeth; there is stony impassivity; there is ribaldry, and vacuous staring. There is confusion. But there is pure gentleness, and it is in this vein that perishing speaks.

Friday, August 7

What a painful discrepancy between the spirit in which I reflect, on some days, and that in which I go about doing other things. It has seemed to me these mornings, as I have thought and written, that I have meant what I said, and that I was not fooling myself in the main. Indeed I have set nothing down except as it came to me in line with a cumulative criterion (implicit, to be sure) of work that is continuous and work that I must be about. But there are days during which I go on from my work, and remembering at least nominally the themes on which I have dwelt earlier in the day, I become something of a mockery to myself, catching such strong hints of inherent weaknesses of mine as force upon me the misery of questioning the very authenticity of my own work. The world as I take it reflectively and the world as I muddle through it then seem excruciatingly worlds apart. What is all this talk of love, of respect, of decision, coming from one who is so often devoid of them? Does one write such philosophy out of compensation for his inadequacy? Is one retreating from his smallness into a realm of sententious utterances? And it is clear enough that the more scholarly phases of my work,

Wittstein - philosophy of language, analytic philosophy
.thinks that was a preparation for this
kind of work = makes him better equipped to
spot bullshit

the inward morning

139

such as go into the preparation of my courses, do not leave me face to face with such questions.

Yet I stick to these considerations:

✱ It was music which first awakened me to the need for reflection; but for the music which aroused and defined a sense of unconditional reality in me, I doubt if I would have found it relevant to reflect on our condition in a way that drew me to the works of philosophers as speaking to that condition. Since those earliest days of philosophic study, I have remained concerned with the works of philosophers, not in themselves, but as helps to the understanding of experience. I study the works of philosophers out of an interest which subordinates theory to understanding. And though I have the patience to thread my way through theoretical considerations as such, I have acquired it only as I have found them to fertilize reflections that are essentially non-theoretical in character. It will ever be important to me to give attention to technical philosophy, but I will never be able to take technical philosophy as the ultimate phase of a reflective life. ✱

During my years of graduate study before the war I studied philosophy in the classroom and at a desk, but my philosophy took shape mainly on foot. It was truly peripatetic, engendered not merely while walking, but *through* walking that was essentially a *meditation of the place*. And the balance in which I weighed the ideas I was studying was always that established in the experience of walking in the place. I weighed everything by the measure of the silent presence of things, clarified in the racing clouds, clarified by the cry of hawks, solidified in the presence of rocks, spelled syllable by syllable by waters of manifold voice, and consolidated in the act of taking steps, each step a meditation steeped in reality. What this all meant, I could not say, kept trying to say, kept trying to harmonize with the suggestions arising from the things I read. But I do remember that this walking in the presence of things came to a definitive stage. It was in the fall of '41, October and November, while late autumn prevailed throughout the northern Canadian Rockies, restoring everything in that vast region to a native wildness. Some part of each day or night, for forty days, flurries of snow were flying. The aspens and larches took on a yellow so vivid, so pure, so trembling in the air, as to fairly cry out that they were as they were, limitlessly. And it was there in attending to this wilderness, with unremitting alertness and attentiveness, yes, even as I slept, that I knew myself to have been instructed for life, though I was at a loss to say what instruction I had received.

Shortly after this period in the Canadian Rockies I got caught up by the war, and during three years at sea I left philosophical studies completely behind, not only by reason of devoting no time to them but also in the sense that they came to seem utterly remote. Indeed I came to think that if ever I had 'known anything about philosophy' I had surely forgotten what I knew, and I could no longer imagine ever returning to a life of study. What I did not realize at all at the time, as it now seems to me, was how philosophy, or perhaps I should say a trend of meaning, continued to take its own course with me. Looking back now, I understand my life at sea as an almost uninterrupted active meditation, continuous, quite, with the walking I had done throughout earlier years. And so continuous was life at sea with the instruction I had received in those mountains just prior to the war, that the sea absorbed me without a ripple of difference intervening to make known to me that everything was as it had been before. But handling a ship at sea is full-time preoccupation, and I lived unwittingly on the breath of life drawn deeply from sea and storm and the unending expanse and the going on and on, living with men, men I can never forget. They were men taking men as they come, but men with whom I lived thoroughly enough to experience the community of men and place; though I did not know it, I lived a meditation of both in communion. The thought which I have been working out in these last three years is definitively based on that experience.

But reflection, it seems, must earn the gift of the essential meaning of things past. It is as if experience must continue underground for some time before it can emerge as springwater, clear, pure, understood. And reflection is a trying to remember, a digging that is pointless if it be not digging down directly beneath where one stands, so that the waters of his life may re-invade the present moment and define the meaning of both. Thus it was that after the war what

governed my thought and guided me in the writing of my dissertation was the instruction of the mountains blended with interpretative
clues from studies also conducted before the war. After four years
devoid of philosophical study, without preliminary ado, I found that
I could sit down and write off in eight months, without hesitation,
an articulate version, at least, of what I had been helpless to cope
with before. And the tools of reflection, derived from those philosophical studies which I had thought almost entirely forgotten, came
readily enough to hand with the resurgence of that which I had
gleaned in the experience of the place prior to the war. The basic
theme was simple enough, indeed it was the theme of simplicity:
Things say themselves, univocally, unisonously, formulating a tautology
of infinite significance.

In my thesis I did some justice to the instruction I had received
from those mountains. But it seems to me that I left man out of
account, and in so doing, falling short of a philosophy of action, I
entirely failed to connect the meaning of existence which I was trying
to bespeak with the experience of acting, of commitment, of standing
forth as a man, as one who is made to stand forth (I use the term
'ecstasis' for this being made to stand forth). The nearest I came to
an intimation of this idea was in what I wrote of Charles M. Doughty
and his *Arabia Deserta.* Here is why I persisted in the naturalistic
thinking of those whose vision of reality I shared. But how hard it is
to learn what it is to think as one who acts, and to distinguish the
turn of ideas which pivot on the development of this standpoint. After
five years of gradual schooling in this mode of reflection, perhaps I
am ready to revert to the experience of life with men at sea, as the
situation defining my task.

Those days give me the courage now to continue this endeavour
in terminal reflection, not as a termination of anything, but as a renewed endeavour in understanding finality more maturely, in rounded
human terms.

I perceive that I am one month out of port. Herman Melville
must be sailing somewhere hereabout, as when he wrote in Chapter
XXIII of *Moby Dick*: ". . . in landlessness alone resides the highest
truth, shoreless, indefinite as God . . ."

What is bound up with this notion of realization, in terms of which I have been thinking more and more of late?

I do not think it can be separated from the thought of a destiny which is ours to fulfill. But the way in which we think the meaning of having a destiny to fulfil seems at the mercy of our actual conduct of life. Thus there are bound to be times when it seems as if having a destiny could mean no more than finding ourselves in a situation not of our own making or choosing, and relative to the standpoint of such moments our situation could be summarized by the theme of contingency: The contingent situation is the situation experienced as devoid of basic rhyme or reason. And it is perfectly compatible with this way of taking things to recognize that things happen in certain regular ways rather than in others. An endless reporting on how things happen and codification of the ways of things seems neither here nor there when it comes to making basic sense of a situation. To be familiar with the way in which things are likely to happen, and not to have one's expectations violated, need not mitigate in the slightest the lack of conclusive meaning in what one is familiar with, or in what conforms to expectation.

On the other hand, it also seems clear that we are capable at times of taking our situation in quite a different vein from that of contingency and an arbitrary course of events. Nor for this to be so does it seem necessary that we assume the position of being in control of our situation, making it answer to our intentions; or that we discern in our situation any intention or plan of which it might be construed as the embodiment. (Though it may be, as Kant's discussion of natural teleology suggests, that we experience our situation in a way that we *think as if* it embodied purpose or plan, and were expressive thereof.)

I will go a step further to say that the notion of finding things to our liking is also quite inadequate to thinking out the vein in which we may experience our situation as non-contingent. We need be finding no conclusive meaning in events that are to our liking. Contingency may still pervade the vein in which we take things as 'good luck' as much as that in which their course is one of 'bad luck.' (Kafka's *Amerika* makes very interesting reading in line with the notion of 'luck.' You can read the fortunes of the boy, whose story this book is, as an absurd oscillation between moments of good and bad luck, yet the book seems an attempt to define a way in which this seemingly senseless alternation of fortunes is undercut by the constant innocent involvement of the boy in his fluctuating situation.)

Participation, active and receptive participation in our situation — this seems the key in which we must think of what it means to have a destiny which is ours to fulfil, and at the same time, of what it means to be involved in a situation that is non-contingent. By 'realization' I mean fulfilment of destiny and appreciation of the non-contingency of our situation, rolled into one. We find that which 'explains' our situation in acting as we must.

In so far as I have been able to think in this manner, I have been led to suppose that reflective clarification of conclusive meaning to be found in our situation, and of genuinely decisive action, respectively, are inseparable reflective endeavours. And I have thought that both metaphysical and ethical reflection must turn on one's actual involvement in reality as an active being, as this involvement fluctuates in depth. This fluctuation in depth on our part marks our condition as ephemeral. Would not the notions of prediction and control be utterly irrelevant to it? If meditative reflection can be construed as a way in which we may reestablish ourselves in a deeper vein of experience, surely it is a way we must take without knowing where we are. going.

For years I have been impressed with the justice of connecting the ideas of meditation and prayer. In true meditation one is opening oneself, there is a deepening of candour without which nothing is revealed, but for which one's thought skims round and round on surfaces. If one's thinking is more like skating on hard ice, it seems doubtful if he can imagine what it might be to be immersed in the fluent medium of meanings drawn from experience in depth. To be shut off, estranged, is not to appreciate what one lacks. As I put the idea before, more ultimate than any attitude which we can be said to adopt is that attitude which is actual, and from which, upon which, we proceed, whatever we may proceed to do. Our actual attitude, or standpoint, esablishes the vein and the level in which our appreciation of possibilities of meaning moves.

There seems to be a purchase right here for a valuable distinction between prediction and prophecy. We can predict at will on the strength of knowledge which we can summon at will. But prophecy concerns a significance of things to come which must be wrung out of a depth of experience which we cannot similarly command. And prophecy has always been thought of as an insight into human destiny sensitized to the significance of trends in human affairs to which we may remain oblivious even in being most knowledgeable with respect to the course of events. In laying aside this distinction between prediction and prophecy for subsequent consideration, I want to set down this cue to follow up later on: Can I not distinguish between predictive awareness of that typhoon which we had to face in September, 1945, a predictive awareness extending to the exigencies which the storm might bring upon us and our little ship, and a prophetic awareness of the coming storm as a trial of mettle? Also consider this: Is not prophetic awareness just what we must take into account and think out in distinction from predictive awareness if we would do justice, reflectively, to the prospective orientation of decisive action? Here is something which those philosophical proponents of the forward-looking orientation, the pragmatists, seem to have left out of account. I doubt if I have taken explicit account of it before.

Wednesday, August 12

destiny/fate

Care must be exercised in working out the idea of having a destiny to fulfil so as to extricate it, for one thing, from the idea of having a fate — of being fated. It seems to me that I am invited by the idea of fate to think from the standpoint of a certain inner paralysis often reflected in speaking of man's helplessness in the hands of

fate = inner paralysis"
destiny = responsibility

fate. On the other hand the idea of having a destiny to fulfil seems
to invite me to think from the standpoint of responsibility, as one
responsive to a call: a call clarifying itself in its constancy as we respond with relevance in multiform situations engendering it; a call
imparting to sustained courses of action a vocational significance
which is at the heart of not acting in vain.

The idea of fate not only suggests that we act in vain; it tends
to controvert the very idea of our acting. The idea of a destiny to
be fulfilled suggests that we are followed wherever we go, whatever
we do, by a basic significance in terms of which our lives must be
construed, and that we act in vain only as we fail to respond consonantly with that significance aligning the otherwise contingent moments of our lives.

The distinction between these ideas brings us to the verge of
human bondage and human freedom. For belief in the idea of fate
would *partake* of human bondage, while realization of the meaning
of a destiny to be fulfilled would partake of human freedom. I see,
too, that our way of thinking of necessity is at stake in this distinction.
What I want to think out is an idea of necessity that partakes of concrete liberation with the advent of finality in experience.

It may help with these ideas to consider an aspect of the story
of Oedipus. Oedipus is confronted with a prophecy of awful deeds
he will do. Wherein is he *fated* to do these things? The key to his fate
(and to the meaning of his being fated) seems to lie in his characteristic way of "assuming responsibility," which is suggested even
in the way he takes steps in the light of the prophecy to avoid what
is foretold. I am tempted to say that if he had been deeply sensible of
a distinction between prophecy and prediction, the prophecy could
not have been made. For it seems that he takes the prophecy as
merely a prediction; he takes it in character, in the character of a man
who supposes his destiny to be just that which he himself can command and control. He takes charge of the situation, and in so doing,
as Jaspers says of him, "always travels an unintended road."[53] Fate
is the way of a man whose assumption of responsibility is an attempt

[53.] Jaspers, Karl, *Tragedy Is Not Enough*, Boston, Beacon, 1952, p. 60.

to take charge of his destiny; no matter that he sets about this with right-minded convictions.

Oedipus' great gifts and developed powers abet his reliance on his capacity to foresee and control the outcome of the matters in which he has a stake by the exercise of sufficient vigilance. Yet the point is not that Oedipus overestimates his powers and goes too far in assuming control of his situation. It is not that he makes errors of judgment to which the most perspicacious of men are liable, or even that he fails to take due account of that liability. In this story I read a connection between responsibility lived as autonomy, however well-intentioned, and destiny which comes to assume the visage of fate. It is in a seeming assumption of responsibility which is really a distortion of responsibility that destiny is converted from a significance which we may fulfil with our very lives into a fatal discrepancy between what we intend and the way things turn out.

Can we not say that necessity is more fundamentally gentle and firm than harsh? And in the case of Oedipus are we not led by the very deepening of honesty in which he accepts what has come upon him to an appreciation of human destiny as transcending fate? Not happiness, but the touch of blessedness comes to this man. Such seems to be the final word enunciated by great tragedy.

Only on the strength of a true responsibility can we hope to form a true idea of necessity; at the heart of our 'metaphysics' must lie the clear strain of responding to call. Otherwise reality will surely pass in endless review before a mind's eye that is helpless to understand — the image of our own deadness.

Sunday, August 16

For the last three days some bearings from Hume, from Spinoza, and from Kant have been coming to the point of convergence.

Hume's discussion of our disposition to believe in necessary connections between events begins to strike me as a glancing approach to the fundamental question as to the disposition in which necessity may assume its basic meaning for us. Perhaps we should hold in abeyance questions about the relevance of an idea of necessity to the course of events until we have clarified the attitude in which necessity may assume the meaning it is to hold for us.

Even when we are referring to the course of events, much of our invocation of the category of necessity has to do with our mode of response in the situation admitting of that reference. We speak of the necessity of taking account of features of our situation; we say they must be acknowledged, accepted, or dealt with. And here we are clearly voicing *de jure* claims that obtain their relevance not only *to* the activity of judging and otherwise dealing with the course of events, but *from* the standpoint of an active being for whom there is genuine necessity in the very grain of active response. All judging as activity implicitly presupposes the category of necessity, and with it the standpoint of an active being for whom *de jure* claims have fundamental force. May it even be that necessity can have no meaning or relevance in so far as we abstract from such a standpoint in attempting its interpretation?

But what bearing might this line of thought have on interpreting the sense in which the course of events may embody necessity? The more I reflect on this question, the more I am led to consider what it is to be interlocked with the course of events in 'a tight spot,' when we find ourselves in a critical situation. In such a situation how integral the meaning of the situation is with the response in which we realize it. If the course of events were to seem extraneous to us, and we to it, that would be akin to fear; but as we meet the situation, it is as if there were one seamless texture of experience in which we reckon with 'must be.' I gather at least one intimation from such experience right now: Necessity must be construed as an *experiential* category; it has no proper place in thinking abstractly about the course of events.

At this point two propositions of Part I of the *Ethics* seem to jump into place with peculiar significance. Proposition XVI has stayed with me for a long time: "From the necessity of the divine nature must follow an infinite number of things in infinite ways . . ." But hitherto it has somehow dangled at loose ends. I take it now with what Spinoza says in Proposition XVIII: "God is the indwelling and not the transient cause of all things." Must we not discover 'the indwelling' from within ourselves? Can we understand things in their necessity apart from acting on that necessity as it governs us? Our actual mode of responding — of assuming responsibility — would seem to hold for us the understanding of reality of which we may be capable. Except as we realize ourselves that necessity pertaining to all things, how will we understand it as pertaining to them?

Once again: We discover what it means to exist in being made to stand forth, in standing forth as we must.

If philosophical truth and active decision are thus akin, it would follow that we are not in a position to demonstrate the relevance to the order of events of the idea of necessity we may form. What enters decisively into the connection of events is to be realized, and not merely observed.

If we fall away from an experiential mode of thought and the urgencies of human existence in which our destiny interlocks with the course of finite beings, if we disorient our thinking from the standpoint of one who acts and assumes responsibility, must we not come to share in the essentials of Hume's point of view? Let finite phenomena merely appear. Cut them to the limit from all that is implicit in concrete response. That would be comparable to taking Spinoza's modes merely and flatly as finite things, in abstraction from their being modes — expressions, that is, of "the divine nature." And note how this would work out in Spinoza's terms: Except as finite beings express the divine nature, they cannot be said to condition one another; there would be no necessity in the order of events if modes were to be taken merely abstractly in their connection with one another, and not as *modes* in Spinoza's sense. For Spinoza 'the indwelling cause' of all things underlies the 'transeunt' causality of modes.

It is now much clearer to me that if we think in the vein of what happens, we can only think that what happens happens — period. Hume seems quite right about this. There is no relevant purchase for an idea of necessity in what we consider merely as a series of happenings. To describe transient causes can only be analysed as an extension of the scope of happenings to be noted, and a subsumption of an occurrence to a series of occurrences of a uniform type. Accordingly, we give up the notion 'must happen.' And we *can* give it up; it does not remain as a persistent illusion.

How is it, though, that Hume confines his thought on the notion of necessity to his eventual account of how we happen to persist in such a gratuitous notion, as he sees it? What could be simpler than to pass from 'must happen' to the consideration of necessity as reflected in 'must do?' Yet how curiously the imperative mood escapes even a most scrupulous thinker. And how easy it is to hand over action with all its fundamental implications into the receivership of the point of view of an observer who busies himself with noting how things happen where men are lurking about.

Since we find Hume in his ethical writings bringing to bear on action, and men in action, the point of view from which he considers happenings, it is not surprising that he fails to reconsider the notion of necessity in conjunction with action. How are "the springs of action" to be construed, according to Hume? How else than as subject-matter for empirical psychology? They can be thought of as nothing but *de facto* conditions of action and appraisal. It is only relevant to inquire how men happen to do what they do. But men evaluate and judge of the rightness or wrongness of what is done. . . . These phenomena also can be studied and described. Isn't that Hume's explicit undertaking in his theory of morals? — the specification of the *de facto* conditions under which men arrive at those 'moral judgments' which they consider to have *de jure* force.

Still, we may always read what a man writes on morals, even if it be dominated by an observational standpoint, alert for indications of the vein in which he would himself appraise. What does he see, after all, in what men are about? In what terms does Hume approach nearest to an indication of the form in which finality lays hold of his thought? Where does he take his stand? we may ask.

With the benevolent and disinterested spectator? In the belief that we must inform ourselves most carefully about situations to which we would refer evaluative judgments? With that paragon of "honour and humanity," Cleanthes, whom Hume embellishes with accomplishments, talents, sensitivity — all traits useful and agreeable in a man, to himself and to others? It is not obvious if Hume takes us beyond the summary terms of this portrait in the Conclusion of his *Enquiry Concerning the Principles of Morals.* Even his own concern for truth, as distinct from his ambition as a man of letters, seems to go its way without informing his ethical thought with any theme more ultimate than can be carried in terms of utility and agreeableness. Where finality is imaged in these terms an idea of necessity that is believed in is not to be expected. What it means to find a stake in a situation on which one *must act* cannot be fathomed in these terms; nor, as it seems to me, from the point of view which prevails in Hume's thinking.

all about Kant

✳ *Tuesday, August 18*

Whatever we may say of the relation in Kant's thought between the dynamic of nature and the dynamic of moral existence, his ethical thought clearly expresses the standpoint of one whose appreciation of action is fundamentally in the vein of genuine necessity. The task in which he instructs us most unmistakably is that of clarifying what it means to act in a way that is not arbitrary. He bespeaks that strain of imperativeness in our experience as active beings which is categorical, and in so doing he seems to me to bespeak *unconditional concern.* Translating Kant's theme of categorical imperativeness into the terms of *unconditional concern* sets off some suggestions which may prove helpful now.[54]

If we take as our task that of thinking out the implications of

54. Editorial note: Tillich's "ultimate concern" may well come to mind in connection with the phrase "unconditional concern" appearing here. I know that I was very soon to begin to profit from Tillich's writings, if I had not already done so by the date when the phrase occurred to me.

unconditional concern, we must be prepared to explore this concern in its actual experiential range, and follow where we may be led by experience in this vein. I would say that we may be led to restore reflective issues otherwise taken too narrowly to the full range of their philosophic implications: I am thinking particularly of issues too often confined within a demarcated reading now of 'moral,' and now of 'aesthetic' experience. There is something not only 'morally' but even 'metaphysically' categorical about our experience of 'the beautiful.' And to experience things as beautiful, the more profoundly we experience them so, is clearly a matter of experiential tutelage in unconditional concern. If we recognize this reflectively, bearing in mind the ethical import of unconditional concern, we might undercut the tendency to interpret aesthetic experience as amoral without falling back on either aestheticism or a moralistic reading of artistic intent. At the same time we may accord due weight to aesthetic experience in our interpretation of reality.

It is time to think again of the beautiful in the vein of gratitude, from experience in which the very soul of the man who acts is informed with grace, and not as if the beautiful were a refuge from the moral life, a sphere of amusement, of holiday from reality. Kant lost much, I think, by failing to link the conception of categorical imperativeness in his ethical writings with the experience of finality which he later touches upon in the *Critique of Judgment.*

Unconditional concern also seems reflected as concern for truth, and the more so, again, the more profound concern for truth may be. If we approach the interpretation of truth bearing in mind the ethical import of unconditional concern, it may restore us to the appreciation of the standpoint of active commitment in which truth is at stake, without which no proposition can be consummated truly in the activity of thought. Accordingly, we may begin to do justice in our reflection to the active — indeed the categorical commitment involved in the very meaning of truth without confusing that with a pragmatic interest in the utility or convenience of true thinking. Unconditional concern cannot be explicated in terms of any kind of result to be obtained in acting upon it, compatible though it may be with an interest in all manner of results. What we think or otherwise do in acting upon it may or may not be convenient; but then, what we find convenient depends after all on what we are governed by — on what we serve. A man concerned to build the foundation of a house right might not think it particularly inconvenient to make a long trip to town for more cement to insure the proper proportions of gravel, cement, sand, and water in effecting his mixture.

What I am trying to suggest for the present is this: Wherever unconditional concern may lead, as into consideration of our concern for truth, the standpoint from which Kant bespeaks categorical imperativeness in his ethics needs to be brought to bear. This standpoint seems definitive for philosophical issues, and not just for those which are segregated as ethical. Thus I would say that in the end reality must be interpreted in the terms to which our experience may lead us, in so far as we may be capable of unconditional concern. The companion ideas of necessity and finality would seem futile to pursue in abstraction from such concern. And devoid of it, will we find conclusive importance in anything, or necessity, let us say, in any way of acting? I think this consideration is to the point in connection with attempts to demonstrate finality or necessity. From what standpoint do we ask for demonstration?

Wednesday, August 19

Both are experiential ideas, there is no demonstrable conclusive meaning in the situation in which we live and move and have our being. And there is no demonstrable necessity about any course of action which we can represent to ourselves. We cannot, then, make good the ideas of finality and necessity by demonstrating their relevance to anything which we represent to ourselves. These ideas must be thought out from the standpoint of unconditional concern, and so far as our thinking is not actually centered in such concern and *informed with it* we are out of position for their interpretation — just as we are out of position for the discovery of finality and necessity in anything which we fail to take account of from the standpoint of such concern.

It seems most unfortunate, then, to try to make out the relevance of an idea of necessity to action by trying to establish a procedure for judging what it is necessary to do. For if a procedure could be established for judging of what it is necessary to do, this would amount to the possibility of demonstrating the necessity of a course of action. Much of ethical thinking seems to have been misdirected along these lines, almost as if necessity could only pertain to action if you could prove to a person what he ought to be doing. Yet when you come right down to it, is it not clear that really believing in the categorical (i.e. genuine) imperativeness of what one is doing, or better, really believing in what one is doing, carries with it the realization that one has not proven, and could not prove the necessity of doing what he does? We can only bear witness to the necessity of what we do, and through that action which is necessary, rather than through showing how what we do fulfils specifiable conditions by virtue of which it must be acknowledged as necessary. Appreciation of necessity cannot be forced.

Returning explicitly to Kant, it seems to me that he confuses the attempt to elucidate categorical (i.e. genuine) imperativeness with the attempt to formulate a procedure by which to determine what it may be categorically imperative to do. It is as if he thought that the possibility of non-arbitrary action hinged upon the possibility of demonstrating wherein certain actions are unconditionally required, and therefore that elucidation of the former must consist in making good the latter. Even the champions of his ethical thought usually fall into the error of following him in this confusion.[55] And most of the adverse criticisms of his ethics obtain their purchase in the hopeless miscarriage of the idea of necessary action which Kant is involved in through his efforts to establish an explicit criterion for the determination of categorically imperative actions — as if the necessity of action might

[55]. Editorial note: For two excellent exceptions see Teale, A. E., *Kantian Ethics*, London, Oxford, 1951, and Gahringer, R., *The Principle of Self-criticism in Practical Reason*, doctoral dissertation completed for Harvard University in 1954.

be represented in the image of the conclusion of a demonstration which one is forced to accept.

It is ironical that in his use of examples (in *The Fundamental Principles*) to illustrate his meaning Kant strays farthest from his deepest intent, and farthest from the vein of experiential thinking informed with the implications of unconditional concern. But Kant suffers, I believe, from failure to distinguish between experiential and empirical thinking. In rightly distinguishing ethical thinking from the latter, he seems to obscure from himself the truly experiential character of ethical reflection: That every ~~emphatic~~ stroke by which our ethical thinking is informed with understanding is a moment of strange awakening into what has already been confirmed in our experience as active beings; that every stroke of ethical 'argument' is futile and fails to engender understanding which is not *ad hominem*. It is strange that Kant, for all his recognition of our capacity to be perverse, failed to underscore and follow up the point that perversity presupposes truth in an aspect not susceptible to proof. For a man in his entirety is the pivot on which realization of essential truth turns.

perverse = showing deliberate desire to behave unreasonably

Thursday, August 20

I have dwelt on the idea of unconditional concern in the hope of positioning ourselves for philosophical reflection. It has seemed to me that we are unable to think in terms of finality and necessity except as our actual mode of concern in the act of reflection be unconditional. It is not an attitude which we adopt or deliberately acquire. But it is an attitude to which we may be recalled; it may reawaken in us and bring us to ourselves. And there are things one may read, such as we have from Kant or Spinoza; there are things one may hear, certain music — it may be; there are men who live again in remembered deeds of theirs which revisit one as true; one may be struck clean by sunlight over a patch of lawn, by clouds running free before the wind, by the massive presence of rock. What untold hosts of voices there are which call upon one and summon him to reawakening. He remembers, and is himself once again, moving cleanly on his way. Some measure of simplicity again informs the steps he takes; he becomes content to be himself and finds fragrance in the air. He may eat his food in peace. He does not wish to obviate tomorrow's work. He is willing to consider: not to suppose a case, but take the case that is. He becomes patient. Things invite him to adequate himself to their infinity. The passage of time is now not robbery or show; it is the meaning of the present ever completing itself. It is enough to participate in this, to be at home in the unknown.

Philosophy is not a making of a home for the mind out of reality. It is more like learning to leave things be: restoration in the wilderness, here and now.

Friday, August 21

By 'leaving things be' I do not mean inaction;[56] I mean respecting things, being still in the presence of things, letting them speak. Existing is absolute. Things are of infinite importance in existing. But as Kant says, existing is not a character of things; it is their givenness. And since the givenness of things is what I take to be the foundation of respect for *them*, I cannot see that emphasis on things of a certain character, as opposed to things lacking this character, affords an ultimate purchase for interpreting the possibility of respect. On this point I have seemed to differ rather radically from a great deal of the thought with which I am acquainted. Thus, for example, I have been unable to follow that tradition of thinking personality to be a necessary character of anything deserving respect. And I cannot see why religious encounter should be limited to the circumstance of encounter

---

56. This point holds me to the study of such works as the *Gita*, the *Book of Tao*, the literature of Zen, Meister Eckhart's recorded thoughts; and I have found some very interesting cognate material in Jung, as in the introductory paragraphs of Chapter II of his *The Integration of the Personality*.

with persons. This is not to say, however, that anything can take the place of persons as capable of testifying in the manner of respect. And it may be well to follow Kant here: in making central for the idea of the dignity of man man's capacity to bear witness in respect. But isn't this a capacity to find and to act upon a meaning of things which is final? And if so, must one follow Kant in thinking of respect in a way that excludes the possibility of respect for things? I cannot follow such a way of thinking. It seems to me to ignore the finality of the existing. And if *denial* of the finality of the existing is pressed, this denial may well turn into an insistent refusal that bespeaks nothing but the impoverishment of experience, a severance from reality manifest as things. What is needed to substantiate affirmation of respect for things as a genuine possibility of experience? What more is needed than experience in which this possibility is clearly fulfilled as genuine, authentic? But the interpretation of such experience, that indeed is a matter for reflection.

I do not think we see how great a risk of idolatry we must constantly run. Both naturalism and idealism *seem*, in a way, to avoid that risk, because both involve the reduction of finality out of the finite. For naturalism the thing is merely an object — that is, for naturalism as a theory of the nature of things. For idealism the existence of things is denied in its ultimacy by making them tributaries of sovereign mind; their existence is construed merely as a giving of mind back to itself. If either theory were true, the upshot would seem the same: Man is left to himself, responsible ultimately only to himself, sovereign over a world of things vacuous in themselves. Neither theory seems to do justice to things as radically unknown; in neither is the dense presence of things preserved in thought. And our togetherness with things is forgotten, profoundly buried. I do not see how either type of philosophy avoids the terminal implication of egoism as a mode of ethical thought.

Of course if my thoughts on these theories are on the right track, then both would tend to what is basic in idolatry, the magnification of the self.

Now, however, I want to identify a subtler risk of idolatry which seems bound up with the mode of thought which I am trying to define.

Perhaps there is only a hair's breadth between the theme of the immanence of ultimate importance in things, which I am affirming, and a heady aberration of this theme in which all semblance of its necessary complement, the theme of transcendence, is lost. The absoluteness of the existence of the finite is then perverted into the absoluteness of something finite. And the individual who acts on this confusion of soul permits conspiracy with an essential inhumanity in himself. This again is a form of 'playing God.' Then the density of things is fostered as a preference for darkness in the soul. Then one calls on things as presences to bear witness to the finality of his insistence. And indeed, things are there; to claim their finality in behalf of one's insistence on them, to draw authority to oneself from the ultimate importance of things — these are liabilities in living out the theme of finality found in things. I was dealing with this before, I guess, when I spoke of seizing upon the power in the thrust of the wave which swiftens the swimmer on his way.

Saturday, August 22

Early in Walter Stace's *Time and Eternity*, which I have commenced to read, I run into an expression of a position which counters the theme of the immanence of finality in the existing. It may be helpful to quote a passage at length in order to clarify by contrast with it the theme in terms of which I am working.

> One thing is better than another thing. Gold is perhaps better than clay, poetry than push-pin. One place is pleasanter than another place. One time is happier than another time. In all being there is a scale of better and worse. But just because of this relativity, no being, no time, no place, satisfies the ultimate hunger. For all beings are infected by the same disease, the disease of existence. If owning a marble leaves your metaphysical and religious thirst unquenched, so will owning all the planets. If living on the earth for three-score years and ten leaves it unsatisfied, neither will living in a fabled Heaven for endless ages satisfy it. For how do you attain your end by making things bigger, or

longer, or wider, or thicker, or more this or more that? For they will still be THIS or THAT. And it is being this or that which is the disease of things.[57]

So long as there is light in your life, the light has not yet dawned. There is in your life much darkness — that much you will admit. But you think that though this thing, this place, this time, this experience is dark, yet that thing, that place, that time, that experience is, or will be, bright. But this is the great illusion. You must see that all things, all places, all times, all experiences are equally dark. You must see that all stars are black. Only out of the *total* darkness will the light dawn.

Religion is that hunger which no existence, past, present, or future, no actual existence and no possible existence, in this world or any other world, on the earth or above the clouds and stars, material or mental or spiritual, can ever satisfy. For whatever is or could be will have the curse on it of thisness or thatness.

This is no new thought. It is only what religious men have always said. To the saint Narada the Supreme Being offered whatsoever boon his heart could imagine — abundance of life, riches, health, pleasure, heroic sons. "That," said Narada "and precisely that is what I desire to be rid of and pass beyond." It is true that the things here spoken of — health, riches, even heroic sons — are what we call worldly, even material, things. But they are symbolic only. They stand for all things of any kind, whether material or non-material — for all things, at least, which could have an existence in the order of time, whether in the time before death or in the time after.

In so far as we cling to things and claim the right to mastery of them, this sense of disillusionment with them cuts with a keen edge. But it seems an appalling illusion to turn the experience of disillusionment with things *mis-taken* into occasion for indicting them. When we proclaim things at naught, do we not utter the word of a stricken soul, do we not bespeak our own incapacity to receive the ultimate gift from things, of themselves, in their infinite meaning? If we turn against the world, do we not shut ourselves off from the realization of eternal meaning in the very existence of finite things? If we think of religion as hunger which nothing existing could satisfy, do we not confuse hunger with burning desire and continue to credit those very

[margin, handwritten] hunger ≠ burning desire

[57]. Stace, W. T., *Time and Eternity*, Princeton, N. J., Princeton, 1952, p. 5. The ensuing quotations are from pages 5 and 6.

[handwritten annotation: awakening = finding meaning among/in the world that is constantly changing]

illusions which persist, with our misery, in burning desire? This undergoing of corrosion may be a genuine moment in our coming to ourselves: the moment of self-estrangement and estrangement from things from which one needs to awaken. But awakening is not satisfaction of craving. The transcendence that is awakening is the transcendence of craving and satisfaction: These are bondage in *Karma*. Awakening does not find the world empty, devoid of a significance that can stand. It is the discovery of a significance in things which stands. *Stands.* Not "stands still;" not as possessed, not as held fast. That again would be the clinging that perpetuates itself in the inconclusive round of burning desire, the emptiness of mere satisfaction, the anguish of burning which consumes us, engendered anew, turning time into the enemy that lays us waste, turning finite things into the image of the fickle, the untrustworthy. And the world is rejected as undeserving of allegiance.

In abandoning the world we are lost; we are lost again and again. We may speak poignantly of the experience of being lost while we are lost; but we cannot be clear about ourselves and our situation in so far as our thinking is dominated by that experience. Disillusionment with the world knows nothing of the sacrament of coexistence. It can find no place for the sacramental act. It can conjure out of itself no philosophy of action, for its ultimate implication is inaction.

If we fail to find finality in the world we will ultimately fail to find it necessary to do anything; and all that we have done will come to seem senseless. But if we can act on faith that is an appreciation of the finality of things, we may come to understand that neither ourselves nor any finite being should be counted at naught. We all stand only together, not only all men, but all things. To abandon things, and to abandon each other, is to be lost.

"Neti, neti!" it is said: "Not this, not this, no, not that!" There are two respects in which this seems true. First, nothing in so far as we are attached to it by craving and satisfaction. Second, nothing, in so far as we can demonstrate its nature. I recall again a saying of Norman Kemp Smith's which can be read so as to accommodate both these points: "Potentially any situation may yield an immediate awareness of the Divine; actually there is no situation whatsoever which invariably yields it."[58]

There are those philosophers who identify clarity with respect to the finite with a conception of the finite strictly excluding the relevance of any ideas to the finite which are not demonstrable as empirical truths about the character of the finite; this is the naturalistic thesis. When they try to accommodate philosophically the possibility of religious experience, they are grooved to think of such experience in unworldly terms, and they can claim the theme of disillusionment with the world so common in all religious traditions as if it bore true and conclusive testimony to the truth of naturalism, and justified the rejection of finite existence as inherently worthless. They take up a theoretically impregnable position. Nothing can be *proven* about the nature of the world contrary to the naturalistic thesis. And it is a thesis, we should note, that claims for itself complete accord with the results of science, as if these results also confirmed the thesis. What could be more comfortable intellectually than to yield over our experience of the world without remainder to what can be demontrated as true about it, and to take from the very mouths of the spokesmen for religious experience not only the denial that there is positive purchase for religious experience in the world, but even an added confirmation for the naturalistic thesis about our experience of the world? A nice clean solution — like rendering to Caesar the things that are Caesar's. The philosopher can then continue to be a good hard-headed, tough-minded character, who needn't be ashamed of himself in any intellectual company, and at the same time 'find a place for' religious experience where our experience of nature supposedly leaves off.

I cannot help saying just what I feel about this: The clarity is false clarity, the tough-mindedness and hard-headedness conceal a refusal (which no proof can dislodge) to accommodate reflectively the gift of the world in the experience of things. And the genuine religious mystery — which is none other than that of the existence

---

58. "Is Divine Existence Credible?" Annual Philosophical Lecture, Henriette Herz Trust, British Academy, 1931, *Proceedings of the British Academy*, Vol. XVII, p. 24.

of things, of ourselves and all finites — is likely to be substituted for by mystification. There may be as many truths as you please; but a philosophy that is thus twofold seems to me unlikely to be on the right track in either of its disparate moments.

I know I am unclear. But I want neither false clarity nor mystification. ⚡⚡ ((. religion = false clarity

I remember that Pierre Emmanuel closes his book of autobiographical reflection with the eating of an apple as the dawn comes on. That I can understand. It sounds right.

finality = individuality + universality

Sunday, August 23

To experience finality in things is to experience things in the vein of individuality and universality. These also are experiential ideas, and likewise tend to evanesce in so far as our effort to think them out more exactly removes us from that vein of appreciation of things which affords their concrete purchase. Concreteness is experiential, and not the specificity of the specimen or example, not the particularity of a member of a class. For the typological frame of mind universality tends to be construed merely as the extension of a concept over the members of the class it defines, and individuality as the particularity of a member instantiating the class. For the typological frame of mind things are taken as if substitutable for one another in so far as they exemplify the relevance of a concept. Existentially, nothing is substitutable for any other thing, and this is quite other than a matter of the infinite specificity of anything actual.

Even as I say this, however, it occurs to me that the attempt to be thoroughly specific in one's characterization of something *may* plunge one into quite a different mode of appreciation of it, namely, that it exists, just as it is, no matter how far short we fall of saying just what it is. But if the existence of things does not echo through one, searching out, evoking, his utmost responsiveness, as a matter to have a reckoning with from within himself, how can he hope to bring his thought into accord with finding anything ultimate? Lacking this experiential anchor, is not his philosophy adrift?

Men have sought the light of eternity, and they have often thought to look away from things. Yet is this light something apparent, or is it a light in which things appear? Are not things dense and dark as it is necessary for them to be to take this light? And what is revealed by this light, to what does it supply relevant illumination, if not to things standing forth wonderfully in it?[59]

In wonder reality begins to sink in. It sets us to a questioning which can only find conclusive answer in terms of a deepening of our response to things, which is the deepening, and not the allaying, of wonder. Last fall it seemed to me that the deepening of wonder is faith, and the deepening of faith is certainty. To this I would add that this deepening throughout is the deepening of our response to *things*. It cannot be an abandonment of them, an ignoring of them, a turning away from them, say, through the disillusionments we constantly undergo in our experience of them, in our way of taking things, in our ephemeral orientation. Those who speak of experience in which man may find conclusive meaning as if this meaning was not a completion of our experience of things and a revelation of them, seem to speak more as men who dream than as men who are awake. Awakening is not finding things illusory, but awakening from illusions into the very reality of things; it is finding finality in them.

I am trying to suggest a way of thinking contrary to modes of thought in which things are treated as devoid of finality. This is not to suggest a method of thinking as a procedure to be adopted, but to define a style of thought in the very act of it, knowing not where I am going or to what it may lead. It seems to me that I want to say we must hold with things to the extent of not invoking anything behind or beyond them of which they are the appearance. As I put it years ago in my doctoral thesis, reality makes its stand here and now

59. Things *exist* infinitely; I do not mean 'on and on interminably,' but something closer to what may be *expressed* in saying: ever and ever, forever and always, it is so. Mahler comes close to it in his way in *Das Lied von der Erde*, the closing song.

in existing things. By the density and opacity in terms of which I think and speak of them, I mean just this inescapable involvement with them from which there is no exit through which thought can make a breach and extricate us from our situation; any beyond and behind things leads to nothing at all. When this comes home as a matter of experience, vast emptiness may echo throughout every last chamber of the soul. Somehow it seems to be the ultimate condition of finality in things; this vast emptiness is not finality itself. Except as we appreciate our utter containment in reality, however, it seems that there can be no release in us of the decisive word, that meaning of things which is simplicity itself. 'Beyond,' 'behind,' are these not more properly construed as images of the obscurity in our souls? But as we learn to take things in their darkness, their utter density and darkness, as we can acknowledge them in the intimation of their finality, then we stand upon the threshold of receiving the ulimate gift of things, and obscurity within us gives way to utter light.

Monday and Tuesday, August 24 and 25

Only as things are dense and opaque do they stand forth in the light of eternity, and take the light. To take that which exists as existing, and not as a symbol for something else; to find something to which one gives full heed, and not merely to push right through it in search of a beyond, or to have from it only a message at once directing the mind away from it and on to other things; such is the experience of things as eternal, in the making. To experience things in their density is to experience containment in reality. But the agile mind and the distraught soul militate against true perception; for true perception requires stillness in the presence of things, the active, open reception of the limitless gift of things.

Moby Dick seems to me an articulate introduction into the presence of things in their finality: After all is said and done, after all attempt at final reckoning has run its course, and shipwreck places a seal on human lips, there is yet a word spoken:

> Now small fowls flew screaming over the yet yawning gulf; a sullen white surf beat against its steep sides; then all collapsed, and the great shroud of the sea rolled on as it rolled five thousand years ago.

•　•　•　•　•

Things exist in their own right; it is a lesson that escapes us except as they hold us in awe. Except we stand on the threshold of the wilderness, knowingly, how can our position be true, how can essential truth be enacted in our hearts? Here is what I miss most in the thought of Marcel — the wilderness theme.

A philosophy of the given misses the point which does not think of things as given in their independence.

Yet the truth of the independence of things should not lead us to succumb to a sense of isolation and insularity among independent existents. The independence of things is no warrant for an objectivizing mode of thought about them, for taking an abstract point of view toward them and ourselves. For concretely, experience of the presence of things is also complete intimacy with them, the opposite of estrangement from them and ourselves. The gift of things in their independence is also the gift of ourselves together with them. And here Marcel seems to me very clear and just right: In the experience of presence that estrangement between self and other, that tension between self and other, which supports the representation of the other as over against the self, that estrangement and that tension are dissolved. To be aware of the other as a presence in its independence is an experience of participation in reality with the other, and such experience concretely resists the reduction of the independence of the other to the terms of objectivity (the German term for objectivity, once again, seems most precise: *Gegenständlichkeit*: "standing-over-against-ness").

All that Marcel has to say in *Being and Having* about the attitude presupposed in attempting to characterize something, as an attempt to reduce what we characterize to the status of a mental possession — along with his analysis of the tension and estrangement inherent in exerting claim to possession — is extremely pertinent to seeing through the confusion of thinking the independently existing other in terms of objectivity. If you follow through with Marcel's thought on the matter, it seems to me that you come smack upon the root of that wholesale rejection of the world of things inherent in seeing in them blind indifference to man, in taking things as objects which remain obstacles to be overcome in so far as man has yet failed to exert mastery over them. So long as our approach to the other is an attempt to make good a position of mastery over it, and even in characterizing the other to render it tributary to us as a mental possession, our very conception of its otherness, its independent status, will tend to reflect the tension and estrangement of such an untenable position. Otherness, then, will seem inherently *contrariety*. And being realistic will be vaunted as an emphasis on the hardness, the coldness, the blindness, the indifference, the resistance, the opposition to ourselves supposedly ingrained in the very nature of things. We might say that for the possessive mind the other is merely an object; and that the characterization of the other taken as object amounts to a taking possession of it in effigy, as Marcel puts it. But here as in all possessiveness a certain dialectic obtains. It is a commonplace that the possession exerts a subtle hold over the would-be possessor, and that this hold becomes tighter the more he endeavours to make his grip on the possession secure. The possessor becomes estranged both from himself and from the other. In so far as our endeavour to know things is an attempt to make secure a hold over them as mental possessions, it is not surprising that we should come to regard their otherness as over-againstness, even to the point of their seeming inherently inimical to man. In the face of things so construed we have placed ourselves over against them, and we are apt to define for man a Promethean role, as Russell does in *A Free Man's Worship*. From this position we are at a loss to understand that ours is a holy place, a universe of things, a wilderness.

That ours is a holy place has ever seemed to me true when I have been most awake, and I take it as a mark of awakening whenever it dawns upon me again as true. But much of the time I cannot remember that it is true, and I cannot understand what such a saying might mean, if it were to occur to me to dwell on it at all. Amidst the noise of my thoughts things appear as an innocuous congeries of items, noted, and so what?

Thursday, August 27

Yesterday it occurred to me to speak of the ideas in terms of which I have been thinking in the image of a reflective harvesting of experience, a binding into sheaves of 'non-properties of things.' As this last phrase suddenly came to mind and I fell to savoring it, I became aware that it smacks of E. E. Cummings, though I doubt very much if I have it from him ready-made. Is such phrasing only a striking and perverse mannerism, or does it suggest a genuine style of thought?

Can I say that empirical thinking is thinking in terms of properties (characteristics) of things, while experiential thinking, in its relevance to things, is a thinking in terms of non-properties of them? This *could* be sheer double-talk. Yet such ideas as existence (independence), finality, individuality, and universality cannot be made out as relevant to properties, characteristics, of things; I want to say this, yet I also want to say that they are relevant to things. They are sustained in experience of things, in which attentiveness to things themselves is indispensable. It is essential to the non-arbitrariness of these ideas, as it seem to me, that we conceive things as supporting them. Yet I also notice that I have been inclined to think of things *in terms of* these ideas, to employ these ideas as primitive on the supposition that their elucidation cannot be a definition of them in terms of more ultimate ideas. In this respect they conform to the Aristotelian conception of metaphysical ideas. But my aim is not to argue back to them abstractly, to enforce dialectically that one must think in terms of them, or that they must be presupposed as primitive in any attempt to define them. For the point of which I am persuaded is that these ideas, so handled, tend to become emptied of concrete meaning, and we exchange thinking in terms of them for thinking in terms that become verbal traces, in which we become trapped into supposing that as we employ the terms at will, so we must be in constant possession of 'their meaning.' But the experiential meaning rendering these ideas concrete and their relevance clear not only does not lend itself to possession; it is actually expunged if in our thinking we attempt to make secure a certain hold over reality and seek to enforce our title to having attained such a hold. Metaphysical thought, I agree with Marcel, is in essence meta-problematic and meta-technical. And this accords perfectly with the failure of the most strictly problematic and technical thinkers to find any genuine and distinctive metaphysical problems along with any peculiar and practicable technique for their solution. Of course it does not accord with the conclusion to which they incline that metaphysical thought is spurious. But it suggests that the conclusion is inevitable from the premises implicit in their mode of thought.

Perhaps it is important to acknowledge that in philosophical thinking, as I am trying to work it out, one keeps getting into problems, and one's thinking trails off repeatedly into moments of speculation. But the consummation of philosophical thinking with respect to such problems is not in 'their solution' but in their dissolution (as a blood clot might be dissolved, permitting renewed circulation). And the restoration of philosophical thought from its moments of arduous and necessary speculation is consummated in contemplation.

It seems to me most unfortunate in Kierkegaard's *Postscript* that he *identifies* contemplation with speculation, and utterly misses the contemplative act as the essence of philosophic responsiveness, of the assumption of responsibility to reality in its plenitude. What bearing has this on his tendency to lump aesthetic experience indiscriminately under a conception of man in his moments of gravest irresponsibility? At the very least, Kierkegaard seems to confuse 'the aesthetic' with its perversion. But a far more serious deficiency which seems linked with his failure to distinguish the act of contemplation from speculation is his failure to find finality, i.e. ground for faith, and the evocation of necessary action, in our very experience of things.

In our experience of things as presences, reality conveys itself and permeates us as a closed electrical circuit in which we are involved with things; the circuit is charged with finality. But in so far as we take things, and think of them, as placed over against us, i.e. objectively, we break the circuit. It is inevitable then that we can find no purchase in things for the thought of finality in them, and fall back upon some conception of intrinsic value as a property of ourselves, or as we are apt to say (objectifying 'experience'), as a property of our experience.

I want neither objectivism nor subjectivisim (which, if I am right, also presupposes an objectivizing mode of thought), but realism, such as Thoreau suggests when he says:

> If you stand right fronting and face to face to a fact, you will see the sun glimmer on both its surfaces, as if it were a cimeter, and feel its sweet edge dividing you through the heart and marrow, and so you will happily conclude your mortal career. Be it life or death, we crave only reality. If we are really dying, let us hear the rattle in our throats and feel cold in the extremities; if we are alive, let us go about our business. [60]

Friday, August 28

The phenomenological image of the closed circuit is misleading if it tempts us to assign priority to a dead circuit, to be characterized from a standpoint outside of the energized circuit. The closed circuit is meant as ultimate. Objectivization in our thinking about the self and the other abstracts from reality as the closed circuit of our participation with 'the other,' and thinks of self and other as poles of a dead circuit, to which the closing of the circuit (whatever that may then mean) can only be something 'which *happens*.' The subject-object distinction converts the genuine mutual independence of self and other *in the closed circuit* into the separateness of dead poles.

---

[60]. *Walden*, New York, Random House, 1937, p. 88.

Self and other both become merely objects for thought, and experience is regarded as something that happens to a subject conditioned in its relation to other objects. To think experientially is to partake in thought of the closed circuit of reality, in which we live and move and have our being. Out of such thinking it can become clear that characterization always involves a measure of abstraction from reality. I do not think, however, that this suggests condemnation out of hand of all endeavours to characterize; we assume a false position, it would seem, only in so far as we presume to reduce reality to something we have pocketed in characterizing things. Not science, but scientism as the arrogation to science of philosophical ultimacy, is the anti-philosophy so troublingly insinuated into present-day thought. Unfortunately that true sense of the mystery of things which may, in fact, deepen in the course of scientific investigation, and which seems at the root of genuine humility in the investigator, finds no articulate place in the articulated results of scientific investigation. Nor is scientific thought a schooling in reflection on things in their mystery. The unfortunate feature of this is that a philosophical interpretation of the experience of the activity of scientific investigation is seldom offered; and philosophers of science are for the most part preoccupied with the method and results of science. Thus the wonder, respect, and love for things investigated, which may be at the heart of scientific experience, virtually escape reflective interpretation and testimony.

One surmises the meaning of the experience of scientific activity from a man like Albert Einstein; he has drawn near to reflective expression of it at times. I can remember hearing Robert Oppenheimer on an occasion, when he was casting about for a way of communicating the 'beauty' he found in the things he had investigated. Those with whom he was talking wanted to go on talking about the quantum theory; how little they reckoned with the look in the man's eye as the meaning of his life's work suddenly overtook him anew, and he stammered with gratitude for the magnitude of the gift, in the appalling newness of essential truth. How shall a man find a word to say it?

Saturday, August 29

" 'Mysteries are not truths that lie beyond us; they are truths that comprehend us.' (R. P. Jouve.)"[61] Such are the truths of our experiential participation with things. They become ideate when we think in terms such as those of faith, of hope, and love, not in so far as we merely employ these terms and cogitate upon their meaning, but in so far as our thinking is born of experience in the vein of faith and hope and love. Such thinking may be comparatively rare, yet, remembering that saying of Spinoza's at the close of the *Ethics* — "But all things excellent are as difficult as they are rare" — it might be well to consider that it transcends the correlatives: easy-difficult. Such thinking is not strictly speaking difficult, even though comparatively rare, and even though much genuinely arduous and difficult thinking may lie in store for us along the way. That which illuminates our labors, in reflection as in other channels of endeavour, that which decisively empowers us in the deed, comes as an unanticipated precipitation of meaning. Thinking dedicated to essential truth seems consummated only as it is *graced*. It therefore transcends categories pertinent to an effort we make. And though many ideas may probe facets for the ideation of truth that comprehends us, must they not harmonize, and if they are to harmonize, is this not by virtue of a oneness of essential truth: the oneness of simplicity?

What but simplicity renders us whole and heals us of our anguish, our anxiety, our grief and our perplexity? Yet when we come upon simplicity in men, would it not be foreign to think of it as something toward which they have bent their efforts, as something in the nature of a difficult accomplishment with which we must credit them? Is it not more accurate to think of simplicity as 'something' which comes to us, with which we are infused, as a precise mode of being contained and sustained in reality? Can we even say that simplicity makes us true (true in thought, in deed, in perception), and defines our position as true?

I can recall men on occasions when they were clearly men of

61. Quoted by Marcel, Gabriel, *Being and Having*, Boston, Beacon, 1951, p. 141.

utter simplicity. First, I mark that this was not ingenuousness about them. Nor simple-mindedness. It involved most wide-awakeness. They were men alert, sensitive, poised in themselves, yet utterly receptive (as distinct from suggestible). They were independent, yet set up no barrier around themselves. Also, they were not trying to prove any-thing, in the colloquial sense. They seemed to be taking an even strain, yet patiently, on the burden of the world's work. They did not seem to be laying claim to the enabling power that was in them, nor effacing themselves, either, before the world.

[margin note: ex of simple men]

Without extending such observations as these, I want to raise the question: What was simplicity in them? It had to do with the manner of men they were, but I do not think it could be rightly re-garded as a property of theirs. We speak of a simple person, as if simplicity might be a property of that person, as this shape is a prop-erty of my table. Yet I want to suggest that simplicity is derivatively thought of in attributing it to persons, and by virtue of a more primi-tive meaning of simplicity which in their action, their demeanor, they express. It appears in a man as something with which he is informed and infused, enlightened — rendering him implicitly trusting (not gullible or undiscriminating). Here is the idea: Simplicity in men presupposes a basic, concrete appreciation of reality in its ultimate meaning; simplicity in men is the incarnation of that meaning.

Or, might we put it this way?: Simplicity is that concretely ap-preciated meaning of reality which purifies men. They become simple by virtue of 'it.'

Again it seems to me that the sense of this thought can be located in the writings of Faulkner, and for me it seems paramount in *Light in August* and in the short stories *Red Leaves, Hair, The Tall Men,* and *Mountain Victory.* But a certain experience also comes vividly to mind right now.

It was in the summertime, at a summer resort, along the North Fork of the Trinity River in California, on a day like so many summer days of bright sun streaming down through the tops of the pines. Most of the length and breadth of that long, smooth, flowing pool lay translucently exposed to the bouldered bottom. Children played on the sandy shores, or splashed along the fringes of the pool. The air was of ambient fragrance of pines, reassuring warmth and stillness, refreshing coolness of moving water, and frank with the murmur of conversation punctuated by shouts of farthest remove from alarm. The roar of rapids below the pool might have been but a ground-bass of contentment, filling us all.

There came a cry for help, seconded with a cry of fright, and I turned toward the tail of the pool just in time to see a young man desperately, failingly, clinging to a great log which had been chained as a boom across the lower end (to raise the water level in the pool). No one could reach him in time. An enormous suction under the log had firm hold of the greater part of his body and drew him ineluctably under. He bobbed to the surface in the first great wave of the rapid below, but there was no swimming or gaining bottom to stay what seemed an impending execution on the rocks at the bend in this mill-race, some hundred yards on down. But it chanced that the river was abnormally high, and as it carried this helpless man doomward it swept him just for an instant under the extremity of a willow which arched far out from the bank and erratically trailed its branch-tips on the heaving waters. With a wild clutch the young man seized a gathering of the supple branches and held. Everything held, that grim grip and that rooted willow, while the rush of the river brought him in an arc downstream and to the bank. He had barely the strength and the breath to claw himself up the muddy slope onto firmament.

I had run across the log and arrived on the opposite side below the willow, where he now paused, panting and on all fours, unable to rise. Slowly he raised his head and we looked into each other's eyes. I lifted out both hands and helped him to his feet. Not a word passed between us. As nearly as I can relive the matter, the compassion I felt with this man gave way into awe and respect for what I witnessed in him. He seemed absolutely clean. In that steady gaze of his I met reality point blank, filtered and distilled as the purity of a man.

I think of Meister Eckhart's "becoming as we were before we were born." I think of what Conrad says of the storms visited on sailors far at sea as chastening them. I think, too, of Camus' remark at the close of *The Stranger* about a woman in her last moments of life before death: "No one, no one in the world had any right to weep for her."

Some ten or fifteen minutes later, as we lay on the warm sand having a smoke beside the pool, I noticed that this young man had commenced to tremble, and I trembled with him. We had returned to our ordinary estate, and I cannot recall anything unusual about him or the subsequent conversations we had.

Sunday, August 30

Three lines of reflection cognate with that of the last few days now begin to open up. Yesterday I touched on simplicity as a basic meaning of reality which abides as the mode of oneness of essential truth, imparting that unity of harmonization to various ideas which may serve as facets for its ideation. Cognate with this is a line of thought which may take up with the ancient doctrine of the unity of virtues in men. My notion would be of this sort: that the simplicity which underlies and unifies ideation of essential truth also underlies and harmonizes human character; it is constitutive for integrity in man. Simplicity is a bed-rock concrete meaning of reality on which men may take a firm stand in thought and deed, and as it permeates them in their thinking and doing it harmonizes the diverse moments of their thinking and doing. Thus we might say that simplicity is the key to integrity in thought and deed; not as a key which we may employ to unlock doors in thought and deed; rather as a key which unlocks doors in us, integrating us in thought and deed. It is more acted *upon* than with; and if the notion of an instrument comes to mind, then it seems closer to the mark to say that we are the instruments with which it can be active in us, than to say that it is an instrument with which we can act. But I would not press this image of instrumentality; it tempts to a picture-thinking which usually lands us in the reification of an agent employing us as instruments with intent.

When I speak of a bed-rock meaning acted upon, and speak of it as concrete, I do not mean to suggest 'a reason' explicit in thought and as thought, but rather the contrary. As Meister Eckhart puts it, it is not necessary to have come to a reflective appreciation of poverty of spirit to act with poverty of spirit; though meditation may be a restoration of us to it. And as Thoreau says: "How shall a man know if he is chaste? He shall not know it." But earlier in this same section of *Walden* (entitled "Higher Laws") he also says: "Chastity is the flowering of man . . . Man flows at once to God when the channel of purity is open." At any rate, here is the point which I am concerned to put: That concrete meaning on which necessary action is possible lives articulately in the necessary act; necessary action should not be conceived as hinged to an act of thought wherein the necessity of an action is 'explained,' even though acts of thought may be involved in any necessary action, and *even* though the giving of reasons may be a moment in the act of thought which is involved in some necessary actions.

A second line of thought pending today conjoins the interpretation of responsibility with the idea I tried to shape in the image of reality as a closed circuit. Our thinking actively partakes of reality as a closed circuit in which we participate with things in so far as we are actually imbued with unconditional concern. Such thinking is in rapport with our experience of finality in things. As we approximate philosophic contemplation we become continuous in our thinking with that mode of experience of things to which I allude as aesthetic contemplation, or true perception. There is an essential truth about both phases of contemplation, common to both, as that which sets us free. And it has seemed to me, again and again, that as reflection approximates contemplation (i.e. philosophic), one tends to relive and complete the reception of the gift of things past, initially received in experience approximating true perception. I have also noticed that the passage from philosophic to aesthetic contemplation (to the immediate reception of the gift of things as presences, in their finality) is without a break.

There seems to be a kind of two-way experiential confirmation of reflection in the vein of essential truth, then: One is in the gift of involuntary recall, wherein one reflectively taps the vein of the experience of things in their finality, and one is restored anew to the closed circuit of reality obtaining with respect to things past; things past are redeemed in their finality. The other mode of experiential confirmation for reflection, by which its contemplative phase may be marked, is our restoration and renewal in the capacity to receive the gift of things present in their finality. We draw near essential truth reflectively in so far as reflection evolves into a contemplative moment from which one moves to contemplation of things present, and is able to find in them that finality upon which one may respond in necessary action. To come at the meaning of responsibility in this way may help us tie in the ideas of finality and of necessity concretely: We respond upon finality found in things in acting necessarily. Therefore the meaning of necessary action, and of the assumption of responsibility, would seem a closed book to us except as our reflection enters that phase of contemplation in which we receive the eternal gift of things past and things present — confirmed alike in the remembrance of things past and in the welcoming of things present in which we are renewed.

I have anticipated somewhat the third line of thought to which I was disposed at the outset today: having to do with a *philosophic* conception of givenness. This is a matter which concerned me very keenly in the spring of 1950, when I was trying to find out the basis of my misgivings about Mr. Lewis' interpretation of givenness. As I remember, I ended up with a conclusion that sounded right, but one which has taken years to become clearer. This is the conclusion: Only reality is given. I was left with the bare conclusion. Let me amplify it now.

Only reality is given. But its givenness is consummated in the reception of things as presences — as we find finality in them. There is certainty in experience in which reality is given; but this does not seem to be a certainty of knowledge about anything we represent to ourselves and describe. The closed circuit of our involvement in reality cannot rightly be abstracted from in working out the thought of givenness. Certainty pertains to the possibility of understanding reality as participants in it, and not to knowledge in which we abstract from concrete participation. Givenness is a philosophic theme correlative with an understanding of reality as prior to and comprehensive of reality-as-known. It drives us back behind the point at which we fall into a subject-object distinction, and behind the point, if you will, at which we institute a distinction between fact and value.

Thus, to use Mr. Lewis' terms, I would say that there is no givenness that is not value experience and experience of fact as well. Givenness is decisive experience of reality, enabling decisiveness in our thinking and in such action as is really decisive. We may have to consider givenness in connection with decisiveness in scientific thought, but I suspect that we misconstrue it in this connection when we try to construe it as the deliverance of nuggets of information of which our experience is an absolute possession. To experience reality as given is to be at farthest remove from claiming certain possession of any truth; for the certainty of understanding is contrary to such a claim. As we come to understand reality, it becomes clear that reality transcends what could be known about it, since, as Mr. Lewis points out, all knowing makes abstraction from the given. Of course he thinks of the given as 'experience,' or 'content of experience.' But if we make *receptiveness* explicit in our reflection of givenness, then it may seem more reasonable to think of experience as the reception (and I stress the active character of receptiveness), not of experience, surely, . . . then of what? To attempt to classify the given would not seem appropriate. But we do not classify the given when we say that only reality is given. I would be content to speak of things as given, but given only in the experience of them as presences, in their finality. They are, then, reality manifest. But you cannot capture reality manifest in your description of those things.

Monday, August 31

Of reality given and eternal: certain night watches at sea.
One needs to be steeped in the round of watches to the point of

believing in it as interminable — an endless on-going of the rhythmical tending of the ship, of want and use, of work and rest, in the cycle of the ship's routine at sea. To be sure, there are ports, and one may make for a port; one may think of a day when a port may receive him back to land for good. But one needs to have reached the point where the round of watches has distanced him from ports, and one's sinews and bones no longer believe in land. One must become undeceived of elsewhere and another time to come, except as they perpetuate the expanse of the sea for the man on watch and the round of his coming and going, and tending and resting, the taking of meals and the weathering all in due time — the life of the ship underway.

With containment in the situation the gift may come — the gift, I dare say, binding men so namelessly to the life at sea, infusing that round of watches with sustaining office in which it becomes the breath of life to partake, and imparting the mystery of necessity to the work needing to be done. It is this gift at sea, I believe, that makes a man a sailor and a shipmate, absorbing the shock of his aberrations, tolerating the slowness of countless hours, firming him through discomfort and fear, healing the breaches arising ever and again between himself and the other men. There is that which underwrites endless hours of patient labor with a faithfulness and a hopefulness and a willingness which can fix on no aspect of the task at hand or of what can be expected to ensue in consequence; yet hours come in which the pledge kept in seemingly senseless labors is made good.

The especial times on which I think now were always times of utter containment in the fastness of the night at sea, in which a certain intimacy would begin to enfold us, and now one or another of us would begin to speak quietly of things far off. The springs of reminiscence flowing upon us, we would find ourselves suddenly living again the long-forgotten, urged to articulate the very quality of what was there and then in relation to our here and now. And we speak of things side by side in the dark of which we are encouraged to speak by the darkness itself, with our eyes roving the sea, or now and again fixed upon stars above, stars in the water, or the phosphorescence of a wave rushing past. We are encouraged by the feel of the sea in the motion of the ship, carrying directly into our limbs in the dark, bathing us with the mutual trust of true communication. Are we not together here, eager to comprehend? Ah the eagerness to comprehend, to sift and cull the meaning of things past, to find ourselves again in the significance that suggests and summons the remote, some far-off place and time toward which we yearn and dream; there, surely, reality dwelt and a man *lived,* or someday will live again. But the treasure of the remote, of the recalled in tenderness, of the place and the time for which it seems that we long, and all that comes to us now from elsewhere and other times — all this that pervades us with a sense of plenitude and an absolute meaning — where does this treasure lie? Is it not the very meaning of being at sea, here and now? And is not all the yearning and dreaming which seems to place this treasure in the remote, spurred by the mystery of the present moment, which comprehends us, now? Restored to ourselves and in communion with one another, we greet in each remembrance the image of the meaning of this present moment, receiving from it the power of articulateness through which we open out to receive what comprehends us. The remote, then, is the image of infinite meaning received and acknowledged, now.

Which one of us who once stood on deck in those far-off watches at sea, reliving them now, perchance, lacks occasion for correcting the impression which we seemed to voice then: that the time in which we really lived belonged to a remote past, or must be deferred until it might revive in some distant future, discontinous with the life we led there and then? What better hours have we known than those there and then, in which we were flooded with memories in which the essential meaning of things past revived and established us in the present moment, opening us to our present situation, to one another, and to a plenitude of significance transcending the capacity of an endless future to exhaust? Even as we spoke of flowering orchards in Santa Clara Valley, did we not *see* the stars and *hear* the wind and *feel* the sea, partaking in a limitless being which charged our very words with a silence out of which they were spoken and into which we returned from speech? And was the meaning of the past regiven, of the inexhaustible future in which we might pledge ourselves without stint, was this other than the meaning of that present, of our communion in silence, and with the sea? What did we learn in such night watches if not this: that nowhere and no other time might contribute more than more of what was there and then, deepened in ourselves, permeating all things?

Let us remember that in such watches we came to affirm our situation with our very selves, and that our actions testified to the affirmation, when we went about our work with a will, restored and renewed in the harmony of our actual situation.

Yet we never knew what the next watch would be like. All that one cannot know comprehends him and silently trails him up the ladders into the standing of his watch.

Wednesday and Thursday, September 2 and 3

I've been thinking of the ship's companies whom I have known. A motley of backgrounds and personalities went into each crew, a job-lot of men into each ship. These hitherto divergent life streams converging at random, to pour into the ship's life. None of us exercised much choice in landing aboard a particular ship. And the life aboard ship itself had little to do with choice either in the company one kept or in the things one did. Furthermore we always sailed under orders merely handed down and subject to alteration without warning; the ship and all hands were snatched this way and that, and we could seldom see that our moves brought to culmination a purpose justifying the errands on which the ship was sent. Supervening upon these vagaries and the nebulous horizons into which our perspective ever trailed off was the senselessness of war itself. Bearing all this in mind it becomes interesting to reflect on how such a situation could make sense.

I would say that I have this situation to thank for being undeceived with respect to the fundamentality of choice. Relative to an atitude of choice our situation was as contingent as you please. Why were any of us where we were rather than somewhere else? Perhaps if the yeoman in some Personnel Office had not been a bit hung over on a certain morning, he would have stretched a bit farther to pick up another folder on men available for assignment, and one would not be just where he finds himself now. And if our communications officer had not spoken some bitter words to the officer in charge of communications back at the base, perhaps we wouldn't be off on this thousand-mile jaunt, escorting a couple of old scows to some God-forsaken dot of land in mid-ocean.

We sail out of a staging-harbor with other ships of our class, heading for an invasion. Suddenly a sister ship breaks down; she needs an engine part no one can supply, which it will take days to obtain. She is out of the invasion, but we sail on. A year later we meet up with her again, and this time we stand out to sea with her in a typhoon. The last we see of her, she is fading into a flying shroud of spray. Not hide nor hair nor plank of her is seen again.

• • • • •

How will you make out the sense of such a situation in terms of something chosen and accomplished? How can you read sense in it in terms of something you foresaw, elected, and controlled into consequence? What ideals would you say you were trying to actualize? What were you trying to make your actions conduce to, that you would say imparted to the course of affairs the drift of sense? By what ends and goals did you shape your life? As you steered the ship, as you overhauled the engines, as you plotted a position on the chart, as you cooked underway, as you cleaned the guns, as you brought the service records up to date, as you passed the coffee, as you signalled another ship, as you ducked the green water combing the bridge, as you scrubbed down the decks, as you directed the ping of the underwater sound search, as you lounged on deck in the twilight off watch, as you wrote letters home or washed your clothes, or fired on an oncoming plane: What had you in mind? What was it you chose? And what did you think to accomplish? By what ideals did you orient your endeavour? Were you striving, perchance, for the greatest hap-

[margin handwritten note:] Life = similar to this ship (metaphor)

~piness of the greatest number, is that what gave direction to what you did, and salvaged you from fate? By what ultimate attainment might you have taken the measure of what you did?

"What questions! Have a cup of coffee, mate."

Friday, September 4

Call it routine: the constancy of the definite task at hand, the never-ending round of variously permuted work, the rhythm of ship's life enunciated in the engines' pulse, the banging of hatches and doors, the shouts on deck, the steady exhalation of blowers, the clamor of pots and dishes in the galley, the shifting, shifting, spasmodic and incessant stirring of the steering gear, the endless dialogue of voices emitting from the radio shack, the querying ping of the sound search inanely reproducing for the ear the unanswering underwater world, the gliding, slithering, rolling, and slamming of the ship in her seaway. Call it inculcation. A monotonal, polyphonic inculcation in here-and-nowness, in on-goingness, in what is so, forever and ever. You do not comprehend it; you cannot comprehend it. But in the long ship's passage at sea you may understand it through acting upon it with a constancy through which it becomes defined beneath the variables of your task and of yourself. You do not choose to be absorbed into the life of the ship at sea, you do not choose your tasks; you become steeped in them, perhaps even in spite of yourself. And the round of definite tasks becomes something from which you can hardly withhold yourself; staying with them you discover staying power. And as you learn to work affirmatively, becoming more or less effectual in your tasks, you are not working on a clear choice of means to some ultimate desideratum which explains to you the significance of what you do. Rather, your routine becomes transfigured into the ritual of a true life at sea. An utterly silent blessing of finality teaches you the necessity of the task in hand, dwelling at the very heart of ordinary work. What need have you, then, for anything in mind but the task at hand? But what a benefactress is the sea in the exigencies she engenders, time and again stealing your attention back to the task in spite of yourself, cleansing you unawares as you are trapped into concentration on holding a course in a heavy sea-way, straining your eyes in her mists, managing your balance as you go for stores in some cramped hold, as you fight against a wave of nausea in the engine-room stench. Who would choose such things? You need not listen in long aboard a ship underway to have the answer, loud and clear. Nothing delights a sailor more than improvisation on the theme of his miserable fate. Probably nothing could fall more afoul of his innermost ear than to have someone solicit his assent to the life at sea as a matter of choice. What bilge. But it is not easy to fathom the offense. Can we say that the offense is against that sense of reality on which the man acts — so inarticulate in him apart from the living deed, that he spurns the risk of sentimentalizing his faith, and takes his stand against the propositions of choice with defiant emphasis on the features of his life that give the lie to the image of choiceworthiness? No man wants to bespeak or to tolerate the bespeaking of his life in a way that cheapens it.

Saturday, September 5

Through unmediated instruction the sea and the ship's work carried us beyond that abstractness of viewpoint, that partiality of participation, that tenacious tendency to suppose a case, that deference to ourselves in the optative mood, that day-dreaming and speculative departure from reality, which engender the impression of contingency and inconclusiveness in our situation. The sea and the ship's work established us, founded us in taking the case that is. And concrete reality dwelt in the sinew of decisive action. Not that this was always so. Not that we did not all falter more or less; not that we did not reject and withhold, again and again; not that we did not dream and speculate, and set our minds athwart the current of ship's life; not that we did not also nurse ourselves along and petulantly draw the line against the unceasing demands that arose. But the sea and the work waited us out. Ineluctably, their instruction told.

It might take years of such instruction, but sooner or later one could feel the sea and the work defining a position that was true; and they took the measure of his aberration, with unhurried thoroughness. In fact it was a lesson in thoroughness, in close attention to detail, in acting on a concrete sense of reality pervading attention to exact detail. If you let things go with less than precision, you learned that your position was untenable. You could not fathom this; you fought against it; it was all a bitter and senseless infraction on your private rights, you might think; you would do no more than someone else might require, to avoid a still more uncomfortable lot. But the sea attends you unremittingly, outlasting your reservations and protestations, until, perhaps in your hundredth, or in your thousandth watch, it has taught you that enduring is truer than withholding. You have learned that you cannot but endure. But from withholding to enduring may be only from bitterness to inanity, and the sea continues its questioning, ever just as before, and so long as you merely endure, going through the motions, as it were, you fail to fit, and give no satisfactory answer to its questioning. But there are traps awaiting you, to spring on you awakening.

Perhaps you are dead, dead tired, dead asleep in your bunk. A hand shakes you and a voice calls you once again to go on watch. The ship is reeling through the night. Wrenched from oblivion, you sit upright, clutching the chain by which your bunk is hung, staring into darkness, swallowed up in the crazed enormity you have been summoned to endure. Sick, sickened and dreadfully alone, you stagger onto the main deck, into the openness, into a darkness, a madness of waves from which one water-laden gust has drenched you before you have even secured the door. If you endure your way to the bridge, you'll never make it; a smash against the bulkhead jolts you out of endurance into fighting your way along. By rushes and hand-holds you reach the pilot house. How is it the ship isn't pounded to pieces? You turn toward the man at the wheel and the ship tilts upward, hanging in air. She pitches forward, throwing you ahead; you grab the man before you and hold on against the shuddering shock at the bottom of the fall. "Don't grab me, take the wheel," he yells. "Course is two-three-five. Steering engine is out; it's on manual." "Two three five," the words come thickly from your tongue. Manual. With the first attempt to move the wheel you have the full weight of the ship's departure from course, backed by the thrust of wind and sea, translated from the rudders to your arms and shoulders and back. You begin desperately, you fight back. But gradually you are drawn into it in the only way it can be done, working with the wind and the waves and the ship. The trap has sprung, and you have no idea.

Your first half-hour at the wheel, it seems, has passed. A look-out has come down to relieve you. You couldn't have said whether it was a half-hour or half the night that had just passed. "Steady on two-three-five," you say, "it's on manual, you know." You climb to the flying bridge, somehow tolerating the night, but feeling the tiredness throughout your frame. Then somehow, in a dash, a figure is beside you and shoving a mug of coffee into your hand. It is scalding hot. It burns your lips and the end of your nose, and it burns your gullet as it goes down. In your stomach it settles to warmth. Maybe the next time you go to steer that watch, you go to steer. Not to fight, nor to endure, but to hold a course in a difficult sea.

In tending the ship an answer awakens in you to the endless questioning of the sea; but not otherwise, it seems. And adequation is never done; the ship's work can make that patently clear.

Sunday, September 6

As I think back to my shipmates, reaching back to them in memory, I find that they elude me, that I cannot really call them to mind, except as I identify them in moments of their earnestness when they were conclusively defined in action. I can remember them when they were in earnest, and until I can remember them so, they do not come back alive to me. And every man I can so remember I realize that I have cared for and respected, and care for and respect all over again. And I see through the unevenness that would inevitably obtain between one's liking for one man and another. Each man had his defining moments — some rarely and some frequently, a few almost constantly. Now they would come singly for this man or that, and occasionally there were moments in which every last man of the ship stood forth revealed, three-dimensionally clear in the flash of a ship-embracing event.

Though I had sailed in other ships for nearly two years before I came to her, my clearest and most complete memory is of YMS 319 and her men, with whom I lived for over a year. It had been her good fortune, in a sense not too perverse, to be assigned to the forward area in the Pacific not very long after her commissioning and shake-down. I cannot but see in that an element of good fortune on the evidence which struck me even as I swung over her side for the first time, as she lay at anchor in the harbor of Manus Island. She had just completed participation in her second invasion and had come through a typhoon. Here she lay, not so far short of half-way round the world from home, and facing no respite from sheer work and risk for an indefinitely protracted period to come. The ships I had sailed in before were seldom away from a liberty-port for more than a week at a time, and had been based on no more austere place than the Hawaiian Islands. But here were thirty-five men who had participated in proving that a 137′ minesweeper and patrol-craft might operate like the larger units of the fleet, provisioning and fueling at sea for weeks of operation on end, with only occasional recourse to casual harbors for staging and repairs. Those men had come to live with a sense of mortal danger sure to come, already well confirmed. They had little to look forward to. Even the mail might be a month or more delayed, and sometimes had surely been lost. They had played a game or two of baseball in the past six months, had drunk a few beers, taken a few swims, and seen a movie or two, but "recreation" was mostly of the improvised hour off watch while underway, or the luxury of eight hours' sleep while riding the hook in an occasional safe harbor. And you could pick up the disc-jockeys of the Jungle Network and the Voice of Freedom, or Tokyo Rose — out of the very air that brought suicide planes.

I came aboard the 319 with trepidation, to join the lives of utter strangers, a man untried by the circumstances they had known. Within my first hour aboard I savored something for which I was unprepared, something I could not really understand until I had drawn of the life of that ship. There was a prevailing cheerfulness and buoyancy about the ship, so marked and strange to me, I must admit, that I almost questioned its authenticity. In one or two of the officers, it is true, I sensed a shade of self-consciousness about it; were they trumping it up? No; I think they were trying to find refuge in the genuine quality that dwelt as a bond in that ship, a refuge from the nervousness to which we are liable when we must call the moves, prepared or not to do so. There had been a shattering explosion in another ship close aboard the 319 a couple of days before. A sister ship alongside had suffered casualties, had been reduced to a shambles as well. A reminder of past scenes, an adumbration of what scenes to come?

During my first hours aboard I discovered a man or two who conveyed exception from the pervasive liveliness; at that time Eddie Jones, the Stewards Mate, was sullen enough, and Soldahl, Seaman 1/c, exuded reticence, a heaviness that hung like an atmospheric nimbus around him; it took quite a while before I came to know Soldahl, discovered the quick in him. But these and possibly two or three others were the exceptions, and I could even sense the prevailing atmosphere the more clearly as it resisted contamination here and there. I have said it was one of buoyancy and cheerfulness, but these terms are not sufficient in themselves. It would be still nearer the truth to say that the 319 was a ship of innocence and hope. I noticed refinement in the tone of speech and comportment here, beneath the stereotypes of the vernacular. I saw that this crew was not going through an act or marking time in the far-Pacific. And I noticed that on the whole the men were good friends. I came to perceive them, sometimes one by one, and sometimes all together.

All together for the first time as we got the ship underway and spent a day in anti-aircraft practice. It was evident that they knew what they were doing. All together in that hour at the close of Christmas Day, of which I will say no more. Then there were times when one man would gather us all, as it were, into an epitome of expression. Such was the time when Chief Boatswain's Mate Johnson met a certain plane on our way to Lingayen Gulf.

Chief Johnson's battle station was in charge of damage control, placing him amidships by the damage control locker on the starboard side. He had long plead for a gun of his own with which he could occupy himself before any damage might occur. During twenty years in the Navy he had never served as a gunner, and some of the crew averred that he would not be able to hit a seagull perched on the tip of his gun. But at last an extra 50-calibre machine gun had been surreptitiously acquired, and here it was installed for him by the rail at his station. We were at General Quarters steaming in a large formation off Mindoro, awaiting the arrival of a group of suicide planes from the direction of Manila. How quiet it was.

Eight planes appeared in our bright and cloudless sky. As they headed for various ships of our group, the rending cannonade began. The danger of ships firing into one another increased as the planes came down. Out of a canopy of chaos a plane swept into range in a long, steep glide, heading for a ship forward of our beam on the starboard side. We opened up. The disciplined gunners on the Twenties and Twin-Fifties pounded away in bursts, and the Three Inch was blasting fast. Then I saw the Chief: his small figure tense between the handles of his gun; his blond beard flowing down over the life jacket around his chest; his fingers frozen upon the trigger, the continuous stream of tracers flying from his gun; his whole frame shaking to the shattering recoil; the searing concentration with which he followed the plane.

Though it was his firing the whole drum without pause that burned out the rifling, it was as if the little man himself were making the prayer of his life and burning out that gun with the white fire of his soul, pouring out, pouring out, flowing toward the plane from where he stood. And I saw the plane brought to focus in the sky by the converging cone of fire from ours and other ships. It kept on and on, and as it came on without deviation toward its target it seemed to be standing still in the sky, hanging, hanging, hanging upon the air. In that hanging moment of the undeviating plane, in that moment when the Chief became continous fire, gun and plane came to seem one, so that we might as well have had the pilot aboard and the Chief might have been at the controls of the plane. In that moment I saw beyond the war. Into this transcendence the Chief carried us all.

Though provided with a new barrel, he never became a gunner. He was a sea-faring man.

I remember Chief Johnson best from times that were not spectacular, which partook of the everyday concerns: setting the watch, considering the scope of the anchor chain upon a rising wind, positioning the fenders while we surged alongside other ships, checking and handling the sweep gear, catching up on a bit of scraping and painting here or there, discussing someone's complaint about someone else, and the rationing of the beer — which he kept from going awry. I remember the gravity in those sharp eyes and his habitually mild-mannered speech. I knew him as a man you could work with, whose basic dignity carried through even his moments of peevishness. Whatever stubbornness might lie on both sides of a disagreement with him, it tended to dissolve in the concern for the ship underlying the judgments he formed.

What account can be given for the authority so unobtrusively present in this key man aboard our ship? He was a competent seaman, but not a brilliant one. From long experience in the Navy he had acquired an ingrained sense of the position and prerogatives of a chief petty officer, and he stuck to them. Yet this of itself was not convincing. Nor did he maintain his authority through being especially clever in handling the men in his charge; indeed some of them seemed a good deal sharper than he. Perhaps in a rear-area ship he would not have proven forceful and commanding enough. Qualities of leadership conventionally stressed were not conspicous in him. What, then, authenticated his position as leading petty officer and preserved his sense of position from seeming false?

In answer to the question I see him seated at his place at the head of the larger table in the galley, taking his food and sipping his coffee in perfect accordance with being just where he was — a man who believed implicitly in the things he did. He was where he was, and not in the least degree anywhere else, his smallest moves a taking of the case that is. In this, then, he surpassed every man aboard: in the entirety of his being in that ship, with not the smallest gap intervening between him and the next thing to be met.

During peacetime Raymond Johnson had never risen above the rate of Coxswain, serving mostly aboard large ships. So it might have continued to be but for those exigencies which uniformly lifted in rate men whom the service had schooled by dint of years. Yet now he came to be a chief so fit for our small ship in war, setting that innocence and readiness with which the life of the ship was charmed, that I'm sure none of us could have put our finger on it at the time, and known our debt to him more than to any other man. The only outstanding feature of Boats was that long beard of his, and he shaved that off in time.

There was a night down in Tulagi when we were in floating dry-dock. We'd spent the day in scraping the ship's bottom. Then, while the others slept, Boats and I fished the whole night through. We fished with hand-lines right off the dry-dock. The fish kept us baiting up. There was little sound upon the passing night; no engines turning over, no sound of waves, only the listening stillness of the jungle along the shores of our narrow estuary and the stars above. I knew, too, that Boats knew of the month-old news of my father's death.

Tuesday, September 8

Chief Machinist's Mate Hill was clear from the very start. He also must have been nearing forty; his hair was a bit thin; he was a deep-chested man and erect, with an air of being settled about him. It is most natural to think of him wiping his hands on a rag and speaking of his engines, of fuel tanks and parts, of the evaporators and the men in his watches below. In the timbre of his voice were mingled the harmonics of the varying situation and the fundamental tone of a man who meant business. His manner was mild and steady and reserved. You could surmise Chief Hill from the fact that the availability of our ship came to be taken for granted wherever she went, though in two years' time he never had the chance for a major overhaul. There were able and experienced men in the Black Gang besides Hill, but it was the mark of him that by the time he was transferred, some months before the end of the war, the others were fully able to carry on without him. He had not merely trained them; he had established among them a tradition of work, a belief in the continous operation of the ship.

It seems to me now that Chief Hill, like the Boatswain, achieved anonymity in the on-going life of the ship — defining concretely and unself-consciously the meaning of transcending oneself. I meet Saint-Exupéry in such men as these. Ordinary, unassuming men.

I think of Edwards, the Quartermaster, and of O'Leary, the Yeoman, both men of lively intelligence, quick and taut, yet of vastly different personality. Everybody knew Jack O'Leary, thin as a rail, of swift and salient wit, never at a loss for a word or a song imparting spirit to the life of the ship. With a sweep his humor flitted from man to man, touching equally and ruefully as much on himself as on the rest. He was always willing and kind, and penetrating in his vision of men and the state of affairs. Right at the tip of his tongue and plain in his mobile face and limbs, was a man whom everyone understood and liked, though there were times, perhaps, when Boats might have found Jack a bit glib. O'Leary could decipher the riddles in reams of Navy literature and dispensed freely among us all magic disclosures of how to keep officialdom at a proper distance, palliated and unsuspecting, while he probed its ponderous utterance for schemes which might bring each or all of us a tour of training duty or reassignment in the States. He gave a fine, bright mythical force to our notion of the future, and went on celebrating the present as fast as it came off.

I liked Edwards just as well as O'Leary, but I rather doubt if many others did. He was just as alert, and had as good a mind, but unlike O'Leary, Edwards was a man who could only be met through his work. O'Leary did himself justice in words precisely as Edwards did not. O'Leary was a warm person and Edwards rather cool. In Edwards wit took a sardonic turn. What interests me in comparing the two is the contrast between the possibility of access to what was essential in these two men — men of similar mental aptitude, keyed to about the same pitch of intensity and alertness, of diametrically opposite personalities, yet basically apiece in their steadfast, active intelligence.

Edwards was usually taciturn. He was slim and dark and sensitive; he kept very clean. The first conclusive thing I noticed about him was that he entered corrections on charts and in lists of navigational aids in a determined effort to keep us up to date on developments throughout the Pacific. He was as concerned about a change off the Strait of Juan de Fuca or in New Zealand waters as he was about those affecting any area we would be likely to move in. Also the weather entries in the log for a period of months would reveal no sign of that filling-in with which observations on small ships are rather likely to be padded. The chronometer record afforded a navigator the most reassuring evidence of our chronometer's rate of change. The sextants were in beautiful condition. Edwards himself evidenced a quiet eagerness about the whole business of taking sights, from the time of making initial preparations, through the calling and recording of the actual sights, to the working out of the lines of position on the chart. He made it a point to be ready with suggestions for the coming morning or evening star-sights. He always left word for the watch to call him in time to participate in the regular sights, if they were to fall due during a watch that was not his. Nothing exasperated him more than those occasions when someone failed to call him in time; for example, in time to take the time-tick from the radio. During periods of protracted foul weather, he had an eye even in the back of his head for the possibility of a fleeting emergence of the sun.

Single-handedly, single-mindedly, without benefit of the schooling or example he might have obtained from old hands in his rating, without the companionship of any other enlisted man in the intricacies of his particular work, and without having to be driven in the slightest by the navigator — under the most trying conditions of such a small ship so constantly at sea — Edwards silently acquitted himself down to the last minutiae of the quartermaster's billet. All the capacity he had for joy and for friendship, so far as he could bring it to words, went into the dialogue of navigation itself.

"Now we'll take Sirius."

"Aye, aye."

"Mark . . . Forty-two degrees, six minutes, twenty seconds."

"Forty-two degrees, six minutes, twenty seconds. . . . Do you want to take Sirius once more, sir, to be sure?"

"All right, Edwards; let's do it once more."

I remember the time when we leaned back at last from the chart, and gazed together at a five-star fix with not a triangle among the lines of position; they all intersected at one dot on the chart. That was our fix.

For critical operations Edwards' station was at the wheel. He was there the time we were forced to take on fuel in a high-running sea. The huge tanker was steaming ponderously into the on-coming seas as we gradually overtook her on her port side. The nearer we drew to fueling position on her beam the more sickeningly violent our rearing and plunging seemed. Could we fail to crash her in trying to get the line aboard? And if we got the line, could we fail to part it in veering to save ourselves? It was impossible to think of twenty minutes or more alongside.

From the main deck Chief Johnson waved his readiness to the bridge. A boom had been swung out to starboard and secured. The inboard end of the boom's whip was carried to the winch, so that the heavy fuel-line might be drawn up clear of the leaping seas. Our fueling detail now stood by, holding on. It was up to those of us on the bridge to enable them to do their work.

The tumult of water between the two ships intensified as the gap closed. In the full presence of the tanker our pitching was even more wild. One moment I looked into faces on the tanker's deck, the next there was nothing but green water and her massive hull. With boldness keyed to desperation we came well within range for a heaving line. Someone on the tanker threw, the Boatswain caught, and in moments the fuel-line came aboard.

Now to find exact course and speed — to maintain the delicate parallel amidst the surging thrusts of the sea. I doubt if Edwards' glance once strayed from the gyro-repeater, the rudder indicator, the wave at our bow. His hands flew to anticipate deviation of the ship's head from the given course. His immediate answer to every word I spoke to him came in a clear voice, raised only enough to be heard above wash and wind from the wing of the bridge. With each exchange of words the confidence quickened between us, until in its embrace the ship herself began to dance from sea to sea.

When the time came, we cast off.

Wednesday, September 16

These are days of fall stealing upon us, especially in the quality of the sunlight and in the stillness now hanging upon the air — no longer the quiet of deep summer-sound. No longer the cicadas in the trees by day, or the full chorus of the night. When the wind stirs, it awakens in the trees a prophecy of dead leaves. From Cambridge, Massachusetts to Arctic tundra is but an unstopped step. This sun now rising will soon set a glow among Rocky Mountain quaking asps.

Lately I have watched the inland winging of gulls high in the turbulence of pre-Equinoctial storm. Many birds in the wooded plot beyond my window seem brisk with preparation. And now among their number I hear one small bird of a kind which only seems to be here on its biennial way through. In northern California it used to be around more constantly, and out there it would utter sometimes two, sometimes three notes, but here I have only heard it utter two. They are in minor key and descending scale. I have seldom seen this bird;

I guess I have not looked for it, for any particular source from which its song might be coming. The song is so pure, so infinitely near and far, so definitive of finality in its very self — as sound to be heard — so much the very heart of anything and everything, so intimate and so utterly other; the song itself invites terminal acceptance. What more is there to be said? And what would be the point of looking for the bird which sings this song? Its song is no more relevant to itself than to the rock and the tree nearby, to the distant hills, and the innermost spring of responsiveness.

There have been times when I waited expectantly to hear the song, only to find that I had mistaken the whole matter. Truly heard, the song comes upon one in a readiness to hear that has nothing to do with getting set in expectation. Such is the clarification of the eternity of things.

Thursday, September 17

Reading in Thoreau just now, in the section of *Walden* on "Sounds," a saying of his leapt out at me: "Every path but your own is the path of fate. Keep on your own track, then." This fits exactly with what I was working out for myself this summer especially on August 11 and 12, but also more concretely in terms of the life aboard ship, as on September 5-7, when Thoreau's notion of "taking the case that is" again came to mind. It would be interesting to discover whether the Intuitionists reflect this in exploring their notion of 'fittingness.' Actions would be fitting for a man, they would befit him, in so far as they were a fulfilment of *his* destiny, and the Buddhist idea of sincerity clearly obtains in connection with this. Again it is clear that our thought cannot move here on the level of rules of action. The Way can be but one unique way for each person. Yet this way is no way, no clear prospect, or marked path ahead: neither straight and narrow nor broad and meandering.

Arthur Miller's *Death of a Salesman* is worth considering at this point. It is an extremely interesting play to reflect upon. In his lecture on contemporary drama given at Harvard last year Miller himself remarked that this play of his failed to fulfill what might be called the intent of tragedy; it was not deeply enough conceived. Yet the makings of tragedy were in it, even though he failed overall to get beneath the level of a dramatization of a social predicament of our times. Left as it stands, the play seems to teeter on the verge of indictment, and might be read as a protest against the milieu which tempted Willy Loman into the artificialities of ambition and even insisted on his conformity to a pattern of life in which he was trapped into betraying himself and those close to him. Yet if the suggestion of indictment in the play had been more squarely settled on Willy himself, would this have deepened that insight into responsibility on which tragedy may be conceived to turn?

Or should we say that tragedy if true enough carries us to an appreciation of responsibility that supplants or undergirds the level at which a fixing of guilt prevails and is rendered acceptable? So far as guilt goes, who stands outside the circle of guilt? What seems central in tragedy is that an understanding of responsibility is wrought concretely. One is brought beyond the image of a human fate settled by choice and contingent circumstance, into the presence of the life of an individual person as involving a destiny to be fulfilled. There are glimpses of things that Willy Loman did truly, with the suggestion of authenticity about them, things done in all simplicity. One such glimpse occurs when he harks back to a time when (as Meister Eckhart might put it) he was what he wanted and wanted what he was (such as a man is before he is born, Eckhart says): a time when he had been pouring concrete for the cellar or fixing the back steps. There is a glimpse of the genuine Willy in his relationship with the neighbor with whom he played pinochle, another in his moments of tenderness toward his wife. Then there is the final moment in which he acted truly, though out of all connection with the daze in which he goes on to commit suicide — when he comes out of his house at night to begin planting a garden. Restitution into the truth of human destiny through simplicity, that theme of tragedy, is at least faintly, but perceptibly at work here. But it fails to interlock with the full course of events in which Willy is shown, and we are left with the sense of a life unredeemed. We are left seemingly faced with the ultimacy of the theme of fate: man caught and brought to naught through conspiracy between impinging circumstance and his own weakness. Does not pessimism name the false note in this play? But as Marcel remarks in his "Sketch of a Phenomenology and a Metaphysic of Hope" (in *Homo Viator*), optimism would be an opposed false note, and cannot take the measure of the inadequacy of pessimism any more than of itself. Indeed no fixed and claimed evaluative rendering of the human situation might.

Are not optimism and pessimism alike a suffering of the illusion of fate, and is there not a complacency of undeepened responsiveness in both? Evaluative dogmatism writ large, each claiming exemption from a reality of which they take possession in a wholesale judgment, with a claim to having drawn up the balance sheet. When it comes to evaluating our situation, who *knows*? Following Shakespeare's own conception of tragedy as Cunningham exhibits it in *Woe or Wonder*,[62] through tragedy we pass through woe to wonder, to a quickened understanding of our situation that must belie evaluation of it set forth as knowledge possessed. We learn something of the meaning of Shakespeare's final word: "the readiness is all."

The appalling thought for a philosopher is this: that the basic questions on which our endless questioning revolves can only be stilled as we make decisive answer from the very center of our lives. We cannot shift the burden to our knowledge of the world. Yet on every hand philosophy is practised as though philosophical responsiveness in depth might be substituted for with knowledge of some super (i.e. "meta") sort.

Again I would say, essential truth seems neither objective nor subjective. Yet even as I say this the case of Kierkegaard comes to mind, to remind me once more that *to an objectively-minded way of thinking,* the connection of essential truth with decisive responsiveness *will seem* to rest on subjectivity, as I think it did to Kierkegaard

62. Cunningham, J. V., *Woe or Wonder*, Denver, Univ. of Denver Press, 1951.

himself. And again I am struck by the fact that Kierkegaard never seems to come out with a true note of affirmation of the infinite importance of finite things. It is as if he did not discover himself being born with them, and so could never really acknowledge them with a love that is their due. The irony of ironies in his thinking is his preaching a *doctrine* of love while bespeaking despair and disillusionment with the world. And yet, . . . that theme of the leap of faith beyond despair can be genuine enough, not as a *recommendation* but as the upshot of reflection based on experience. But should it not bear with it the recognition of a redemption into which finite things are assimilated, from which accordingly they are born out anew?

Friday, September 18

Today has been a day of prowling in books. I have read and reread not a little in diverse books, and found much to engage me in each. Yet the ideas in the interest of which I have sought out the help of these books seem to move today in a kind of merry-go-round fashion, each like a horse in the merry-go-round, bobbing to the music and coming round again and again. Too familiar, perhaps; too much looked at — thought *about*. I hear the music that unites them yet still I look on, not infected to the point of paying my ten cents and taking a ride. What is this being a kind of watchful, attentive, nonparticipant, musing on the round of thoughts, but waiting, waiting, waiting for what? Waiting, at least, which will not cease until thinking is no longer like choosing to ride an old familiar horse, with a somewhat artificial look. To get on a merry-go-round one must approach it with an understanding that finds it real — to the life.

Among the things I reread today was this:

A wood-cutter was busily engaged in cutting down trees in the remote mountain. An animal called "Satori" appeared. It was a very strange-looking creature, not usually found in the villages. The wood-cutter wanted to catch it alive. The animal read his mind: "You are now wishing to catch me alive, are you not?" Completely taken aback, he did not know what to say, whereupon the animal remarked, "You are evidently astonished at my telepathic faculty." Ever more surprised, he conceived the idea of striking it with one blow of his axe, when Satori exclaimed, "Now you want to kill me." The woodman felt entirely disconcerted, and fully realizing his impotency to do anything with this mysterious animal, he thought of resuming his business. Satori was not charitably disposed, for he pursued him, saying: "So at last you have abandoned me."

The woodman did not know what to do with the animal as well as himself; altogether resigned to the situation he took up his axe and paying no attention whatever to the presence of Satori, he vigorously and single-heartedly began the cutting of the trees again. While so engaged, the head of the axe flew off its handle and struck the animal dead, who with all its mind-reading sagacity failed to read the mind of "no-mind-ness."[63]

Perhaps this is a good day for chopping wood; there is a brisk, cool wind bearing down clouds out of the northeast.

Saturday, September 26

I've been thinking of responsibility as our mode of involvement in reality, and groping for a conception of truth in terms of our being true in responding. This would be a non-specialized conception of truth, and it might lead to the conception of a non-specialization of the self in responding truly. There seems to be a level of responding, we might say, that defies reduction to the category of expertise, a level underlying *knowing*, on which a person may *be* arbitrary or not. What does it mean to serve the truth, in contradistinction from claiming the truth? Does the meaning of truth get exposed exhaustively in forms in which it may be claimed (as in truth-claims), or is there a sense in which truth is such that it can only be served — defining, perhaps, the very meaning of service? From the point of view of a specialized conception of truth, this coupling of the basic meaning

63. Suzuki, D. T., *Zen Buddhism and Its Influence on Japanese Culture*, Kyoto, Eastern Buddhist Society, 1938, p. 88.

of truth with the idea of service would probably seem strange and vague. Yet if service is properly extricated from servility, with which it may be unfortunately confused, it seems precisely indicative of a meaning of truth that pertains to our being true, whatever the differentiated modes of response in which we are true, whatever is being non-arbitrarily done. Still further, however, I think of reality as understood in being true, and reality understood is the essential truth of reality as grounding us. Accordingly essential truth might be defined as the non-specialized truth in all true response, and as that which a man serves in responding truly. It would follow that except as essential truth is served, it could not be understood. The experience of reality as grounding us in what we do, even in whatever thinking we may be doing, thus seems more basic for the conception of truth than any of the features of what we do and think by which we may attempt to distinguish what is non-arbitrary in thought and deed. Reality as grounding the possibility of non-arbitrariness in man is presupposed in all that is responsibly thought and done. Therefore no idea of reality can consistently *supplant* that of reality as grounding responsibility. This, at any rate, seems a fair statement of the line of thought which I have been following up — suggesting, as it does, the need for coarticulation of the ideas of responsibility, of understanding, and of reality.

Herzog's *Annapurna* is an interesting study in connection with this idea of being true. The book rather bears out his saying: "I saw that it is better to be true than to be strong."[64] But then, the idea of power here supposed seems a relatively unreflective one.

Sunday, September 27

It is just in respect to the advent of essential truth that I have conceived our condition to be ephemeral, and precisely because es-

---

[64] Herzog, M., *Annapurna* ("First Conquest of an 8000-meter Peak"), New York, Dutton, 1953, p. 12.

sential truth seems yielded in a way that controverts the possibility of making good a hold over it. Its advent does not place it at our disposal. On the contrary, its advent seems bound up with our being disposably oriented within our situation — with our mode of responsiveness to the world around us. And it is clear that being responsive cannot be a matter of falling back on what one has made secure. This is not to suggest that in responding truly the resources at our disposal would not be drawn into play, but it is to suggest that capacity for true response cannot be defined in terms of the resources at our disposal, even though the availability of our resources to ourselves, and the very richness of the resources at our disposal, may be intimately proportional to the truth or falsity of our mode of commitment. Since I have been thinking of knowledge in terms of the resources which may be conceived as at our disposal, I have been led to reject the identification of capacity for true response with any knowledge we might possess, however much knowledge we possess may enter into true response, and however much the acquisition of knowledge may align with a genuine fulfilment of our destiny. The link between an ultimate claim to *know* what is right and the tendency to unresponsiveness on our part in so far as we assert such a claim, is often noted.[65]

In the course of my own reflective concern with essential truth, emphasis on the theme of ephemerality has been sharpened by the experience of conflict in the attitudes in which one may persist with reflective inquiry. I find that as I become the more grasping in my thinking, what I am concerned to understand eludes me the more. And at times I have discerned that the explicit disavowal of the possibility of possessing explicit criteria, to be invoked with ultimate assurance in evaluation, may cloak an implicit claim to the possession of an implicit criterion in the name of which one is speaking. This would be akin to what might be called a certain spiritual pride, perhaps even more insidious than the moralistic pride called in question. I have suffered through the experience of this quite vividly at times

---

65. *The Book of Job* is a fine study in this connection. Do not Job and his 'friends' assert a claim to know what they lack the responsiveness to understand?

when I have argued in behalf of an indemonstrable groundedness pertaining to action as if I 'had the word.' But the whole climate of expectation with which philosophic reflection is received in professional circles conduces to the clearing of ideas in the form of theses which one claims to have thought through to the point where he defends a position stated in terms of them. The expectation is that philosophy be consummated as knowledge in a strict sense. Largely in reflective response to this expectation, now in succumbing to it with pretension, and now in restoration to the sense of essential truth, philosophy has become for me a distillate experience of our condition as active beings.

I have spoken of moving from philosophic to aesthetic contemplation without a break. Perhaps one may also experience no break between what it means to respond more or less falsely in reflection and with respect to matters with which one is otherwise involved. It seems to me that the life I lead is continuous, in and out of periods of reflection. If reflection culminates in moments of regeneration, one experiences in such moments an informing of the will which is clear in its relevance to the entire scope of one's relations and actions, and it becomes clear that the essential truth informing the will in such moments of reflection is akin with essential truth as it may permeate the will in moments of non-reflective action.

One of the most instructive points which Zen Buddhism has suggested to me is that essential truth, as man's ultimate concern, may lead us into endlessly inconclusive reflection, only to dawn on us entirely unexpectedly in moments of non-reflective action. I cannot follow Zen, however, in the tendency to regard reflection merely as a kind of preparation through disillusionment for the non-reflective advent of essential truth. This brings me to a further implication of the thought that as it is with us in action generally, so it is with us in reflection: Faithfulness is possible. And it is faithfulness that makes possible constancy in philosophic reflection, just as in doing anything else which we may come to do understandingly in good time. Zen emphasizes the swift advent of essential truth. It does not seem to me to place an equally deserved emphasis on the slow increment (gestation?) of swift truth (by increment I do not mean acquisition).

No doubt Zen does emphasize the all-alongness of that essential truth into which we may suddenly awaken, and it may even bespeak a kind of confirmatory retroactive blending of decisive insight with antecedent presentiment suggesting continuity in the *way* one has come, and imparting a certain wholeness of meaning to one's life. But like so much of literature in which the non-theoretical character of essential truth is stressed, Zen seems to bespeak the futility of reflection in a way that is apt to overlook the relevance of faithful reflection to the possibility of reflective understanding. Neither intellectualism nor anti-intellectualism, at any rate, seem to do justice to full-fledged reasonableness in action and in philosophic reflection. If either viewpoint were sound, the 'life of reason' could be neither practical nor philosophical, it would be exclusively scientific and technical. As I write this, I hope I speak a word which George Santayana would wish to confirm.

There is much that goes by the name of mysticism, as a reflective interpretation of the advent of essential truth, with which I disagree rather deeply. The themes which seem most adequate to the advent of essential truth are not those of the rare and special experience, discontinuous with daily life, the ineffable transfiguration of the one who is seized (in effect isolating him from the bulk of men, who cannot share his experience), and abandonment of a stake in the everyday world. They are more nearly those of a belief in communication unbound, and a sharing of essential truth in all loyalty, all steadfastness, and all simplicity, just here and all along in the everyday world.

Monday, September 28

A day of Indian Summer, and a good day for the trail.

There has been much uneasiness about making philosophy pivot on theory of knowledge, an uneasiness that has grown with perspective on modern Western thought in which this tendency has prevailed.

intelligence) knowledge

The uneasiness seems thoroughly justified, yet the tendency often persists even where the uneasiness is acute. Isn't Pragmatism a particularly instructive movement of thought in this connection?

What has struck me most vividly in reading William James and John Dewey is the sense of a struggle to revive and articulate a more basic philosophic theme than that of knowledge: the theme, let us say, of intelligence, and of intelligence as commensurate with the full range of our fulfilment of responsibility, and therefore perhaps above all, of intelligence as living and proven in action. In both these thinkers there is marked determination to resist the thinning out of intelligence, its consignment to the realm of purely theoretical endeavours, its identification with the attitude of the non-participant in everyday life. And both would reinstate intelligence as the quick of a life worth living, active in all the affairs of the world — in art, in politics, in artisanry, in religion, and not merely in inquiries which make abstraction from man's stake in life. Of William James in particular I would say that no philosopher has shown himself more open to suggestions of *wisdom,* from whatever quarter they might come, and no philosopher has striven more earnestly to uncover the pre-doctrinally-disposed experiential soil of truth by which men might live. *there is truth in experiential knowledge*

I am tempted to say that when all the paraphernalia of Pragmatism are removed from the foreground and one strikes through to its basic significance as a movement of thought, it may be reviewed as a recall of philosophy to the love of wisdom, and an affirmation of the basic affinity of essential truth discovered in action with essential truth as a matter of reflective concern. Perhaps I would not say this if I had not discovered it crying out from the utterances of C. I. Lewis to which I have attended with great care over the last five years. It is clearest when he has spoken without technical mediation, when he has spoken without having anticipated what he was going to say, when he has expressed thematically something of what he feels philosophy should mean and be.

Yet if I am not amiss in thus surmising a greatness in Pragmatism, I would have to add that its greatness is far from being understood, and the chief difficulty lies with the Pragmatists themselves.

For in spite of themselves, they have tended to betray their theme. In attempting to work out their idea of intelligence they have taken knowledge as their theme, and they have tended to rejoin Aristotle in his explicit emphasis on the conception of intelligence in terms of scientific and technical thought. Thus for Dewey intelligence is pre-eminently problem-solving, and truth in action comes down to the application of a correct solution to a problem of 'what to do.' Truth, then, is that which can be experimentally verified. So, as I see it, Dewey entirely misses the conception of essential truth as subject to experiential realization and confirmation, where the heart of the matter is that you cannot really understand what requires experiential, as distinct from experimental, substantiation, apart from the substantiating experience.[66]

Essential truth is experiential and it turns on what a man is, in whatever he may be doing. It is such that he can never appropriate it to definition in terms of conditions which he may deliberately fulfil by a chosen method, abstracting, as it were, from himself. But the essence of experimental truth is that it can be appropriated to definition in terms of conditions which may be fulfilled by a chosen method, abstracting entirely from the manner of man one may be. In fact you've got to understand what you set out to verify experimentally apart from that which is necessary to its substantiation, in order to choose a relevant method of experiment. But with respect to essential truth, we *move* in relative clarity or obscurity with respect to it, and its clarification and substantiation are one. You do not define "what might be essentially true" and then proceed to prove it, having understood already "what would be true."

Right at this point the basic similarity between Dewey and James, in the miscarriage of their efforts to reflect in line with the love of wisdom, is something I would like to consider. For Dewey intelligence has taken on the aspect of man's gradual mastery of the practical situation through experimental truth. In James intelligence takes on the aspect of mastery in a less obvious way, for James is less caught

66. November 1, 1953: Today I have run across an explicit distinction between experimental and experiential "verification" in Paul Tillich's *Systematic Theology*, Vol. I, p. 102, Chicago, University of Chicago, 1951.

up in outlining a programme for active reform in the world, less pre-occupied with a methodology of practical intelligence.

The crucial subject in James seems to be that of belief, and again the emphasis on action is conceived as an emphasis on verification, *implying* that truth enters into what we do only in connection with beliefs *which we have* on which we can act successfully. Thus again, truth enters into what we do only *deliberately* through beliefs which we choose to act upon. More freely, beliefs are treated as tools with which we enter upon action, to be chosen and shaped for their ef-ficacy. Action is necessary for testing their efficacy, but the ideas or beliefs themselves are consummated in abstraction from the actions in which they are proven. Intelligence in action is thus instrumental to action. The intellectualism here is subtle, and it is blurred by the emphasis on action as the test of the truth of ideas as tools employed in action. The ready-made character of ideas so conceived is easily overlooked. But the upshot still seems to be this: that no truth is realized in action that is not understood in advance; action cannot enhance understanding, it confirms or disconfirms ideas already un-derstood and imported as understood into the action in which they serve as tools. The give-away in James, to me, is his conception of the *optional* character of fundamental belief, as if what were funda-mentally believed might be the sort of thing one could understand well enough, but for which one sees that he must lack substantiating or disconfirmatory evidence. As if fundamental belief were akin to a scientific hypothesis, understood well enough, but lacking in obser-vations which would tell the story, not of its meaning, but of its truth.

What I would suggest is this: In the realization of essential truth, meaning and truth are hand in hand. The reclamation of the idea of intelligence seems to require testimony to truth discovered through service in action and reflection, which cannot pertain to anything we deliberately import into either. So far as realization of essential truth is a matter of ideation, ideation does not break into separate moments of understanding and of substantiation. There is no greater clarity of meaning than there is immediate substantiation for what is understood.

No doubt the Pragmatists have felt the limitation of that explicit Aristotelian analysis of practical intelligence which emphasizes the fixed end and construes practical reflection as deliberation in the selection of means for its attainment. They have wished to redefine practical intelligence as flexible, and relevantly so, with respect to ends. Dewey especially, as in the latter chapters of *Human Nature and Conduct*, subsumes all possible ends within the scope of practical intelligence, and emphasizes their evaluative revision and formation as expressions of practical intelligence. Dewey even goes so far as to conceive the consummatory aspect of intelligence in terms of a growth of meaning in experience which would, I think, defy analysis either in instrumentalist terms or in terms of deliberate production. That is, intelligence as realization of growth of meaning could not be construed as merely instrumental or as a result of intelligence aiming at such growth. Nevertheless, as philosophy of action (and of intelligence in action), Pragmatism mainly bespeaks the prospective orientation of practical intelligence, and to a corresponding extent slides over the depth of intelligence in action, as a matter of groundedness discovered in acting. This matter of groundedness in present action tends to be lost upon reflection in so far as reflection is dominated by a concern to find reason for action in future attainment, and in so far as the ruling preoccupation is with the definition of aims. It even escapes reflection prepared to acknowledge the consummatory phase of practical intelligence, such as we find in Dewey's *Art as Experience*, in so far as consummation is not also reflectively explored as steeping man in moral obligation.

My point is that every true consummation is enabling and demanding with respect to continuing responsibility. Every appreciation of finality is charged with imperativeness for an active being, and becomes a liability to him in so far as he fails to fulfil its potential in active commitment. How near is this to what Meister Eckhart intends in the following remark?

> Many good gifts, received in virginity, are not brought to birth in wifely fruitfulness by which God is greatly pleased. The gifts decay and come to nothing, so that the man is never blessed or bettered by them. The virgin in him is useless when it does not ripen into the wife who is fruitful. Here is the mischief![67]

[67.] *Meister Eckhart: A Modern Translation*, p. 208.

Tuesday, September 29

To continue with this point, for a moment: Pragmatism seems to share in a difficulty more easily discerned in Utilitarianism, and in spite of such suggestive criticisms of Utilitarianism as we have Dewey to thank for. Both philosophies suffer a misfortune of teleological ethics. When they think of the necessity of action as requiring explication in relation to the realization of finality, they think of the necessary action as necessary in relation to a subsequent realization of finality. This forces them into the reduction of practical intelligence into the aspect of technical intelligence. It also leads to an impasse and a paradox: The impasse is that responsibility to other persons and the necessity of action in relations with them embodying concern for them, get translated into a concern for the realization of finality as an achievement, terminally justifying the action necessary to that achievement. When this is done, there is no way of avoiding the conclusion that only the eventual realization of finality by me can justify for me what I will have done; and the consequence of such ethical egoism should be practical egoism, namely concentration on the enhancement of my own realization of finality. And it should follow still further that bending every nerve to such enhancement would actually enhance my realization of finality, at least in the long run — the less I leave it to chance or to others, the better. Yet, and from this point of view utterly paradoxically, it seems that he who is governed by concern to preserve and enhance his own life defeats himself. It must be a strange prudence that can advise transcending a merely prudential orientation.

What I wish to suggest is that true realization of finality is ever the *spring* of necessary action, and not an achievement which renders action necessary as means to it. Present realization of finality informs the will with concern in the imperative mood, and necessary action is the working out of the implications of informed will, ever renewable and subject to clarification in further realization of finality. And true realization of finality is to be marked in the readying of the will for what is yet to come — come what may — and for what yet needs to be done, as long as one may live.

To act with ultimate concern we must be charged with the ultimate significance of the situation in which we act. The essence of practical intelligence is in constancy of response in consonance with such intimations of finality as silently and gently press upon us — now faintly and distantly like echoes from afar, now near and vividly clear.

It seems to me that the ultimate practical importance of philosophy is the lifting up in us through reflection even to the point of clearer understanding of the very ground of faithfulness in action. Thus we might say that philosophical intelligence is indeed the reflective moment in the clarification of practical intelligence. As we become the more deeply sensitized through reflection to what it may mean to be true, we must also become the more deeply sensitized to the depth and extent of our capacity for betrayal. In the former respect we are informed of our common human nature, and partake of an unshakeable ground of loyalty to men; in the latter respect we are informed with compassion. Communion in reflection, as in non-reflective action, seems to have these two fundamental aspects — in the words of Buddhism, "Great Intelligence" and "Great Compassion."

Finality construed as a consequence justifying what we do renders no action necessary, and carries practical intelligence no further than its aspect as technical and prudential. For instance, it cannot fit the fact that it might be necessary for a man to risk his life for another, or the practical intelligence in that.

Sunday, October 4

Finality dwells in faith, and clarification with respect to it is the deepening of faith into understanding. It seems to me that our thinking is informed with finality just to the point of the depth of our reflective appreciation of our communion with one another. And

though it might be a tougher thought to think through, I am impelled
to add that our communion with one another must be fathomed within
communion with finite being. The Chinese scrolls sometimes give a
clear sense of the coemergence of everything distinct. Finality grounds
our standing forth; in standing forth we receive the gift of all existent
things: coexistence in communion. The sacramental act, and the sacredness of all things — it is to these that reflection on finality must
ultimately come. To perceive something truly is to be alive to it in
its sacredness; such, at least, is the full implication of the idea of true
perception to which I have been led. And the individuality and universality of whatever is so perceived are clarified in the finding of it
sacred. The mystery of each thing is the mystery of all things; and
this — not generalization or the broadening of our scope of attention
to wider and wider complexes of things, is the foundation of the idea
of universe: the omnirelevance of the experience of something as
sacred.

Monday, October 5

Sometimes, indeed very often, in speaking to one another, we
call upon one another by name in a way that intimates we have something to say — inviting attention and readiness in the one whom we
address. And we pause before going on; and the one whom we have
addressed may say "Yes," before we proceed with what we have to
say. There is a way in which that "yes" may come, quite without
anticipation of what we may be going to say, charged with quiet
intimacy and the willingness to consider, suggesting that our respon-
dent is completely at our disposal and trusting toward us, yet also
prepared to accept the responsibility of an independent person in
relation with us: This "yes" of readiness and disposability, this offering
of fair and open attention in which a person extends credit to us in
advance of knowing what may be asked, sealing the bond of mutual

reliance — does it not seem a far cry from anything we could adequately conceive in terms of the alternatives of either an objective or a subjective attitude?

Let us consider men as we would find them; with what manner of man would we deal? What shall we say of a man whose attitude toward us is consistently objective? Is he not the man who withholds himself, who speaks to us over a wall and asks us not to bother him too much? Is he not the man who receives us as a kind of specimen or instance of humanity, to whom he is prepared to extend the rights which he claims for himself, perhaps, because he is concerned with the consistency of his position far more than he is concerned with us? Is he not the man who fails profoundly to respond to *us?* Is he not one who insists on treating us abstractly, who sits over against us with the reservation of one who assumes the role of our judge? What intimacy and open reciprocity can there be with a man whose attitude toward us remains only objective? What invitation does he extend to us to call upon him, beyond the limits of those claims of ours which he is prepared to acknowledge as defining his duty 'in our case?' Perhaps we are an interesting case to him, and in that event he may deal with us protractedly — accordingly. Who among us has not been through the abdication of responsibility and the sterility of the objective attitude in human relationships? If it be urged that much of the time we can do no better than a kind of objective fairness in our relationships with one another, let us not suffer the confusion of taking this as a paradigm of what it may mean to be responsible by reason of insisting that "we cannot be held responsible for more than this." Because a *profound* concern of man for man cannot be legislated into us does not mean that anything short of such concern can guide us into an adequate interpretation of the meaning of responsibility.

With what manner of man would we deal, then? With one who is indulgent toward us, with one who makes a doormat out of himself, with one who caters to us, with one who clings to us, with one whose attitude is that of bias in our favor? Is the responsiveness we want even that of sympathy and benevolence? Are these the fundamental modes of *withness* of the man who is with us? (I will not speak of attitudes more obviously "subjective," in that they are a matter of

being so wrapped up in oneself that they do not bear the semblance
of responsiveness to another person.)

These questions, sketchy though they may be, suffice to bring
me face to face again with issues I have derived from Hume, from
Kant, from the Utilitarians, and from Lewis. For some time Hume's
"benevolence" and "sympathy" have struck me as not ringing true,
and in the same respect Mill's "fellow-feeling" may be conceived
without the discrimination to see through the inadequacy of the subjective attitude so far as it amounts to being merely favorably disposed
toward our fellows. Kant's entire critique of inclination, including
what he calls "love from inclination," may be read as a critique of subjective attitude. But Kant's failure, as I see it, and that of Mr. Lewis
as well, lies in formulating his critique of subjectivity as a defense of
objectivity. Hume, Kant, and Lewis all seem to fall short of reckoning
with the possibility of the transfiguration of man; yet in that possibility the full meaning of responsibility must be sought.

Thursday, October 8

For the last couple of days I have been considering Kant's ethical
thought again, and finding Teale's *Kantian Ethics* very helpful and
suggestive even though I often fall short of comprehending what
Teale means by his central idea of perfection. It is interesting to find
Teale speaking in exactly the phrase which has struck me so power-
fully of late: "informed will." And there seems to be in Teale a precise
analogue for the thought I have been trying to work out, of finality
as informing the will, both as enabling and demanding action in fulfilment of its implication: True action clarifies the unconditioned condition of its possibility. Thus action in its consummatory aspect must
be understood, not in terms of an objective extrinsic to action — and
to which action is necessary as means to its attainment — but as the

fruition (to use his term) of that seed in which both the necessity and the enabling power of necessary action must be conceived to lie. We can only pass to blessedness through honoring in action the intimations of that by virtue of which we are blessed, demanding and enabling action of us; we are only free in so far as we do what we must do. Teale clearly and courageously rejects attempts to conceive freedom in any other way, in any other sense. Only in being grounded are we free, and the essence of being grounded is partly revealed in the will's being informed in a way that cannot be construed as the will's informing of itself. As Marcel points out, neither autonomy nor heteronomy suffice to the interpretation of the groundedness of man in action, just as neither egocentricity nor heterocentricity suffice to the interpretation of true interest (and ethical egoism and altruism therefore both fail).

Again I return to the idea of disinterested interest which laid hold of me three years ago, and I mark again the point that nothing which we can describe as falling within the focus of interested attention can suffice to define the meaning of disinterested interest in it. When I have spoken of inclination transfigured, I have had in mind 'the same thing.' If one does not reflect in this vein, but preserves as Kant does an appreciation that no specifiable interest or inclination is of itself authenticated, the result is apt to be, as in the case of Kant, a diremption of the capacity for well-doing and well-being, respectively. And when it is appreciated that an utterly uninterested man is one for whom inaction obtains, the result is apt to be, as in the case of Kant, an attempt to define some peculiarly moral interest set over against all other interests (inclinations) with which men may be imbued. (I think an analogy between Kant and Kierkegaard might be drawn here, in that Kierkegaard tries to substantiate the conception of an absolutely precedent interest really disorienting men from the world.) When these steps of thought have been taken, one has let go of the possibility of thinking human integrity, and of wholeness relieving the ambiguity and internal conflict otherwise written into the condition of man. And a further consequence is liable to ensue, as in the case of Kant.

Human happiness, or well-being, is thought of as if it required no careful reflective interpretation; as if anyone, any old time, were adequately informed with respect to its meaning. (How little this accords with Aristotle's observation that agreement on the subject of happiness tends to break down as soon as reflection gets beyond the nominal stage.) Thus in Kant happiness is naively associated with the requital of interests and inclinations, with no sensitivity to the possibility of our being mistaken in thinking ourselves well-off. Any old 'satisfaction,' such as self-satisfaction, or complacency, or the living death of mere comfortableness, or the requital of any interest or inclination, may pass muster as disclosing the meaning of happiness. In failing to follow up the possibility of disinterested interest and transfigured inclination in thinking out well-doing, Kant also misses their centrality for a critical conception of human well-being. It seems to me that if we think through either well-doing or well-being, our thinking must converge upon an interpretation of generosity from either direction. But Kant would be right in insisting that we refrain from conceiving generosity as a *mere* inclination. Perhaps we understand the meaning of generosity no better than we understand the meaning of eternity. For is not the latter incarnate in the former?

I keep trying the shape of these thoughts. How strangely they alternate between seeming more or less precise and concrete and seeming almost utterly tenuous and abstract. If I can only fathom what keeps me going. . . . Is this not so for everyone?

Friday, October 16

I have now reviewed Aristotle on practical reason once again. His conception of practical wisdom seems suggestively modified through the interpretation of intelligence as a function of character. But this in turn seems vitiated by his definition of "moral virtue" in terms of states of character *concerned with choice*. For the concept of choice then becomes central, and plays back into the hands of an intellectualistic version of practical intelligence, and one which is not in the least revised by maintaining that correct choice governing right action is only possible on the actual condition of certain states of character distinguished from the selective deliberation which they make possible. Would it not be proper to say that Aristotle's conception of character is fatally naturalistic? Perhaps the deepening of the conception of character must evolve with the deepening of the conception of practical intelligence: The two conceptions might meet in something like the notion of 'informed will.' But this notion must be thought out experientially if it is not to degenerate into a theoretical sleight-of-hand.

I also reviewed Hume's discussion of excellence in man. The purling smoothness of his thought on this, as on many other matters, invites me to plunge beneath the level on which it moves. How inadequate it seems to attempt to conceive excellence in men in terms of qualities, or talents, or skills, or resources which they may be said to possess — marked by utility or agreeableness to those possessed of them, or to other persons. Such are the 'excellences' through which "fate" may stalk us in the end. None of them incorporate definitively that central self-transcendence and that controlling simplicity which make of excellence in men something to which praise would be ultimately irrelevant.

Saturday, October 17

For over a month I have been thinking more than might appear from the foregoing about where I stand with regard to aspects of the Christian tradition, the spirit of which I have deeply imbibed from such expressions as the Twenty-Third Psalm and the Lord's Prayer, from an early age. At the same time I have been turning over the idea of active agency with two references in mind: One is the question which is like a refrain in Epictetus, What is and is not in our power? What should be the construction we place on this phrase, "in our power?" The other is a notion which Professor Nikam brought out in his discussion of the *Gita,* that a profound delusion may lurk in the way we assume our agency; he sees it expressed in the saying "I am the doer."

I have already articulated the thought that as I presume to command my destiny, then I experience destiny as fate; but that as I fulfill my destiny without presuming to command it, I am freed from such bondage. And I have already come to consider the key to reflective interpretation of reality to lie in the thought of the possibility of responsibility. Still further, I have come to take responsibility as the central definitive concept for the interpretation of personality.

Now I face this question: Does the idea of human agency dissolve, or must the idea of agency be kept in alignment with what it may mean to act truly, as a *man* may act truly? It is at this point that explicitly theological questions must be reckoned with by anyone whose sensitivity to the possibility of our groundedness has evolved within the framework of the Christian tradition. For instance, if one is inclined to reject autonomy and heteronomy as I would follow Marcel in doing, what will one say of the idea of theonomy so familiar to us, at least nominally, in the expression "Thy will be done"?

In considering the matter I have kept in mind Tillich's *The Courage to Be,* and I have been studying with great interest sections of his *Systematic Theology.* I have also kept in mind that tendency in Buddhist thought to dissolve human agency, and to construe true action as that of the original agent, who is one and one only, acting through us. Indeed from the Buddhist standpoint it may be even a kind of rhetorical question to ask "Who am I?". The finite "I" is dissolved. Whether I am right or wrong in thinking to discern this aspect in Buddhism, I would say that I cannot follow it. If you reject the notion that 'I am the doer' in *every* sense, you reject the possibility of a philosophy of human action, and you lose all experiential purchase for reflection on reality as sustaining responsibility in an inexpugnable sense: namely, the possibility of responding, of *our* responding, in a way that is not arbitrary. Abstractly stated, man is a finite center of response. And now I would go on to say, he encounters personality only in relation with other finite centers of response. Since this has always seemed to me so, in so far as I have thought about the matter, I have not, in fact, ever been sufficiently implicated in personal theism to the point of reacting against it. The peculiar importance of personality seems to me to lie in the capacity of responsible beings *to bear witness* to the groundedness of the finite. But from this I cannot derive anything but mystification if personality is conceived to ground responsibility. The conclusion which has become clearer and clearer to me is this: No agent can ground agency, and the delusion in 'I am the doer' cannot be because I am not agent, but in my misconstruing what it means to be a doer, a finite responsible being.

Tillich's movement beyond theism seems reflectively true to his central experiential theme of the groundedness of man as a responsible being (through which alone we discover our union with all finite beings).

Monday, October 19

Yesterday I resumed reading Tillich's *Systematic Theology*, and while engrossed in it, the whole day slipped by. I hear the timbre of his voice, which so impressed me on hearing him speak, and it is in the style of his thought on nearly every page. Great the profit of his immense scholarship and the integrity with which he carefully thinks out ideas; great the discernment to which he may help one in his interpretation of our major Western tradition; but solidest and truest is the tone of that voice, which seems to keep his constant use of "ultimate concern," for example, from settling into a drone. I follow him when he says that every theological thought can only live in what he calls "existential correlation." Yet to me this would mean that it must take the form of experientially hewn reflection, and it seems to me that much of what Tillich says would remain fatally abstract except for the tone which is constant in his utterance. What I find in this book, at any rate, I would not be inclined to consider a system of knowledge, though there is much systematic knowledge in it. I find, rather, a configuration of ideas tending toward harmony and interilluminative interpretation of human experience; the ideas, that is, are interilluminative. And one sees that they derive confirmation from their power to yield historical perspective. In particular, Tillich does more than anyone I can recall to bring out the latently religious character of philosophical issues. For my own part, it has become clear that the philosophers whose work is in itself of the most constructive value are those who appreciate this fact, and whose work brings out more than latently the religious character of the issues which concern them. Of course I do not mean men who merely use 'religious terms' as Berkeley often does.

Tuesday, October 20

Let me see today what I may do by way of reflective interpretation of 'ultimate,' or 'unconditional' concern. Can such concern be differentiated in terms of conception of what it may be concern for? I recall some comments of Richard Niebuhr's near the close of his course last fall in 19th and early 20th Century religious thought. He questioned the tendency to be marked, for example, in William James' *Varieties of Religious Experience*, to concentrate upon religious attitude to the exclusion of its 'objective basis,' as I believe he put it. How can the religious attitude be understood properly without placing it in orientation to God? — that seemed to be his question; and he also seemed disposed to demand a conception of God, with whatever necessary qualifications about its analogical or symbolical character, as *object* upon which religious attitude must depend, if religious attitude is not to degenerate in the end into something subjective and gratuitous.

Much as I concur against the psychologizing interpretation of religious attitude, and with the belief in the possibility of religious attitude of a non-gratuitious character; much as I think such attitude must be interpreted as having relevance, and relevance to what can be referred to; I cannot but think that the very notion of object incorporates a mode of thinking with respect to reality which is cut loose from religious attitude. No 'object' can serve to explicate the non-arbitrariness of religious attitude. If it could, there would be no element of faith requisite in religious understanding; and I mean, for example, that element of faith in the experience of finite things which has led me to consider 'the object' as abstract, and to attempt a reevaluation of the conception of things in distinction from the conception of objects. Thus, too, I have questioned the interpretation of the 'otherness' of other finite beings in terms of the 'standing-over-againstness' which seems inherent in the notion of objectivity. What I should wish to call religious attitude challenges the ultimacy of any interpretation of reality which is 'objective' in the sense of abstracting from the depth of our experience as responsible beings. Thus to demand that we conceive the groundedness of religious attitude with reference to the objectively conceived, no matter what qualifications are placed on the possibility of an adequate conception of the religious object, seems to me tantamount to a request that religious thought be undertaken from a standpoint not merely independent of religious attitude but also tending to oppose it.

Is this to say that religious attitude is not one of concern *for*, since it cannot be objectively differentiated? No. I think, rather, that religious attitude is one of truly universal concern for things, of concern informed with the universality of finite things. I do not mean concern for 'things in general.' I mean, on the contrary, a concern which is concretely an experience of things in the vein of individuality, for this is precisely the vein in which they are experienced as universal. And here, I feel, is the direction I must take in answering the question: How is it that if ultimate concern, in so far as it is concern *for* anything which can be referred to, is concern for the finite, that such concern is not idolatrous? The question cannot be dealt with in abstraction from the standpoint of one whose concern for things is infused with ultimacy, or apart from that understanding of oneself

at least implicit in experiencing things in the vein of individuality
and of universality. That standpoint always seems to involve humility,
the position of a self as participant in the infinite importance of things
in contrast to a would-be appropriation of such importance. I have
already tried to take account of the suggestion that for each of us
there can actually be only one idol, obscured, no doubt, by obsessive
interests which point away from himself.

Things which inspire us with reverence teach us respect for themselves; but reverence seems to be a matter of accepting their ultimate
gift, and not reverence for them. Reverence is a being embraced by
a significance that is all-embracive; as a significance found in them
uniquely and originally it is the essence of their individuality; but as
all-embracive, it sweeps us into ken with them as coparticipants in
a universal situation. It both emphasizes and deemphasizes any and
all finite beings, infinitely. Every other in which we find a significance
which deepens our reception of that other into reverence is experienced as both absolutely other than ourselves and in communion with
us; and the counterpart of the otherness of everything other than ourselves, so understood, is our own independence. In reverence is it not
clear that our independence can mean neither isolation nor assertion
over against other beings? And in reverence, who clings to privilege
for himself or any other?

If there are leads in these utterances worth following up, perhaps one of them would be to suspect an ambiguity in 'ultimate concern' which might be cleared up a little. As concern *for*, might not
respect for finite beings be a definitive aspect of it? But is reverence
concern *for*? Or is it more concern *from* a significance which embraces
the finite, and which we may receive from things in responding to
them most profoundly? Reverence might be thought of as implying
respect for things, but not as identical with it. It might be put this
way: Religious interest in things includes respect for them and transcends it in so far as it involves receiving the ultimate gift of things
with reverence. Reverence seems most clearly an attitude in which
we are neither autonomous nor heteronomous as active beings. It is
omnirelevant as an appreciation of the universal significance of finite
being; but the realization of that significance seems utterly bound up

with 'the act of faith,' which is none other than responsibility in its fullest depth and meaning, becoming actual.

Can we think of reverence as understanding of reality supervening upon the decisive act of informed will? The full flowering of human consciousness. . . . A discovery of 'raison d'être' which is no reason at all, a funding of intelligibility, the fulfilment of a life of reason worthy of the name. These are possible phrasings of the matter.

At the risk of putting the question prematurely, and perhaps awry, I ask myself if there is not a kind of 'logic of responsibility' at least vaguely discernible in the configuration of ideas in which my thought has been revolving. I have thought of faith as sensitization to intimations of finality in things. And I have thought of faith as deepening decisively (cf. 'act of faith' above) into contemplation, into reverence, into the creative reception (Marcel's phrase) of the ultimate gift of things in their finality, in a universal significance which embraces them, and which, in embracing us, transfigures us and renders us whole. And I have thought of this understanding of reality consummated in reverence as understanding-communion with them. But from this understanding in turn we are restored to a destiny to be fulfilled so long as we may live and act. Thus the implication of contemplative understanding lives in generosity as the soul of necessary action. Are not both reverence and generosity charged with the dual communal potential of respect and compassion, both ultimate modes of participation on our part with other finite beings?

I confront myself, then, with a movement in thought, at any rate, from faith, into reverence, and into generosity (with its two moments of respect and compassion). As abstractly stated this seems very lame. It invites one to a tidiness from which the experiential weight of these ideas is liable to drain away. But I must reflect on this schematization of a 'logic of responsibility' for a while. There is something in it of the logic of the thinking I have been actually doing, whether or not the movement of these ideas genuinely reflects what might be called evolution of spirit, the 'logic of responsibility itself.'

Friday, October 23

"The readiness is all."[68] Disposability as the key to our alignment with a destiny to be fulfilled and continuity in finding our way (tao); the vocational character of true action: These themes return to me freshly this morning. I think of reality as ever questioning, calling upon us, as if in syllables shaped from a mouth, which issue almost soundlessly. In a noisy soul this call is utterly ignored, But as true stillness comes upon us, we hear, we hear, and we learn that our whole lives may have the character of finding that anthem which would be native to our own tongue, and which alone can be the true answer for each of us to the questioning, the calling, the demand for ultimate reckoning which devolves upon us. As Carlos Williams perceives: "Do we not see that we are inarticulate? That is what defeats us."[69]

Not merely in verbal response, but in all our doing there seems to be this aspect of learning to make answer and of groping for articulation which may thread us on a central strand of meaning capable of bearing the weight of all the disparate moments of our lives. But we are more or less locked in ourselves and at a loss how to make answer with our lives, to sing a true song. Frenetic questioning is of no avail, restless questing in itself aside from the point; these still suppose a case, however necessary they may be to the discovery of

---

[68.] The key sentence in *Hamlet,* and a far cry from Hamlet's earlier "O cursed spite/That I was born to set it right."

[69.] *Autobiography,* p. 361.

their irrelevance. It is in and out of silence, a deep stillness, that the full honesty of the true human spirit is born — and born to sing in word and deed that demand their own increase. This, this song that each of us must find his own voice to sing, and this alone, can incarnate for him explanation of his life. Its active testimony is the consolidation of belief. True response, then, is from silence, the still center of the human soul, and the corollary to this is patience. For the readiness is all. But patience is not postponement, not falling away from on-goingness; it is the readying to step clean forth (ecstasis), and there ever comes a time when the question sinks home: *when, if not now?* This seems to be what Zen is driving at when it demands, say a word, quick! This present moment.

Is it not more accurate to say that we participate in creation than that we create? Is not creation as it touches us in what we do an interlocking of the resources with which we act, an interlocking of them with that which firms them and claims them as a province assimilated to incarnation? To participate in creation is to be relieved of undue emphasis or accent placed upon ourselves. The truly creative deed of man seems that of which he becomes lucid to himself as the creature of creation; and the very deed in which his creatureliness is clarified is itself creaturely participation in creation. The deed is no more his creature than he is the creature of himself. But this raises the question of agency again. And again it seems to me futile to attempt to invoke an agent other than the man who participates in creation. Strange as it may seem, I cannot follow through the idea of creation in terms of a creator. Nor can I strictly think of man as creator in creative action; for the groundedness of creative action which liberates us is not 'something' with which we endow it; nor can I transfer the notion of agency to reality as grounding agency in us, in an attempt to comprehend the groundedness of the creative act. I am prepared to think of act and agent as co-creaturely, but I can find no illumination in attempting to conceive a creator to which we and our acts may stand in relation as *products* of its agency. Such a conception of creation, as many theologians have observed, reinstates the notion of heteronomy.

One suggestion which I take to heart at this point, then, is that of the inadequacy of attempting to interpret creation in terms of arti-facture, manufacture, invention, production, in all of which the *ulti-macy of agency* seems to be taken for granted. Now agents are indeed artificers; they manufacture, invent, produce; and one thinks of them as in a *controlling* position, disposing and endowing products thus and so. But as I cannot think the meaning of creation in terms of production, so I cannot think the meaning of being creature in terms of being produced. This is not to rule out the thought of our produc-tice activity actually being 'creative' in the sense that it may be action in which we participate in creation. It is only to suggest that we avoid the trap of supposing that production considered merely as such can embody for thought the meaning of creation. To suggest the distinction more clearly, I can follow Marcel's 'vocabulary of reflec-tion' by endorsing the idea of encountering and solving problems in so far as we are producers, makers, inventors. But in so far as our acting as producers, artificers, and inventors is also to be construed as 'creative,' it evades conception in terms of problem-solving, making, and inventing, even though such conception is also relevant to it. The stress on the agent as ultimate is lifted, and agency must now be con-ceived as meta-problematic, meta-technical, meta-artifactual, even though it may *also* be conceived as involving the solution of prob-lems, technique, and artifacture. Thus poetry may always be a mak-ing with words, but it should be more than this. And though we speak of a phase of a man's life, say the years he put in in a cannery, as "the making of him," let us not be taken in by the phrase.

No doubt what I have been leading up to may seem extremely disappointing: It is the proposal that creation is inexpungably mys-terious, and can only be understood through participation in it. But this does not amount to a rejection of the possibility of reflective par-ticipation in creation, nor does it seem to me to underwrite the mys-tical emphasis on the ineffability of our basic experience, an emphasis which I must say has seemed to me at times perilously close to abdi-cation of responsibility and a kind of paralytic seizure of the will. True, we may ever fall short of adequacy in whatever realization of the meaning of creation we may act upon. But the theme of the in-exhaustibility, and thus of the unfailing relevance for active beings, of that meaning, as demanding fulfilment in action, seems more to the point than the mystical theme of ineffability. Sometimes I think that the latter affronts the appreciation of our creatureliness, and the patience which that seems to support. By what extravagant standard of articulateness shall we obscure from ourselves that the *will to communicate*, and thus the relevance of communication, can be boundless? Sure, we do not imagine how we can begin to do it justice. If we could, our participation in creation would be in essence no more than the solving of a problem.

Not out of this world, but in this world, we are. In and of this world, as fellow creatures. (Jaspers on the will to communicate comes to mind; on this theme he rings very true.) We cannot *know* in advance what we must do. With whatever knowledge we truly stand forth, we stand forth beyond the frontier of knowledge, beyond, indeed, where we have been. Only so do we find out where we have always been, in all creation, a true wilderness. That is the home in which things other than ourselves may be welcomed as guests, where innocence is sacred, and helplessness moves us not to abandon the helpless, in spite of our not knowing how to help. I think of Terray simply holding Herzog in his arms, unable to do anything for Herzog except to be *with* him while Herzog's life was reduced to a feeble flicker in the gusts of mortal agony. (See the chapter, "The Retreat" in *Annapurna*.) How far we are even from our own innocence so much of the time, and so from the acceptance of ourselves.

Again I feel that optimism and pessimism alike move on a false level, or plane, of interpretation of human destiny; both seem severed from faith and hope, and in both there is still the supposing of a case. They seem to propose an evaluation of our situation in abstraction from the answer always unfinished so long as we live, that answer which each of us alone can understand as it is fashioned in terms of his own response and which cannot be relevantly questioned by him beyond the sphere of his intimacy.

In this connection we touch on what have been familiarly alluded to as the problems of evil or of theodicy. Marcel seems right about this, that our thinking may move here on a problematic plane which it behooves us in reflection to question. And Tillich puts the same point in saying:

> All theological statements are existential; they imply the man who makes the statement or who asks the question. The creaturely existence of which theology speaks is "my" creaturely existence, and only on this basis is the consideration of creatureliness in general meaningful. This existential correlation is abandoned when the question of theodicy is raised with respect to persons other than the questioner . . .
>
> If we wish to answer the question of the fulfillment of other persons, and with it the questions of theodicy and predestination, we must seek the point at which the destiny of others becomes our own destiny. (. . . The question of theodicy finds its final answer in the mystery of the creative ground.) [70]

I have included the sentence in brackets (not in text) for its own interest. But the quote as a whole *suggests* something cognate to what I mean by not supposing a case when it comes to a basic evaluative reckoning of our situation.

What do we make of the thousand and one fatal accidents of which we may read by following the newspapers for a week or so? What do we make of armed conflicts here and there over the face of the earth? What do we make of drought and flood and starvation, and the sun shining on all alike? Was it William James who had recourse to some news report of one person butchering another in his sleep, as if this of itself were an ultimate consideration when it comes to basic evaluation? Appeal to such a reported fact may be enough to counter optimism, a kind of wholesale euphoria about 'the state of the universe.' But does one conclude upon reports, however well-informed, or upon acquaintance, however thorough, when it comes to the question, what do you make of this? Not *such* as this, but *this*. So long as this is taken as *such as*, one is not yet beyond supposing a case; one has not yet responded to *this*. *This*, indeed, only sinks in as we are involved with it at a level or depth appreciative of its mystery. I think of the suicide planes which I *witnessed*; oh! they still call out to me, and what I make of them, of the lives perishing in flames, is still unfinished business which I feel I shall have to take upon myself until my dying day. What, what, indeed can I make of them? Oh, I must *be* answer for these men. Men I never knew. Living men. How can I find answer except as I can articulate a true prayer? Is it not true that we were not enemies? And who will believe this, how can it be believed?

Saturday and Sunday, October 24 and 25

These have been days of study, in Tillich, in the book of essays about his work, and I have read the Fourth Gospel and the Book of Job, rounding up, on this day of cold and driving rain, with the opening chapters of *Moby Dick*. How much of *Moby Dick* is Melville's heeding of the voice out of the whirlwind in the Book of Job? In both it is the meaning of the independent thing which seems to emerge, and the presence of the thing is the cleansing of man. In both the word of awe in all things is served in terms of the leviathan; in Job:

> Lay thine hand upon him:
> Remember the battle, and do so no more.

Might not the sound of a stream of running water, too, call a man to his senses and out of the intricacies of a "wisdom" in which he may only be propounding a fixation and a preoccupation in which he is stuck? I think of the instruction of walking on a beach; a long walk of a stormy day, on a day like this.

Friday, October 30

Going through the Asiatic section of the Boston Museum of Fine Arts on Wednesday, of all the Chinese and Japanese and Indian art which we saw, nothing impressed me so much as certain paintings

from the Sung period of Chinese painting. These paintings seemed
to be purely *born*, whereas most of the others, by comparison at least,
seemed to be *painted*. I would say they are primordial, but not primi-
tive; mature, but not sophisticated; direct, but not naive. Theirs seems
to be an emergent, rather than a projected simplicity. The refinement
of detail did not leave me with an impression of delicacy. To what
extent may the greatness of these paintings have been an impediment
to subsequent generations of painters in whom their style took on
self-consciousness? This is hardly a black-or-white question, and I'm
in no position to answer it.

We turn to what we have received with reverence even in a
slightly forced manner, and that sweet-edged knife of reality manifest
(of which Thoreau spoke) tends to blunt; it does not lend itself to
our use. Thus, even as I was musing on how a style of painting might
degenerate, a flock of wild geese passed over our house — geese such
as I have often attended to most cleanly before — and I rushed to
the window all-eagerness for them, but with a slightly spoiling expectation. I counted them all before they disappeared in the storm-
clouds downwind — there were forty-five. On telling of them and
their number I met with a true question: If you counted them, how
could you have seen them?

Sunday, November 1

For some days I have been considering how the idea of finality
might be amplified and thought out more carefully. I have already
considered finality in terms of "the informing of will," and in connection with faith and reverence as distinguishable 'moments' of our
being informed with an unconditional significance embodied in finite
beings, by virtue of which they are experienced as intelligible. And
I have thought of the experiential advent of finality as discovery of
ground upon which the necessity of acting depends (including that

of active reflection). Still further, finality seems to permeate us with demanding and enabling power, or *as* both demand and promise upon which we may act hopefully. It would not be imprecise to think of finality as 'the soul of affirmation,' and in so far as 'its advent' makes possible affirmation-in-spite-of, its advent is literally encouragement (a line of reflection on which Tillich's discussion of courage is very helpful). There is also the aspect of terminal, but not terminating, fulfilment for the person in the advent of finality; this might be called its consummatory aspect. Yet I should wish to reiterate that its consummatory aspect depends on its authority, and its authority must be kept in mind as the imbuing of the person with ultimate concern of continuing relevance in his manifold relations with the ongoing situation in which he must participate as an active being. It gives the force and meaning to this "must participate," and at the same time it gives guarantee of the possibility of participation. If one takes the consummatory aspect of the advent of finality as constitutive of finality, and as the source of its authority, one's thinking is then at the mercy of every seeming consummation, which so far forth must be adjudged final, and one utterly misses the point that the only conclusive consummation for a person involves his appreciation of a universal significance realized by him in his concern for finite beings and his affirmation of them. Thus it seems to me that the consummation of the human being should not be construed as justifying human action, and that it can only be understood if conclusive consummation is appreciated in relation to the non-consummatory aspects of the advent of finality, such as the aspect of demand on us as active beings, and the aspect of concern for finite beings with which the advent of finality imbues us.

This much of the idea of finality seems by way of review of what I have thought explicitly in these pages before. Now I want to try to relate the idea of finality more explicitly to the meaning of having a destiny to fulfil. Is there not a 'telic' aspect to the advent of finality, along with its deontological aspect? And what may be said of the advent of finality as it touches the person's orientation both to the past and to the future? And I mean, especially, to his past and his future? Thus, for example, I ask myself, why it is that your work has this fundamental aspect of a trend — a tendency? How is it that each moment or period of comparative discovery also carries with it the suggestion of its own incompleteness? How is it that each moment of reflective affirmation also seems to call for its own criticism?

Monday, November 2

The sounding of bells often seems the very enunciation of finality, defining and reminding us of ultimate meaning for man.

In the Harvard Yard there is a large bell installed over the chapel; it rings out the classes that are come to an end and rings in the classes about to commence. Often I have paused on my way to meet with a class, and watched its hangingly slow movement even as it tolled and tolled. Sometimes it seemed as if its sounding were dissociated from the moments of the impact of the clapper upon the body of the bell, there being a lag between the seen and the heard. A lag? Rather an *anticipation*, it seemed — as if the sounding proclaimed each next seen strike and pause in the movement to and fro. Thus a curious impression would come over me of witnessing events being born out of the eternal meaning that 'explained' them. And it would seem to me that the bell spoke a final word in the soul, the meaning of coming to be and passing away, perennial, always and always, ever so, just as now. How deeply this bell used to fill me with gratitude. How often it gathered me together and inspired me with the trust and the commitment to speak forth in the coming hour, beyond the pale of anything I might have arranged to say. It seemed to key me to the vein of ultimacy in which philosophical reflection must move; many times, I know, it summoned me into the attitude of prayer, teaching me the namelessness of that which a man must serve.

At Stanford there was a carillon on which melodies were played at noon. I will not say what a carillon might mean and be when played upon and heard, but only that it took a tolling bell to instruct me deeply in the meaning of responsibility, to search out with its lingering reverberations the decisive response of an active being upon the meaning of things in passage. It need not be a deep-voiced bell, a great bell, as it were. And this I learned in Taxco, Mexico, a dwelling place of many bells. The bells in Taxco never played tunes. Sometimes, indeed frequently, they were all being rung simultaneously, yet not in rhythmic accord. At first these occasions struck me as bedlam, and the bells seemed to be gainsaying one another. But gradually I became familiar with their respective tones, and when they all broke out together, they came to seem a paean from which no voice was withheld, and it was as if they expressed the acceptance of all moments of human life and rendered them up pure, all laughing and crying, all shouting and murmuring, all phases of the lives we lead assimilated to a sense not requiring any pervasive rhythmical or melodious pattern. At times I was sensible of the possibility of taking these bells demonically, but also that if so taken they would take the direction of degenerating into noise.

What a clamor of sounds prevails almost unremittingly in Taxco; day or night, dogs bark incessantly, pigs squeal and scream, donkeys are braying, and there are roosters who crow through the night. Juke boxes in the cantinas and loud speakers advertising places of amusement keep churning out an assault on the privacy of the soul. And there might be fireworks any time. What made it all supportable, I came to ask myself? Partly the silence visible in the stone, in the massive hills, in the adobe huts and the earthenware, in the deepbedded lives to be read in passing countenances, now grave, now enduring, now mobile with joy and courtesy. Partly the life-giving light and air so constantly playing over leaping colours, or softening into the shadowed recesses of the night. But I remember awakening once in a rare moment of what was really the dead of night, when of a sudden one rather high-pitched bell uttered a single casual sound, and then all again was still. No more than a reminder, ever so slight — no lingering reverberations, no overtones — a reminder of purity tossed off by the night. Then I knew how I had come to love the place, and understood the bells in full peal: the alembic through which Taxco's noise is supervened upon and assimilated to sound. Even the fireworks seem natural there.

Tuesday, November 3

We are taught finality in the once-for-allness of events, so clear in the presence of death, and in the givenness of things to which we reach out with infinite receptivity. Is there not a depth in which joy and sorrow meet? Do we not live to learn the untruth of elation and depression? Finality instructs us in the way of essential truth, positioning us through our sense of universe. How *universal* is the music of Handel, how deeply it explores responsibility. The wonder and glory of the firmament made music: the spirit of true decision.

When thinking of finality, remember the resiliency, the gaiety, the tenderness, the neither personal nor impersonal character of this music. Here you get the suggestion of an attitude, and concretely, that cannot be placed within the framework of thought laboring on the level of the distinction between the correlative alternatives of subjectivity and objectivity. If such music as this of Handel were to be allowed to keep our thinking to careful usage, it might regenerate and reclaim from sentimentality and disparagement the sense of the term 'spiritual' to suggest that attitude which could only be wrongly construed as either subjective or objective. I acknowledge a reluctance in the use of this term, yet I am not sure that my reluctance is any more a scruple against opening a floodgate through which the spawn of sentimentality may pour, than it is a deference to the derogation of 'spirituality' which is so easily accepted among us as token of a hard-headed concern for truth in opposition to phonies, quacks, obscurantists, and would-be personifications of 'a Message.' There is, in Stace's phrase, much "hogwash of spirituality" abroad.[71] There

---

71. For the context in which this phrase appears, see Stace, W. T., *The Gate of Silence*, Boston, Beacon, 1952, p. 34.

could also be much inverted sentimentality in the branding of spirituality as "hogwash," if uttered as an ultimate dictum. As Marcel has noted with unusual care, it is a constant part of a philosopher's job today to guard against the degeneration of basic ideas which have come to traditional embodiment in certain terms, through which they may then suffer inflation and debasement. The language of testimony may always be taken in vain.

Thursday, November 5, 1953

I have noticed that of late I have felt much freer to study than I did during the summer months, when the urgency to write was so paramount. I look back upon my summer's writing as an escape from the perils of diffusion, of which I was so sensible to begin with. One needs defined limits within which to work, not limits imposed in advance, I felt — not arbitrary limits — but the limits of actual thought defined in the act of its taking shape.

I am not content with what I have worked out; but I have worked out enough, perhaps, to be content to consider more carefully as I move along, and to welcome all manner of thinking other than my own.

INDEX

COMPILED BY ANDREW FEENBERG

Breinigsville, PA USA
01 August 2010
242790BV00001B/109/P